Fighting in Canyon Country

Native American Conflict, 500 AD to the 1920s

Robert S. McPherson

Portions of this book were previously published in Robert S. McPherson, *As If the Land Owned Us: An Ethnohistory of the White Mesa Utes* (Salt Lake City: University of Utah Press, 2011) and are reprinted by permission of the publisher.

First published by Dog Ear Publishing
4011 Vincennes Rd
Indianapolis, IN 46268
www.dogearpublishing.net

dog ear PUBLISHING

ISBN: 978-1-4575-4889-5

This book is printed on acid-free paper.

Printed in the United States of America

Contents

INTRODUCTION

Then and Now
Considerations in Writing about Culture and Conflict

The Four Corners region—where Colorado, New Mexico, Arizona, and Utah share contiguous boundaries—has some of the most dramatic landscape in the United States. Large sinuous canyons and towering red-rock formations; laccolithic mountains and colorful sandy deserts; clear mountain streams and brown roiling rivers; and vast skies with their shifting cloud patterns all draw the eye while fostering admiration for ever-changing vistas. As a young itinerant philosopher and artist, Everett Ruess wandered about this land in the early 1930s, writing of his extreme love for it and the safety and reflective peace he felt. Camped upon Navajo Mountain at War God Spring, he mused about "the wind roaring in the tops of the tall pines" as the moon rose "on the rim of the desert" with the "stars gleam[ing] through the pine boughs and the filmy clouds that move across the night sky. . . . The beauty of this place is perfect of its kind; I could ask for nothing more. . . . The perfection of this place is one reason I distrust ever returning to the cities. . . . There one walks in the midst of ugliness and mistakes. All is made for man, but where can one find surroundings to match one's ideals and imaginings?"[1] Not long after writing this, the poet-philosopher disappeared, never to be found, eaten by the land he loved.

As intelligent and sensitive as Ruess was, he missed the irony of his own statement, given where he sat to write his missive. Below him were Anasazi (ancestral Puebloan) sites: one on Cumming's Mesa at the foot of the mountain and the other on Pottery Pueblo on Paiute Mesa—both defensible sites. To the southeast sat Betatakin, Keet Seel, and Kayenta, with their rich archaeological record and Native American stories of conflict.[2] In Navajo thought, Navajo Mountain is viewed as a place of protection provided by the twin mythological warriors, Monster Slayer and Born For Water, who through bloody deeds rid the land of creatures plaguing the people. War God Spring was an important site for Monster Slayer. The mountain shielded many Navajos during the Long Walk period; became a refuge for them and Ute fighters and raiders; and was a place where two miners were killed, and the cavalry came to investigate.[3] What seemed so peaceful was actually a place where human interaction, to include violence, had existed for well over a millennium.

None of this is to fault Ruess for his lack of knowledge about the past, but only to point out that like so many people who come to southeastern Utah to enjoy the landscape, there is a multiverse of events and perceptions tied to its prehistory and history. Few tourists would go there to investigate conflict, but rather to seek peace and explore their own inscape matched against the beauty of the world before them. Human emotions exalt and exult over its majesty, never realizing the stories buried about that give a far different picture of the land and its people. From prehistoric times to the twentieth century, there has been conflict, ranging from individual friction to small-scale warfare, that has convulsed the land in strife. The topography of Canyon Country has played a major role in what events unfolded—and how. The land, in all of its many facets, is the first leg of a triad upon which the theme of this book rests.

There are few places in the United States that could tell a similar or as complete a story as the one found in the Four Corners area. Starting with the Anasazi, where else could one find a prehistoric culture so well-preserved because of the dry climate and large alcoves that protect fragile ruins built of mud, rocks, and sticks—with associated artifacts? Scholars have studied the people in this region for close to a century and a half and continue to do so. A rich and bounteous literature has sprung forth, with archaeologists and others adding to it each year. The past continues to yield its secrets as techniques for gaining the information become more sophisticated, but in the end, it is the land that yields the data. Certainly there are other regions that have a rich prehistory—the Mississippi River and tributaries with its Mississippian cultures, as well as the Iroquois around the Great Lakes—but none have left such an extensively preserved material culture or been investigated more than the Anasazi. Isolation and lack of development in the Four Corners region has also made this possible.

Once one enters the historic period, this region offers an exciting story provided by two major tribes—the Navajos and Utes—who practiced very different lifestyles. The Utes, as hunters and gatherers, shared elements of the Plains and Great Basin culture areas, travelling about in a seasonal cycle and harvesting the fruits of the land. The Navajo, on the other hand, lived a more sedentary or transhumant life, basing their economy on agriculture and livestock, while much of their worldview rested on a rich philosophical and religious experience. The land, central to both groups, was imbued with power and shaped by the cultural lifestyle that each practiced.

Joining them on this land were cowboys, miners, settlers—Mormon and gentile—and the US cavalry, who maintained peace. The rugged topography, limited resources, and general isolation from major hubs of Anglo activity ensured a unique evolution in the affairs of each of these groups. The population's slow growth, struggle for livelihood, and diversity fostered opportunities for conflict as each group competed to make a living. With all of the ingredients that Hollywood and Western novelists later called upon for exciting tales of bygone years, these same stories instruct the reader about fighting in a difficult terrain. How did these different people use this region, and more specifically, during times of conflict, what role did the land play in protecting or challenging those people involved in strife?

The second leg of the triad is culture. Southeastern Utah has been home to a variety of inhabitants with different beliefs and practices adapted to their life here. Culture is the means by which the objective universe is shared and filtered through a group's teachings and worldview. The reader will find that conflict waged by the Anasazi was different from that of the Ute, which was different from that of the Navajo. In each case, it was shaped by the traditional teachings that make each culture distinct. Many of the following chapters explain why different groups chose to wage warfare as they did. Conflict, as a manifestation of cultural values derived from religious and social practices embedded in traditional teachings, assumes its own unique characteristics. By understanding what each group believed and practiced, a clearer understanding of why it assumed the qualities and character that it did becomes more clearly defined. What emerges is ethnohistory, where the understanding of a people informs their approach to a historic event. In the pages of this book are explanations about how war was waged, the role of the supernatural, what the values of a people were, and why the event was important to a particular group. The backdrop of culture explains what might otherwise seem impractical from another view.

The third leg of the triad is conflict and warfare. As paleoanthropologist Robert Ardrey noted, "Human war has been the most successful of our cultural traditions."[4] Cherokee entertainer Will Rogers agrees: "You can't say civilization don't advance. . . . For every war they kill you a new way."[5] The Four Corners region has had its share of conflict, as well as innovation. One important consideration is *scale*. For the person looking for full-on military engagements at the level of the Custer battle or the annihilation of the Pequot in Connecticut, he or she will have to look elsewhere. Native American warfare in this region was characterized as low-level, small-scale conflict rather than climactic battle. Closer to the norm was a tit-for-tat seesawing between opposing aggressors. Indeed, Anasazi conflict appears not to have been waged against a force from the outside but rather was an internal struggle. On that level, *conflict* may be a more appropriate term than *warfare*. On the other hand, when one considers some of the fights between the cavalry and Indians, the scale greatly increases, and the term *warfare* is more appropriate.

By understanding the triad—land, culture, and conflict—one can better appreciate what this book sets out to accomplish. It is not a text on local history, although its examples are tied primarily to a specific region. Instead, it is a study of principles that can be applied in understanding not only conflict and fighting but also the roles of culture and geography in that conflict. The United States military has consolidated important concepts found in both large- and small-scale fighting into nine Principles of War.[6] Each of these principles can be applied to examples found in the history of southeastern Utah as encountered in this book.

1. *Mass*: concentrating combat power at the decisive time and place.
2. *Maneuver*: placing the enemy at a disadvantage through the application of combat power.
3. *Objective*: clearly defining a decisive, attainable goal.
4. *Offense:* seizing, retaining, and exploiting the initiative.
5. *Unity of Command*: unifying effort under one responsible leader.
6. *Security*: preventing the enemy from acquiring an unexpected advantage.
7. *Surprise*: striking the enemy at a time, place, or manner that is unexpected.
8. *Simplicity*: providing clear, uncomplicated plans and orders for thorough understanding.
9. *Economy of Force*: applying minimal essential combat power to secondary efforts.

There has been discussion of adding a tenth one to the list: *Leadership*, in which personality, knowledge, and skill of those directing forces during a conflict have resulted in a decisive victory.

Many of these principles are applicable to battles fought in the Four Corners area. Take for instance an incident of a Ute and cavalry conflict that will follow in greater detail in Chapter Four. Captain Henry P. Perrine, F Troop, 6th Cavalry, pursued a group of hostile Utes who had had a dust-up with some cowboys in early July 1884. He followed them into unknown territory, ran out of water, lost his supply train, had two men killed, failed to retrieve their bodies, and suffered from rocky relations with the large contingent of cowboys accompanying him. The Utes, on the other hand, enjoyed the benefit of early warning, knowing the land, being well-armed, and stymying the cavalry by fighting from a sheer cliff through which only a narrow trail existed. The outcome was simple: Perrine and his force had to abandon the pursuit. Applying the Principles of War to this situation, one can see how the principle of *mass* was negated by the Utes controlling a narrow pass at the top of a ridge. No matter how many men were down below, in this open terrain there was no chance of a successful assault. Indeed, the large force proved to be a disadvantage since the July sun dried out man and beast to the point that all that mattered was precious water. There was no water for the cavalry and cowboys, while there was a sufficient amount for the Utes. *Maneuver* was impossible for the attacking force, which could not get over the tall rock escarpment, while only a handful of Indian riflemen (*economy of force*) held them off as the Utes' families escaped in a number of different directions. The troopers could not maintain the *offense*, there was no *surprise*, and there were a few incidents that showed their *security* was easily breeched. There was *unity of command*, with Perrine in charge of both cavalry and cowboys; their *objective* of bringing in the Utes was clear; and the orders were *simple* ("get them"). But the military had no success.

Not all conflicts share all of the principles, but they do present a way of thinking about engagements and what should be considered for success.

The Principles of War are based in offensive action, which the military believes is the only sure road to victory. A fluid battlefield with maneuvering units presents the opportunity for commanders to make their own decisions, as opposed to being hunkered down behind a protective wall, waiting to be attacked, and giving the enemy free rein to pick the time, place, and method that will lead to the defeat of a static force. Still, there are things that need to be considered when defending, and the Utes just mentioned applied many of these principles summarized in the acronym OCOKA. Their ability to observe (*observation*) allowed them to keep the troopers and civilians pinned down while watching any movement approaching or on the battlefield. Their *cover* (protection from direct fire) and *concealment* (hidden from observation) were excellent, since as soon as they lay flat on the top of the rock ridge, no bullet could find them. The whole escarpment was one big *obstacle* that stopped maneuver and prevented any type of flanking movement. The narrow pass at the top through the rock formation was *key terrain*, or a critical part of the land that controlled the outcome of the battle. If the soldiers had seized it, the Utes could have been pursued and captured. There was only one *avenue of approach*, or way of attacking the objective: straight uphill and in the open. So from the Utes' perspective, their defensive position was ideal because it removed much of the flexibility to operate against them. The defensible communities of the Anasazi also employed many of the principles summarized in OCOKA, as will be discussed in Chapter One.

Each chapter in this book presents a different aspect of conflict as it has occurred during the last 1,500 years of occupation of southeastern Utah. A brief synopsis is offered here to delineate what to expect. The first chapter concerning Anasazi warfare is unique in that, heretofore, most analysis of their fighting has been from the realm of the archaeologist and the material remains left from conflict. Everything from defensible structures to cannibalism to weaponry to pictographs and petroglyphs focus on what those objects indicate. This is invaluable information. In support of what this offers and to add to the discussion, however, this chapter examines Hopi and Zuni mythology and historical practices that suggest why the Anasazi appear to have taken the approach they did. A new look at prehistoric warfare results.

The second chapter on Ute and Navajo modes of warfare establishes a basis for five other chapters concerning specific instances that range chronologically from 1855 to 1923. Its premise is that both Native American groups have different cultural beliefs that determined what they emphasized in preparing for and conducting combat. For instance, the Utes stressed early warning, fighting for material possessions, and a unified force that came from a village community, while the Navajos were more dispersed, placed a heavy emphasis on religious and supernatural preparation, and depended on small-scale raids and ambushes, as opposed to larger-sized confrontations. There are, of course, exceptions, but in southeastern Utah, the Utes predominantly worked collectively. This becomes very apparent in the third chapter, in which we discuss the period during the Long Walk when the two tribes fought each other. There is no denying the effectiveness of the Utes—a fact that remains in the tribal memory of the Navajos to this day.

Chapters Four, Five, Seven, and Eight examine a flurry of confrontations between Native Americans and Anglo-Americans from 1875 to 1923. The discussion of this fifty-year span highlights a number of points. First is the difference between the types of conflict that each group waged as it evolved over time. The introduction of new technology, diminished land space, differences in leadership, and encroachments on culture are placed against the timeless human dimension of warfare. Chapter Six examines the cavalry operating in this environment during the last quarter of the nineteenth century. It is a careful look at what it took to keep an army in the field in the Four Corners region at a time when the military delivered everything by mule train or wagon. Questions concerning organizational jurisdiction, where and when to build a post, how pay was handled in the field, and what it took to keep supplies rolling when there was a shortage of transportation were just a few of the concerns that field commanders had to address while keeping the cowboys and Indians under control. Fort Lewis in southwestern Colorado became central to maintaining the peace and solving these questions.

The first quarter of the twentieth century opened by closing the book on some of the old issues not yet settled during the nineteenth century. Indeed, the last cavalry charge against "hostile Indians" in the United States took place in southeastern Utah, as did chasing recalcitrant Utes in a Ford Model T. The barbed-wire stockade built in the center of Blanding in 1923 to house Indian prisoners was yet another anomaly carried over from the era of World War I.

At this point, the theme of this book should be apparent. It is that the land of southeastern Utah has served as an important backdrop for the people who have lived and fought in this area for over 1,500 years and that each of these cultures offer lessons worthy of contemplation concerning the human experience. The ugliness that Everett Ruess so badly wanted to escape is part of that experience. Anthropology, ethnohistory, and military science provide the keys to opening the door of understanding different lessons learned from home front to battlefield.

What do I hope the reader will take away from this book? For thirty years I have been writing about the history of southeastern Utah, some of which is duplicated here as noted in the endnotes of various chapters. My intent is to take these scattered writings and put them under one cover as a single topic, thus connecting different dots to create a fuller picture of what has transpired over a long period of time in the Four Corners area. Each person will approach this text differently. For the tourists enamored with Canyon Country and on their way to Lake Powell, I hope they will peek beneath the beauty, stop below Piute Pass, and contemplate what Captain Perrine felt in the middle of July 1884, with sweat running down his back while staring at two dying men just feet away from an entrenched enemy. Hike the trail to the top and see what the Utes saw and what a perfect ambush site and defensive position they held. While no one expects to return to the 1880s to be a cavalry unit short on water, there are still principles to be learned that help us understand problems from the past. The land, its people, and their approach to conflict over fifteen centuries provide a unique opportunity for understanding man's conduct of conflict as part of life in the Four Corners region. From the earliest archaeological remains to events in the twentieth century, southeastern Utah offers an interesting case study of how a rural area can provide valuable lessons in certain aspects of the human experience.

Chapter Endnotes

1. W. L. Rusho, *Everett Ruess—A Vagabond for Beauty* (Salt Lake City: Peregrine Smith Books, 1983), pp. 158–160.
2. See Robert S. McPherson, *Viewing the Ancestors: Perceptions of the Anaasazi, Mokwi , and Hisatsinom* (Norman: University of Oklahoma Press, 2014).
3. See Karl W. Luckert, *Navajo Mountain and Rainbow Bridge Religion* (Flagstaff: Museum of Northern Arizona, 1977).
4. James Charlton, *The Military Quotation Book* (New York: Saint Martin's Press, 1990), p. 40.
5. Ibid., p. 107.
6. Center of Military History, *American Military History* (Washington, DC: Center of Military History, United States Army, 1969, 1989), pp. 6–7.

CHAPTER ONE

Close Combat in Canyon Country: Prehistoric Warfare in Southeastern Utah

Southeastern Utah's Canyon Country and adjacent Four Corner's region offer a dramatic landscape filled with scenic vistas and evocative Anasazi ruins that draw tourists' eyes and capture their imagination. Within a day's drive, one can reach Mesa Verde, Chaco Canyon, Betatakin & Keet Seel (Navajo National Monument), and a multitude of lesser-known sites that are equally interesting. While the earliest Native American inhabitants in this area, the Paleo-Indian (10,000–6000 BC) and the Archaic Indians (6000–1000 BC) did not leave a great deal of material remains to study, the next group, the Anasazi, did. Indeed, from ruins to potsherds, arrowheads to petroglyphs, and skeletons to woven materials, their rich culture has been studied for well over a century, with surprising results that explain parts of their lifestyle. The literature concerning these people is vast, sometimes controversial, and ever growing. Much of it lies in the domain of the archaeologist, who discovers, classifies, and interprets the material culture, then postulates what social practices caused its rise and decline. For the awaiting public, each explanation brings them closer to a greater understanding of these people.

Even to give a cursory view of what is known about these Native Americans, who occupied southeastern Utah from 1000 BC to 1300 AD, would take far more than this chapter can allow. Instead, its purpose is to discuss the limited topic of waging warfare in southeastern Utah and examine the earliest forms of combat in the region. In order to do so, however, and given the long period of occupation in this area, a basic timeline with associated shifts in activities and material culture provides a useful context for the more interpretive discussion that lies ahead. A particularly helpful approach for this purpose is the masterful study by Steven A. LeBlanc, *Prehistoric Warfare in the American Southwest*.[1] LeBlanc focuses primarily on the Anasazi but also brings in neighboring archaeological traditions such as the Hohokam, Mogollon, and Mimbres. He divides the time periods into large chunks, starting with the Basketmaker and Pueblo I eras (1000 BC to 900 AD). This he characterized as a fairly violent period, where large groups of warriors fought in an organized manner using at first the *atlatl* and dart with a fending stick to deflect an oncoming projectile and later the bows and arrows that technologically changed from *self*, or the single stave of wood, to sinew-backed. Ambushes, raiding, and surprise attacks on villages were the desired modes that minimized casualties for the aggressor. Line formations with champions in front to start the initial combat are also suggested. Individual homes, hamlets, and villages varied in size, number of dwellings, and their defensive nature. Some sites had stockade walls, and some were built on hilltops to provide early warning and an advantageous fighting position. Other structures ranged from pit houses to free-standing jacal and masonry dwellings. In general, Leblanc characterizes this long evolutionary period as rife with warfare.

The Middle Period, which includes what archaeologists call the Pueblo II and Early Pueblo III times (900–1150 AD), is generally characterized as a much more peaceful era, especially within the influence of power emanating from Chaco Canyon (Chaco Interaction Sphere) over the larger part of the Anasazi domain. Site locations were less defensive, populations were widely spread across the landscape, and general prosperity reined, as evidenced by the increased carrying capacity of the land, long-range trade networks, and decreased violence when compared to the preceding or following eras. Some archaeologists named this era the *Pax Chaco*, when warfare was present but minimal. Yet the physical record on the ground is slow to yield a definitive answer as to why and to identify the forces—internal or external—that made it so. Leblanc summarizes this phenomenon by stating, "It is wrong to view this peaceful Middle Period as the norm for the Southwest. It was exceptional, and should be understood as such. This period is reminiscent of other times and places when there appeared to have been widespread cultural interaction, new forms of expression, and little evidence of warfare."[2]

Not so for the next phase, Late Pueblo III and IV (1200–1500s), which witnessed the Anasazi departure from the San Juan drainage on the Colorado Plateau, massive clan and group migrations, and the eventual establishment of locations where today's Puebloan people now reside. Warfare, or fear of it, appears endemic, with populations clustering into large communities that were highly defensible and inaccessible, often mutually supportive, and if possible, with enough food and water to be self-sustaining when under siege. Donna M. Glowacki characterized this period at Mesa Verde as a time of strident ideological and sociopolitical conflict, resulting in violence and warfare. She writes, "Although the buildup of change and tension was long in the making, the transformation happened quickly in the latter half of the 1200s, and in less than a generation the revolutionary tides of change and emigration could not be stemmed. The collapse was precipitous, turbulent, and beset with endemic warfare."[3]

The remnants of this chaotic time at Mesa Verde are now part of the archaeological record left open to interpretation. Both there and in the surrounding region, one finds dramatic sites that serve as classic examples of strategies to keep an enemy at bay. Multi-storied dwellings, defensive walls, restricted access, and line-of-site visibility between pueblos tell a physical story of a people concerned about protection. Many of these excavated sites have burned kivas, towers, and dwellings with body remains showing a violent death. The introduction of the shield as portrayed on pictograph and petroglyph panels also adds to this story of conflict. By 1300 AD, the Anasazi had vacated southeastern Utah and were on the move, seeking a new life with better conditions.

This cursory overview gives a foundation for what follows. The archaeological record, as valuable as it is, supplies only part of the answer as to how warfare was waged and why the participants fought as they did. Factual evidence is evaluated according to stringent scientific process that serves as proof and a basis for interpretation. Take for instance the issue of cannibalism, a topic that reached fever pitch following the publication of *Man Corn: Cannibalism and Violence in the Prehistoric American Southwest* (1999) by Christy and Jacqueline Turner.[4] This husband-and-wife team applied six criteria to judge whether people at a given location practiced cannibalism. They then examined individual or group remains from various sites for indications of violent deaths among Anasazi men, women, and children, many of whom lived and died in southeastern Utah. The Turners found that according to cut marks on bones and other criteria, a good number of these ancients had been butchered and eaten. A firestorm of protest arose from Native American groups, as well as fellow archaeologists, who refused to accept this interpretation for a number of their own reasons. Additional information and examples since then have been offered so that now many agree with the Turners' thesis. Even if one does not accept all six of the criteria or the interpretation about cannibalism, the Turners have verified archaeologically that violence was an important part of life in the Southwest.[5]

In recent years, the Native American voice has sounded strongly that its views on understanding Anasazi behavior be considered. Since archaeology demands concrete, measurable, and reproducible physical proof, the realms of ethnographic interview, oral history, mythology, and tribal perspective can fill in missing gaps and provide a different perspective from cultural explanations. The world of myths, dreams, visions, supernatural power, and other intangible elements that are common fare in the Indian world can be brought to bear in answering questions raised by the archaeological record. This chapter, therefore, builds on the good work of LeBlanc by looking for further explanations—some physical, others intangible—in identifying and recreating aspects of the Anasazi world. Every effort will be made to support what archaeologists have found on the ground, but there will also be times where the native view should be accepted as just as real, valid, and important as those physical elements discussed by archaeologists.

The power that comes from this position of combined archaeology and ethnography is illustrated in Deni J. Seymour's recently published *A Fateful Day in 1698*, the earliest written account of Native American warfare (Apache and O'odham) in the Southwest, as recorded by the Spanish and witnessed by the Indians.[6] This remarkable study looks at many of the topics considered in this chapter: attacking and defending motivation; tactics employed by both sides; religious beliefs and cultural practices that shaped the battle; the use of champions in combat; the importance of alliances; trophy-taking and its significance; and the effects of the environment. In this account, the written record is paramount in understanding what and why events unfolded as they did. In this chapter, the ethnographic account is dependent on the traditional teachings of two tribes.

Rather than list a series of caveats and justifications, suffice it to say that two peoples—the Hopi and Zuni—are used here to provide the information used for comparison with elements of the Anasazi culture.[7] While archaeologists recognize these two groups as likely descendants of the people formerly called Anasazi, there are other contemporary Puebloans who make similar claims. These two tribes were chosen because of the early ethnographic material collected by well-versed anthropologists such as Jesse Walter Fewkes, Alexander M. Stephen, Frank Cushing, and Matilda Coxe Stevenson, who had access to elders who shared traditional beliefs. The Zuni and Hopi also have a rich symbolic culture: mythology; traditional teachings and practices; intense ceremonial knowledge; and a system for passing this information on in an unbroken chain to succeeding generations. While variation does exist, what has been transmitted orally over the years is the intellectual lifeblood of the tribe and provides understanding as to what is important in preserving those cultural beliefs. What follows is an explanation from two worlds—that of the archaeologist and Native American tradition—as to how the Anasazi practiced warfare in Canyon Country.

A basic premise underlying this and the next chapter is that traditional Native American thought and practice centers upon the teachings found in tribal mythology: a code of beliefs that are both sacred and true and as such, are acted upon accordingly. While archaeologists use science and their own cultural beliefs to evaluate physical evidence, for the Hopi and Zuni, reason and truth reside in deities and associated spiritual powers, in the stories about these gods, in a religious understanding that explains how the world works, and the pattern that comes from these teachings that defines proper behavior. Invisible powers permeate their world, can be approached for assistance, or may harm because of neglect. Safety and correct conduct is achieved by following the patterns established at the time of the creation of this world and through interaction with supernatural beings, termed *kachinas* by the Hopi. These beings are ever-present, ever-powerful, approachable, and involved in the activities of humankind. Thus, both tribes have a complexity of thought concerning these forces, recognize an extensive pantheon of beings with diverse powers and responsibilities, and acknowledge different ways of obtaining their assistance.

The challenge here is to look at some of these beliefs and see if they can be matched with archaeological evidence and recorded historic incidents. Only recently have the Hopi and Zuni recognized the dominant culture's use of time classifications such as Basketmaker and Puebloan periods. The Hopi called their ancestral Puebloan forebears the Hisatsinom, among other names, while the Zuni used the name A:shiwi. For simplification here, the Navajo term *Anasazi* is used because it is widely recognized in the sources used and is all-encompassing to indicate the general population of ancestral Puebloans in the Southwest.[8] Archaeologists are cautious about identifying specific contemporary tribal ancestors when discussing Anasazi sites, while at the same time, conflating Hopi and Zuni ancestry, beliefs, and practices can create its own problems when dealing with specifics. The intent here is to show that deep-seated in the cultural roots of these Puebloan peoples lie specific teachings and references that allow for ethnographic comparison. When applied in this way, how might Anasazi warfare appeared, why was it waged as it was, and how does this accord with the archaeological record left behind?

For most traditional Native Americans, everything starts with the gods. The creation of the world, of its people (whichever tribe that might be), and the establishment of a way of life all set a pattern for behavior. Early anthropologist Frank

Cushing, who lived with the Zuni for five years (1879–1884), learned early on the importance of myths in explaining everything from behavior in daily life to the most esoteric religious belief. He was in an excellent position to evaluate the influence and power of myths by obtaining the Zunis' respect, learning their language, recording their cultural practices, and being initiated into their powerful Bow Priest Society. He wrote of these teachings, "With them all these various myths are held in brief and repeated in set form and one sequence as are placed the beads of a rosary or on a string, each entire, yet all making a connected strand. Here, then, we see the rudiment or embryo of a sacred epic." Later, when stressing the importance of myths in ceremonial performance, he wrote, "This may best be done, perhaps, by contrasting the drama of primitive peoples . . . with civilized people. While the latter is essentially spectacular, the former has for its chief motive the absolute and faithful reproduction of creative episodes—one may almost say, indeed, the revivification of the ancient."[9] This adherence to myths is equally true of the Hopi.

An example of the "revivification," or bringing to life of these gods that Cushing refers to, is found in the teachings about a major Hopi deity associated with war, death, and the underworld: Maasaw. The linguist and ethnographer Ekkehart Malotki, in introducing Maasaw's involvement in warfare, notes that "war lore at one time constituted a sizable part of Hopi cultural fabric. . . . [and that] the whole realm of war, with its tangible as well as intangible aspects, is conceptualized to a highly sophisticated degree, and for that matter, lexicalized in great detail in the Hopi language."[10] Even during historic times, Maasaw's representative appeared on the battlefield.

Unlike many tribal peoples who use war as a test of bravery and an opportunity to exhibit skills in defeating the enemy, the Hopi, along with Maasaw's help, take a more pragmatic view of killing their foe as quickly and safely as possible. Thus, Maasaw becomes a real protector by sapping the strength of the enemy so that his people remain unharmed. The Hopis pray to him only at night, fashion prayer sticks (or *pahos*) that carry their messages and prayers to him, and visualize him walking around the perimeter of a mesa or village as a sentinel during the hours of darkness. When conflict occurs, his job is to weaken, confuse, and stun with fear the enemy by throwing his club at their legs, allowing the Hopi to dispatch them quickly.[11] "Maasaw's club, known as *maawiki*, is believed to render any mortal unconscious when only touched by it."[12] The Hopis today still follow suit in ceremonial mock battles by "killing" opponents with clubs.

Another means by which the enemy is frightened and weakened is through a container or "gourd of ashes" that Maasaw carries. When either a gourd or clay pot containing these ashes is thrown, it explodes on impact, the ashes and other ingredients scattering and demoralizing the enemy. Malotki attests that clay pots have been made for this purpose since prehistoric times. In 1891, some cavalry men arrived at Oraibi to gather children for boarding school, an action that the Hopi resisted. During a confrontation, Maasaw appeared and gestured against the intruders; a woman soon followed him with a gourd of ashes that was dashed on the ground, the intent being that the white men "would be helpless to resist being clubbed to death."[13] While it did not have the desired effect, a number of accounts taken by different individuals confirm the presence of the jar with the war god and belief in its use. Ashes were also tossed for protection from witches, smeared on children's foreheads for protection, and applied at the end of some Hopi ceremonies to ensure evil was not present.[14]

Other deities associated with war are the "twin war gods"—more appropriately referred to as Elder and Younger Brother. Many of the different pueblo groups have these two beings. The Hopi call them Pöqqangwhoya and Palögawhoya; the Zuni call them U'yuyewi and Masai'lema. In Chapter Two, a more detailed discussion of the twins' role in Navajo culture will illustrate their closely followed cultural patterns by these people. Many Puebloan groups believed that the sun is their father, their birth was through miraculous means, they passed through a series of bloody challenges overcome through supernatural efforts, and they exist now to help mortals with waging war.[15] For the Zuni, they also play an all-encompassing role in the formation and operation of the Bow Priesthood Society; the Younger and Elder Brothers are believed to have initiated a direct line to the mortals who hold that position today. There are, however, ways of installing the leadership that is not dependent upon heredity.

Historically, induction into the society was possible after a man killed an enemy, showed bravery in combat, and took a scalp and article of clothing. Central features of the ceremony are the cutting of a scalp with a stone knife, a triumphal parade, and a reenactment of some of the twins' activities. At one point in the ceremony, there is a symbolic attack on an enemy sitting around a campfire. Arrows are shot into an enemy scalp, and soon the officiator pronounces, "You have met the enemy. He will nevermore inhale the sacred breath of day." That is followed by four war whoops, and "the enemy is destroyed."[16] The fourteen-day ceremony continues with song, dance, and prayers given to strengthen the Zuni and weaken the enemy. Each night the warriors gather together, sing songs, and brandish their war clubs, the original ones having come from the warrior (Great Star) in charge of the heavens. Clubs and hatchets play an important part throughout the ceremony. Each warrior is armed with one, moves it in rhythm with the songs, and changes it from his left to right hand, symbolically indicating there is no fear of the enemy. There is also a guard—the oldest member of the Bow Society—who stands with his club at the foot of the ladder in the underground ceremonial chamber, or *kiva*, to prevent intrusion.[17] While all of this is part of ritualized performance, one cannot lose sight of the symbolic importance of the club, one of the most ancient forms of weapons, and how its use is institutionalized as part of defeating the enemy.

At one point in the ceremony, "The scalps are rubbed with kaolin, for rain, and a bit of the scalps are taken into the mouth, that the Zunis may have brave hearts and that the Gods of War will empower them to destroy the enemy."[18] The foe is again symbolically eaten on another day of the ceremony, when the successful warrior and a man representing Elder Brother carry on their heads a basket filled with wafer bread, which represents the enemy. As they run in and out of a line of dancers, they let the baskets fall to the ground, indicative of killing the foe, then they exclaim, "We have destroyed the Navajo." The bread is next picked up off the ground, and as the dancers pass, they "catch at the bread with their mouths" before the basket is placed next to the scalp pole.[19]

A detailed description of the dress of the Zuni twins by Cushing provides not only an excellent example of the traditional equipment used by these gods, but also that used by the Anasazi. Everything mentioned was available to these ancient people.

> Lo! Dwarfed and hideous-disguised were the two gods . . . the Beloved Twain who Descended—strong now with the full strength of evil; and armed as warriors of old, with long bows and black stone-tipped arrows of cane-wood in quivers of long-tailed skins of catamounts, whizzing slings and death-singing slung-stones in fiber pockets; spears with dart-dealing fling slats, and blood-drinking broad-knives of gray stone in fore-pouches of fur-skin; short face-pulping war-clubs stuck aslant in their girdles, and on their backs targets of cotton close plaited with yucca. Yea, and on their trunks, were casings of scorched rawhide, horn-like in hardness, and on their heads wore they helmets of strength like to the thick neck-hide of male elks, whereof they were fashioned. . . .
>
> Twain Children of terror and magic were they, and when they called with the voice of destruction the smitten warriors of these Twain Children stirred and uprose, breathing battle-cries as echoes answer cries in

deep canyons, and swiftly they roused those who still lived, of the deep-slumbering people. . . .

[The twins speaking:] "Know ye our chosen: Lo! not long shall we tarry; Prepare as for journeys; Season wood for thy bowstrings and face-breaking war clubs; Plait shields like to our shields; And fashion strong garments—For in such hard apparel shall consist thy adornment . . ."[20]

This Zuni description from the myths parallels nicely one record of Hopi war gear written in 1935. The weapons carried by a warrior included a bow and arrow, a quiver made from mountain lion skin capable of holding thirty arrows, four throwing sticks that were each three feet long, a stone club or axe, a five-foot lance used for close-in thrusting, a crook-stick for tripping a fleeing enemy before dispatching him with a club, and a hide shield. The warrior would wear a white ceremonial kilt with sash while "his body above the waist was wrapped with as many layers of buckskin as possible."[21] Adults taught youth at an early age how to use this equipment, since war was always imminent. They also encouraged physical training to build strength and endurance, praying daily for divine assistance and skill.

Fig. 1—A Basketmaker warrior (right) faces his Pueblo III descendant across a thousand-year time span. The Basketmaker is armed with an *atlatl* and fending stick to deflect hurled darts, while the other warrior is armed with a bow and arrow and a painted basketry shield. The man crouching behind is brandishing a knife and one type of war club that became popular by 1200 AD (Courtesy Edge of the Cedars State Park Museum, Utah State Parks; Winston B. Hurst, artist)

Each item had its own religious significance and particular means of employment. For instance, the bow had an effective range of seventy yards. The arrows were straightened with the horns of mountain sheep, fletched with eagle feathers, painted with specific colors for good luck, and had a zigzag indentation on one side signifying that it "was to go straight to its mark with the speed of lightning."[22] Body armor proved effective against arrows, and two different types of armor were used in the Southwest. Warriors wore armor made of leather, a practice found widely spread from Canada, the Northwest Coast, and California through the Great Basin and the Southwest. The Hopi used this type. The other was that of quilted, plaited cotton popular in Mexico and further south. The Zuni, for instance, used this, as well as leather. When Francisco Vasquez de Coronado encountered different pueblo Indians in 1539–1540, many of those warriors wore leather jackets for protection; no example of prehistoric armor has yet been found, but it is mentioned in the mythology.[23]

The Anasazi appear to have adopted the use of shields relatively late, during the 1200s. While the shield described above was leather, some of the earliest ones were made of basketry. Three early prehistoric shields made from coiled willow and yucca fiber were found at Mesa Verde, Aztec Ruin, and Mummy Cave in Canyon del Muerto. Shields have also been depicted in petroglyphs, pictographs, and wall murals at Awatovi, Betatakin, Defiance House, Mesa Verde, Grand Gulch, Mule Canyon, Chinle Wash, Cow Canyon, and many other sites. Coiled shields, while thirty-six inches in diameter, would not be as effective in stopping arrows as the later hide shields were, but they would have been useful against clubs, thrown or slung rocks, and knives. During historic times, Cushing noted that the Zuni carried "shields of yucca or cotton cord, closely netted across a strong, round hoop-frame and covered with a coarser and larger net, which was only a modification of the carrying net . . . [taken] on hunting and war expeditions."[24]

Large hide shields, introduced after 1300, may have been used as the Pima did in historic times: held out in front at full arm's length and twisted rapidly to distract an enemy marksman.[25]

Beyond the physical protection provided by the shield, there was also the more important aspect from a Native American view of supernatural power. Frank Russell describes the erratic movements of a Pima warrior on the battlefield with his shield moving back and forth as part of his "magic" and then comments, "It is not the strength nor the intelligence of the [enemy] Apache that they fear, nor his arrow with its sting, but his magic—a creation of their own imagination.

And so the shield, with its magic symbols in brilliant colors, is kept in rapid motion not only from side to side but also revolving by the reciprocal twist of the bearer's forearm."[26]

In summarizing archaeological knowledge of the use of the shield, Helen Crotty suggests: "The adoption of Fremont militaristic imagery around the mid A.D. 1200s by the Kayenta Anasazi appears to be a response to the increasing hostilities between neighboring groups as they withdrew from their northern expansion and gathered in larger settlements in the homeland areas. . . . Shield bearer images are more prevalent at Anasazi settlements in the drainages of the right bank of the Colorado, however, than they are in Tsegi Canyon, where the display of large shields in a preferred location on the right side of the alcove may have been perceived not only as a warning to enemies but also as a protective device."[27]

One of the most important artifacts associated with Anasazi combat is the club. As already mentioned, it figures heavily in ceremonies associated with war in many of today's Puebloan groups. Cushing, speaking of the Zuni, notes: "Their hand weapons were huge stone knives and clubs shaped like potato-mashers, which were called . . . [a term meaning] to knock down finally or fatally, and in ceremonial allusion (rather than name) to the old-fashioned and sacred war clubs [known as] . . . knocking-down billets, otherwise called face-smashers or pulpers."[28] Many mythological accounts discuss their use, such as the one shared by Matilda Coxe Stevenson, who, writing of the Zuni twins, tells of their meeting a beautiful woman. They ask her to accompany them on their journey, and she agrees to do so, spends the night with them, and upon arising, asks where the three are going. She receives the answer that they are just going to see the country, but as they prepare to depart, the older brother strikes her on one side of the head with his club, and the younger follows suit, hitting her on the other side with his club, then taking her scalp. There were no underlying reasons for their action other than trickery and deceit, with death as the outcome. The gods continued on their travels until they eventually entered the ceremonial chamber of the ants, only to hear the dead woman's voice. The ghost woman was then invited into the chamber, where they clubbed her again and discarded her remains. The men next learned what they must do to not be bothered by the dead after taking an enemy scalp: "fast from animal food, grease, and salt for the period of ten days," a practice Zuni warriors historically followed after returning from war.[29]

Zunis and Hopis, like the Anasazi, made clubs and hand axes from wood and stone, then fastened the heads to a wooden shaft with hide or sinew. Clubs made of only wood or heavy elk antler have been found in Bullet Canyon, White

Canyon, and Allen Canyon in southeastern Utah, as have the remains of stone axe heads apparently used for war. These double-bitted axes were carefully crafted and do not show signs of heavy use for chopping wood.[30] While there is no record of how the Anasazi used these clubs in fighting, there is a historic account of Gila River Pima warfare that explains how shield and club came together in combat. The Pima divided their warriors into two groups: those armed with bows and arrows and those employing a shield two feet in diameter and a club that looked like a potato masher. Although all warriors carried a club, those equipped solely with one were considered the bravest and best because of the strictly hand-to-hand combat they engaged in.[31]

In 1933, historian Arthur Woodward interviewed Evanico, an old Pima warrior, who gave the following description of shield-and-club warfare.

> Desert fights were generally fought at close range, when the stubby war clubs and knives were brought into play. Shields were held at arm's length by a wooden handle. . . . Usually the warriors armed with such shields carried only knives or clubs. In a fight, the shield carriers leaped nimbly about, twisting the shield constantly until, seen from the front, the disk presented an illusion of colors, making it a difficult target and a distraction to an opposing bowman. . . .
>
> A warrior fighting with a knife or club at close quarters would never strike an overhand blow; it would have been too easy to block with the shield. A man always struck sideways and upwards. Such a blow would have come under the enemy's shield and hit the wrist or arm that carried the knife or club. That is a man's way of striking.[32]

The Mojaves and Maricopas used different techniques with a club, grabbing an enemy's hair, pulling his head down, and then either smashing the back of the head with a downward thrust or hitting the face with an upward blow. They would also throw an enemy over their shoulder so that a Mojave behind could strike his head.[33] The point to understand here is that there were different moves in striking a blow to kill an enemy, and as in European warfare, with its manual of maneuvers with a sword, there was just as much technique to learn and employ with a club.

A final advantage in using a club is that it is quiet. Many Puebloan stories tell of early dawn attacks while residents in a village were asleep. The wielded club has the advantage of being relatively noiseless so as to not awake others, easy to employ, and deadly in effectiveness on a prostrate body. The pre-dawn attack of

April 30, 1871, on a group of peaceful Apaches by ninety-four Papago Indians, forty-eight Mexicans, and six whites resulted in what is now called the Camp Grant Massacre. The husbands and fathers of this unsuspecting group were hunting and so had left all of the women and children and a handful of men behind. Within a half hour from the start, 125 Apaches died, mostly clubbed by the Papago. William H. Bailey, one of the attackers wrote, "Men, women, and dogs were clubbed. . . . Some Apaches that escaped the clubs of the Papagos tried to climb the side of the gulch. They were shot down by the Mexicans and Americans."[34] While the Papagos could have been armed with many different types of weapons, for this early morning attack, they preferred the club.

The results of fighting with a stone axe and club are preserved in the skeletal remains of the Anasazi dead. In the winter of 1893, Richard Wetherill, a rancher turned archaeologist, unearthed ninety-two skeletons from a primarily Basketmaker II site in Cave 7 in southeastern Utah. The mass grave, comprised mostly of mature males, offered concrete proof—many faces smashed at time of death, some with dart points in or among bones—bearing witness of violence. Other *atlatl* dart points were ceremonially arranged around the skeletons. Wetherill concluded that the site was the burial place of people involved in an intense battle or community massacre.

One hundred years later, Christy Turner re-examined sixty-one of these individuals and concluded that although there was serious breakage of arms, legs, and heads, it was the facial bones that sustained the most trauma. "Faces receive [sic] the most identifiable damage, and mutilation such as stabbing the face or smashing the mouth can sometimes be inferred. There are fragments 'blown out,' or ruptured, upper anterior tooth sockets, indicating heavy blows directly to the mouth region. . . . Stone tool cut marks occur most often on the head and suggest trophy taking of scalps, ears, and sometimes the entire head."[35] A more recent re-evaluation of the remains concludes that "[a] single-event mass killing [provides] the most likely interpretation for around 58 individuals, mostly adult males (at least 35) but also adult females and children. This incident occurred between cal. AD 20-80 . . . ."[36]

In terms of smashing craniums, removing heads, or scalping, one might ask if the findings in Cave 7 reflected typical Anasazi practices. Ethnologist Ernest Beaglehole, while interviewing Hopi informants, determined that "[s]calps were taken by any man, whether initiated warrior or not. At times the whole head was severed; usually the hair was held in the left hand and the scalp removed by cutting across the forehead, above the ears, and across the base of the skull."[37] There is every indication that this was a fairly common practice. A quick perusal of Turners' summary of research evaluating human remains gives additional proof that the club and stone ax were just what the Zuni called them: "face-pulpers." While the following list is not exhaustive, it gives an idea of what has been found in or adjacent to southeastern Utah. Take for example two bodies discovered on Alkali Ridge: one, an eighteen-year-old male, had his "right frontal region broken in, apparently by a blow from some heavy cutting instrument," and another, an older male, had "the left side of the head broken in. . . . Deeply stained scratches in a position indicative of scalping are also found." In Monument Valley there were seven bodies that sustained mutilating damage to the faces. At Green Mask Cave there was a woman's skull that had received a crushing blow both before and after death, with the same injuries sustained by an adult male in Red Canyon. At Kin Kletha near Navajo Mountain there was "an isolated skull (probably female). . . . The forehead of this skull had been bashed in, and there were two clear cut marks on the skull, one at the top and the other at the back." Most recently, excavations at Cowboy Wash, south of Sleeping Ute Mountain in southwestern Colorado, unearthed the remains of twenty-four men, women, and children, many of whom had their skulls crushed and heads removed.[38]

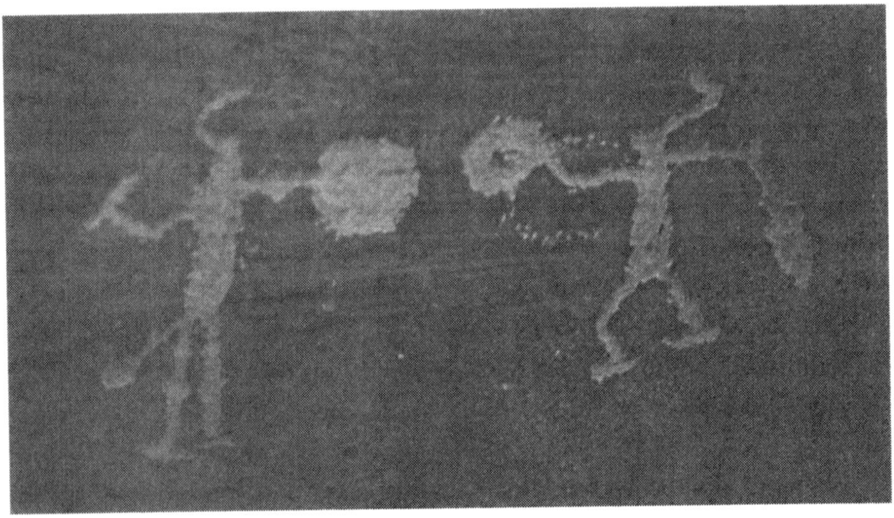

Fig. 2—This rock art image located in Chinle Wash, southeastern Utah, depicts two anthropomorphic warriors fighting with club and shield. While some people might consider a club the most primitive of weapons, historic accounts testify that as in dueling with swords, there were techniques and moves necessary for effective use. (Courtesy Sally Cole)

To better understand these practices—scalping, beheading, and "face-pulping"—one must turn to the traditional teachings of the people. The Hopi twins, for instance, watched a group of cannibalistic monsters (termed *So'yokos*) eat their own children. The twins killed them, then cut off the monsters' heads to show their grandmother. Just to give her a scare, each placed a head over their own. Once the grandmother got over the fright, she and the boys went to Oraibi, with the monsters' heads stuck on the end of their bows. The people of the village thanked the twins and took the two trophies, which they kept at Oraibi.[39]

The Zuni have a very similar tale of their twins, who killed the cannibal Atahsaia. They cut off his head, twirled it around, then cast it into the heavens, where it became the Great Lying Star that rises in the summer at midnight to suggest that morning is near when it is not. The twins used their great knife to disembowel the torso of Atahsaia and tossed his intestines into the air to become the Milky Way, then took the rest of his body and "threw it down into the chasm whither the old demon had thrown so many of his victims."[40] Before doing so, they had removed all the skin and made an effigy—somewhat like a puppet—with which to frighten their old grandmother. After being terribly scared then discovering the ruse, she berated the boys and departed. No one knows where. One wonders after reading the story if the disembowelment and tossing of the remains into the canyon does not in some ways parallel similar treatment of bodies found mutilated and dumped in kivas, later to be discovered by archaeologists.

An abbreviated version of a Hopi tale tells of a time when a group of runners from the village of Qa'ötaqtipu challenged the nearby village of Matsonpis to a race. Matsonpis won the event and peacefully took the presents offered for winning. The two villages held other races but feelings hardened, and eventually, the people at Matsonpis challenged their rival to select their best runner with the understanding that the loser would have to submit to having his head cut off. Through supernatural means, the Matsonpis runner won and without hesitation forced his opponent to lie down, then "grabbed him by the hair, pulled his head back, and cut it off."[41] Next ensued a series of events that culminated in the destruction and eventual evacuation of both villages. Jealousy and pride had resulted in warfare and death.

Another point raised by this story is what constitutes warfare as opposed to a single homicide. Does the killing of one individual or the skeletal remains of one or two people constitute warfare? Not necessarily, but it certainly might be the first act in a series that results in war. Revenge, grudges, and feuding serve as primary reasons for social conditions that intensify friction and result in open warfare. These feelings provide a common theme in many of the Hopi and Zuni stories, as found in the traditional teachings. Part of this is due to marriage relations and settlement patterns in which groups of kin live together. Villages often view themselves as single entities so that an affront against an individual is an affront against all. Witchcraft is as much a group action as an individual problem and so is handled on a number of social levels.

A second Hopi story tells of a hopeful lover from the village of Koechaptevela. The lover is rebuffed by the girl he wishes to marry from Sikyatki, and so he kills her. The girl's father enlists the aid of her brother, who orchestrates a race between villages. He successfully runs—after insisting that the winner gets the prize of cutting a lock of the loser's hair. This was not considered a polite or good thing to do, but everyone agreed to the terms. He continued to race and win, then cut hair from those he defeated, until the last race, which he also won. He vaulted into the crowd of spectators, made his way to the daughter of the Sikyatki chief, seized her hair whorls, cut off her head, then made his way to the edge of the pueblo roof "and waved her head to the people standing below."[42] Both villages were shocked and mourned the loss of one of their daughters, and although war was averted, the people of Sikyatki fell on hard times and eventually abandoned their homes.

All three of these stories involve scalping or beheading an enemy as a trophy: a means of expressing victory. There are yet other stories that have a similar motif. Elsie Clews Parson believed that the enemy who lost his scalp would, after being taunted and humiliated, return to his hair and became an adopted friend of the people who possessed it. The hair is "fed" and kept in a special home for care. Parson gives a lengthy list of who has this responsibility and where the trophy is housed in many of today's pueblos.[43] One of the most dramatic and well-documented of the incidents of beheading took place at Awat'ovi (to be discussed later).

Certainly, face-bashing, beheading, and scalping are very personal ways of appropriating an enemy's identity. While other body parts are important, the head—with its various functions—is the part of an identity most unique to an individual. Just how personal this becomes is illustrated in Hopi war practices. During their twenty-five-day victory ceremony and cleansing, warriors fashioned a bandoleer from an enemy breechcloth taken from the battlefield, whose material had been cut with a stone knife. The bandoleer, worn on the right shoulder, was loosely attached at the ends, so if an enemy were to tug on it, the attachment would come undone, and the enemy would fall over, so that "the Hopi warrior would close with him and split his head with the axe."[44] If the enemy had been valiant in his fight, he would be scalped, but if he were slow and cowardly, he was left alone. "During the twenty-five days of ceremony, the women took the scalps and scraped off, with their fingernails, shreds of the adhering flesh and gave these shreds to their male children to eat; they put the shreds in the mouths of the children, this to make them brave-hearted."[45]

The importance of obtaining a scalp is described by Frank Cushing with his initiation as a Zuni Bow Priest. He tells of passing through Apache country with some Zuni warriors in 1881. The group spotted tracks of horses and mules belonging to raiding Apaches, and so they went on alert. After making camp and acting as if all were normal, the men retired to bed at dusk, waited for their fire to die down, and then crawled away from camp and down an arroyo, only to circle back and wait in ambush. After a while, Apache fighters entered the camp and only too late discovered the ruse. The Zuni opened fire, killing one, whose scalp was all that Cushing needed "for [his] initiation into the Priesthood of the Bow or order of war magicians."[46] When the victors arrived home, they left the trophy outside of the pueblo but returned to it when the morning star appeared in the sky. Cushing and others were "dressed and painted as warriors, with skull caps of thick hide and cuirasses of doubled elk skins, bows, arrows, and shields, [they] silently stole out to the plain where my scalp lay. We went through all the manoeuvers of surprising the enemy, of offering hasty prayers, then shooting one of their number, finishing him with war clubs, and finally with elaborate rituals and ceremony taking his scalp, this time with flint [not metal] knives, with which we were provided."[47] After praying "through the favor of the Sun Father," Cushing took this "token of friendship," spent the day seated on a hill of fire ants, then in the evening bore the scalp into the pueblo on a wand to the cheers of its occupants. Next started an intense initiation process of sleeplessness, purification, pilgrimage, and meditation, which eventually culminated with his entrance into the society.

The causes for warfare among the Anasazi, as with those found amongst the historic Puebloans, were likely many and multifaceted. Whereas the more contemporary groups faced non-Puebloan enemies like the Apache, Navajo, Ute, and Comanche, there is no concrete proof of invasions or conflict with external groups during Anasazi times, although it still remains a possibility. More likely is friction amongst themselves as different Puebloans traveled on tribal migrations, then vied for territory with other groups. The migration stories of both the Hopi and Zuni are extensive, but a short example from the latter will suffice. In their creation story, the Zuni speak of the Bow Priests as their leaders, following the teachings of the twins, "whose breaths of destruction each one of them breathed in due part."[48] They traveled in "clan-lines" with the elder twin in the lead and the younger in the rear, serving as "shields of the people, makers and destroyers of pathways!" Those too lazy or unfit were left behind as the others traveled "from country to country [as the] priests and the keepers of the mysteries, with women and children in their midst . . . [as] the Bow-priests swept danger away."[49]

During these travels, the people encountered "great towns built in the heights," which in their poverty caused them to act "like fierce creatures of prey." War between the haves and have-nots ensued. "Great were the fields and possessions of this people for they knew how to command and carry the waters, bringing new soil; and this too without hail or rain. So, our ancients, hungry with long wandering for new food, were the more greedy and gave battle." At first the "dwellers in the mountains and cliffs" prevailed due to their supernatural powers that controlled the elements, but the tide of battle turned as the Zuni appealed to their gods, made bowstrings of yucca fiber unaffected by weather, and eventually "over-mastered" the town. There, they found survivors hiding in the kivas, covered with soot and "their own war magic." They adopted the survivors into the Black Corn clan and learned of these people's powers. After a respite, the Zuni divided in half and continued their migrations, some heading south and others north.[50]

Other causes for warfare are found in the stories previously discussed. Internal friction within a group of people, between villages, inside the same village, and between individuals led to jealousy, pride, revenge, witchcraft, and general social disintegration.[51] A fundamental concept underlying a need for peaceful, caring relations is embodied in the Hopi term *koyaanisqatsi*, generally glossed as social chaos. When these social conditions occur, respect for elders disappears, religious practices are forsaken, interpersonal friction ignites, love is gone, destructive competition reins, families fall apart, self-indulgence rules, and everything lapses into turmoil and chaos. A graphic example of this is provided in a Hopi description of what took place at Awat'ovi before its destruction (to be discussed later). In the description are most of the elements found in many narratives describing the social unrest that is characterized as *koyaanisqatsi* and caused by evil-doers or sorcerers.

> People began to change in their ways. There was no mutual respect any more. They were constantly arguing and fighting one another. People were

robbed of their food. A woman would be taking piki [wafer-thin bread] somewhere, only to have others snatch it away from her. No one had any concern for his fellow man. For all kinds of reasons people would get angry at each other. Men and boys would reach under the dresses of women and girls and rape them. People seemed to be blind to what they were doing. They got worse and worse. For example, if children encountered an old person relieving himself, they would smear excrement all over him. They showed no compassion for anyone. The leaders of the religious societies, too, grew increasingly negligent of their ceremonial duties. Everything was completely insane. The life the inhabitants of Awat'ovi were living was one of utter chaos. They were all pitted against each other. No one displayed any fondness for his fellow man.[52]

To the Hopi, this practice becomes embodied in a person who uses sorcery and witchcraft. Their name for a sorcerer or witch is *powaqa*, which carries with it the idea that he or she is either angry, jealous, and selfish enough to try to change that which is beneficial into something evil for his or her own purpose and pleasure, therefore disrupting harmony. Individual turns against individual, clan against clan, and village against village until problems erupt and peaceful relations shatter. Death and destruction follow. Albert Yava (Big Falling Snow), a Tewa who lived among the Hopi all his life, commented on a recurring theme in Hopi narratives where "the story, sorcery, and knowledge were sort of linked together. A sorcerer was supposed to know how to do things that ordinary people couldn't do. I suppose that in the old days they would have said that he was a man with powerful medicine."[53]

Whether conflict erupts inside or outside of a pueblo, the people have two choices: to fight within the village and use its walls and other characteristics for defense or to meet the enemy outside, preferably far beyond the town in which the women and children and food stores are located. Anasazi battlefields away from their dwellings are almost impossible to identify and reconstruct, since all that usually remains are the stone points, and those have mostly disappeared into private collections. On the other hand, fighting in and around dwellings is much easier to detect because of the ruins in which remains are found along with visible signs of combat. Both types of warfare, however, need to be considered.

Effectiveness of a particular tactic is based on knowing the characteristics and habits of the enemy. The sneak attack found in the ambush and raid is successful particularly when the opponent is unsuspecting and vulnerable. Snatching women and children when they go for water or are in the fields working on crops; ambushing men returning from a hunting trip or religious pilgrimage; and gaining entrance into a pueblo when its occupants are not expecting it all create vulnerability for those on the defense. These informal confrontations were probably some of the most effective means to gain women, booty, and food. Surprise for the attackers was crucial.

If the defending village knew of the approach of an enemy, it had to decide whether to engage in defensive warfare that depended on the military strength of their position or to keep the fighting away from home and seize the offensive. The Hopi combined religious means with physical force by challenging an approaching enemy away from the pueblo and drawing a line of corn pollen or meal across the trail.[54] If that did not intimidate the enemy, then a fight ensued. What that engagement might look like is provided by Yava. Exactly when this battle occurred is not given; the Utes, however, are mounted, and both sides are armed only with bows and arrows—no guns. Yava starts by pointing out that the Hopis of Walpi had been constantly raided by Utes, Apaches, Navajo, Comanches, and even other Hopi villages. The raiders seized food, women, and children, while many of the men died defending the village. The people were in desperate straits and so sent a message to the Tewa on the Rio Grande to come and join them, settle down, and help fight their battles. After much discussion and hesitation, a group of about 400 Tewa agreed to do so.

Once the new guests arrived, Walpi sent out a challenge to the Utes, who obligingly responded. The Tewas dispatched scouts, who detected the enemy camped at Black Mesa. The Tewa leader, Agaiotsay, decided to use "our tried and tested tactics" of dividing forces so that one group could fight in the front while the other hit the enemy from behind. He instructed, "Get the Ute leaders first. After that, watch to see who takes command then get him. Aim for the heart. If you can't get the man, get his horse."[55] The Tewa then split forces and used the terrain—one part moving behind boulders, the other walking and crawling down a wash—to complete the encirclement of the enemy. In front of the Tewa position were two brothers armed with bows and arrows. They shot and killed the Utes' war captain and then the one who took the captain's place. The Utes rushed forward on horseback to lance the hidden enemy, only to be knocked off their horses and killed by club-wielding Tewas. The Tewa force in the rear placed pressure on the Utes but was unable to complete the encirclement, allowing the enemy to escape behind some rocks. By the end of the fighting, only three Utes were alive.

The Tewa called a truce and received a promise that their opponents would not return to Walpi to bother its inhabitants. To seal the pledge, the surviving Ute spokesman gave his elk-horn bow to Agaiotsay. Later, the Tewa took scalps from the fallen and split the chests of the four bravest enemies and removed their hearts. They buried the hearts in a deep hole surrounded by stones, signifying the victory and the bravery of the men. They then returned to the Hopi and offered some of the scalps, which the Hopi declined. These scalps are still used during the Tewa-Hopi midwinter ceremonies. To further commemorate the battle: "Someone inscribed the record of the fight with the Utes on the cliff wall below. . . . There's a Tewa shield and a long row of marks indicating the number of Utes that were killed. Underneath that pictograph is another one referring to a battle the Tewas and Hopis had later against the Apaches."[56] The site of this inscription is important today for initiates of the One Horn Society, who go there to start part of their physical testing before being inducted.[57]

There are a number of important points derived from this example. First is the enlistment of the Tewa by the Hopi as warriors. Alliances with other villages and even other peoples are a common theme in many Hopi and Zuni stories that reach back to Anasazi times. For instance, the Kokop Clan (Firewood Clan) is one of the "ancient societies among the Hopi villages" that came from Jemez Pueblo and "after living for different periods of time at a variety of locations . . . settled permanently at Sikyatki during the fourteenth century."[58] These people asked to be accepted into Oraibi but were refused until they agreed to serve there as warriors. They went on to found the Warrior Society (Momtcit) and are connected to other clans by ceremonial observances tied to warfare.[59] Yava points out that much of this integration with different groups of Native Americans occurred during the time of migrating clans, or prehistoric times, associated with the Anasazi dispersal from the Four Corners region.[60]

Second are the tactics employed by the Tewa. Frank Secoy, in his study of changing military patterns of warfare on the Plains, describes the pre-horse/pre-gun era of Caddoan and Apache fighters as very similar to what Yava explained. Drawn up in line formation, massed infantry forces armed with bow and arrow, lance, and "especially the war club" operated in groups of up to one hundred men in a line formation with a concave middle. The longer and deeper the line, the greater the chances of closing its ends, encircling the enemy, and preventing a breakthrough. Mass or sheer manpower could be a deciding factor for both sides. As with the Tewa, "another variation consisted in dividing the force and making a succession of timed attacks. Several sections of the army would creep around the

Fig. 3—Jailhouse Ruin, a Pueblo III defensive position located in the Grand Gulch drainage, as photographed in 1891. The three circular forms painted on the rock above may represent protective shields. Accessible only by a ladder entering one controlled entrance, the three-and-a-half-foot-high wall enabled defenders to shoot arrows and drop rocks below on attackers. (Courtesy The Field Museum Neg. #CSA8017, Photographer F. E. Leeka)

enemy and lie hiding, waiting until the main force had fully engaged the entire enemy army before delivering an attack from the rear. Still another practice was to divide the force, usually into two bodies, and then make a simultaneous assault from different directions."[61] The Apache used similar tactics, starting with a barrage of arrows and followed by an attack with club and lance for shock effect, with ensuing hand-to-hand combat.[62] Once this took place, the battle's outcome was usually quickly decided.

A final point to consider is that of champion fighters. An example is found in the Tewa-Ute account, where two men were chosen to stand in front of all the others, representing their side. Perhaps the Utes did the same, since their leaders were easily spotted and killed during the battle. War leaders very well could have been selected for the purpose of challenging rivals from the enemy's side before the commencement of general hostilities. The "champion" would show his men exactly what was expected to triumph. This David-and-Goliath approach is very much in keeping with the combat leadership principle of "follow me."

As a segue from offensive to defensive warfare, a Navajo attack on Oraibi offers lessons for both. The Hopi received word that a large group of Navajos were making their way to the town for their usual purpose of seizing corn and sheep. The men made more arrows, put on their tough buckskin armor, set out across the mesa, then formed a skirmish line—some hidden behind rocks, and others in the open. After recognizing that their enemies were skillful horsemen who would probe the Hopis' line of defense, the war leader gave the following instructions: "When they are in range of your arrows, shoot. . . . If you cannot hit the riders, shoot at their horses. Let us hold fast here like a wall to protect Oraibi. Do not let them break through. If it seems they will overrun our position, fall back and form another wall. . . . We will meet them here. If they break through at this place we can fall back. If they break through at the village we have no place to go."[63]

When the Navajos saw that the Hopi were in a line that stretched from one cliff to another, their war chief and a small group of men rode out to them and fired a fusillade of arrows, then returned to the main body, all attacking together. The Hopi line, as well as those hidden behind the rocks, opened fire and successfully turned the Navajo charge. A second attempt was against one end of the line; a third one swept parallel to the Hopi line, the men being protected by their armor. Following more unsuccessful Navajo forays, the Hopis went in pursuit of their retreating enemy and chased them until, this time, the Navajos formed a battle line. At the end of the day, both sides withdrew, but during the night, the Navajos received reinforcements. The next day, they launched an attack from high ground, broke through the Hopi line, and made their way to Oraibi, where they proceeded to ransack half the village. The Hopi warriors returned to the village to find that half of it had been barricaded with logs to keep the Navajos out of the central plaza and prevent them from taking the other half while the Hopi women and children fled on back trails to places of safety. Oraibi warriors were on the housetops, firing arrows at the enemy and monitoring their advance. Because they were on this height, these were the only men to see the twin warrior gods chase out the enemy with lightning arrows that sounded like thunder. Navajo dead lay strewn over the battlefield, while those still living hastily retreated. Never again did the Navajo attack Oraibi. [64]

Looking at the defensive side of Anasazi warfare, archaeologists have found ruin after ruin that suggests concern with limiting enemy access, structuring the environment so that it favors defenders, and storing enough food and water to outlast a siege. Especially during times when warfare appears to have been endemic, the Anasazi employed a pattern within defensive structures that utilized techniques such as hilltop defenses; difficult-to-reach alcoves; tower structures around springs and at the heads of canyons; stockades and other types of defensive walls; clustering of populations; line-of-sight communication between homes or village clusters; restricted passageways into a site; firing loops within walls; and utilizing height to fight downward instead of upward.[65] It is interesting that the Zuni name for an outer village wall interprets as "cliff-face wall," hearkening back to a protective barrier "descriptive of the encircling rear wall of a cave village, [but which] continued to be applied to the rear but encircling or outside wall of a round town, and hence now designates even a straight outer wall of a village, whether at the front or the rear of the houses."[66] The name for the outer wall of a house, however, is different and simply signifies an adobe enclosure. This linguistic relic of the past, as well as the techniques and principles just mentioned, refer to elements of defense understood and applied by the Anasazi in southeastern Utah.

What does the ethnographic record say about the reason for defensive structures and the thinking behind them? Both the Hopi and Zuni readily admit to a bygone era where raids and ambushes were a common occurrence. Ekkehart Malotki, an expert in Hopi mythology, affirms that "[a] quick glance at the available corpus of Hopi folk tales reveals that cruelties, atrocities and death are among the most frequent themes and motifs encountered."[67] One Oraibi man put it this way: "We walk down into that valley to plant our corn. 'Perhaps an enemy will come and kill me while I am working in the valley,' I think. So while I am working, I look all around. I do not work very long; I come right back; then I sally down again. That is what I have to do all the time."[68]

When the Hopi Coyote, Fox, and Fire clans reached what they believed to be the end of their migration, they established a village named Sikyatki at the base of a cliff. The people prospered, and since this was before the Utes, the Paiutes, and the Navajos lived in the Southwest, the clans gave little thought to defending this large village. They soon realized their mistake:

> Sometimes strangers came to the edge of the cliffs above Sikyatki and shot arrows or hurled stones into the village. The people said, "We need a guard post on the top of the mesa to warn us of enemies." So they built another settlement up above on two large mounds that are still visible. They built houses and kivas there, and a little to the south where the finger of the mesa was very narrow, they built a wall extending from one edge to the other to give them security from the Koechaptevela [other Hopi] people. They cut steps in the cliff side also, so that they could go from the lower village to the upper without difficulty. Their guard post on the heights was called Koekuchomo. From that spot the whole valley to the east, the south, and the west could be seen. . . .
>
> [Sikyatki grew, becoming larger than their neighbors.] The people of Koechaptevela were uneasy about Sikyatki. Sometimes there were quarrels between villages over the springs, or about the gathering of firewood on the mesa top. And for a while the wall that the Sikyatki people had constructed across the narrow part of the mesa created hard feelings.[69]

As previously discussed, friction between the two rivals eventually resulted in Sikyatki departing the area: not because of military defeat but as a means of leaving their problems behind and joining the people at Oraibi.

The effectiveness of many Anasazi/Puebloan defensive positions under attack is part of the traditional teachings, as well as the historic record. When speaking of the cliff dwellings of the Mancos, San Juan, and other canyons of Utah, Colorado, and northern New Mexico, Cushing sees Zuni town structures and patterns as just an extension of what he encountered during his stay with these people. As for the Anasazi, he noted the shallow footholds and ledges that limited access into the ruins and the dwellings in the alcoves. He reported that small children were often placed in granaries at the back of these sites during attacks. "Thus the folk tales which modern Pueblos tell of children left in the granary rooms and surviving during the destruction or flight of their elders by subsisting on the scant store remaining therein (later to emerge—so the stories run—as great warriors-magicians and deliver their captive elders) are not wholly without foundation in the actual past of their ancestry."[70] These metaphoric stories most likely describe prehistoric events and justification for future retribution.[71]

Fig. 4—Many of the characteristics of a defensive position as described by the historic Hopi and Zuni are found in this Pueblo II–III site in Butler Wash. Entrance into the alcove can only be achieved by a twenty-foot ladder, while firing/observation ports in the stone-and-mud "cliff-face wall," as well as two painted shields (not visible), add to its protective qualities. Defenders had the advantage of "fighting down." (Courtesy University of Colorado, Comb Ridge Heritage Initiative Project)

During historic times, the defense of San Ildefonso Mesa gives a well-documented view of Puebloan techniques to keep the Spanish at bay during their reconquest of New Mexico. The following events took place during two weeks in March 1694, but the mesa "had been used as a temporary refuge and defensible site since remote times."[72] Certainly, the techniques and many of the events could as well have occurred with the Anasazi in an earlier period. On March 4, 1694, Governor Diego de Vargas, along with 115 Spanish soldiers and an unknown number of Indian auxiliaries from Pecos Pueblo, arrived at the base of two mesas known collectively as San Ildefonso Mesa. Atop the mesas were a collection of

Puebloan peoples, primarily Tewa, from Santa Clara, San Ildefonso, Jacona, Cuyamungue, and Pojoaque villages. All were ready to resist the invaders' demands to desert their defensive position, descend, and submit to Spanish control. In response, the Indians jeered from above, gave war cries, and insisted that many allies from surrounding tribes were on their way to assist the resistance. Vargas realized that due to the snow on the ground and the defensive positions, he could not assault the fortress. The Tewas, however, descended and attacked, then retired to the mesa tops, where they continued to send smoke signals to their allies. During the night, reinforcements arrived and ascended the mesa, bringing the number of defenders to an estimated 1,000. That morning, the Spanish prepared for a frontal assault up the main path of the mesa, while another group tried to distract the Tewa by going to the back side and ascending a smaller path. Defenders hurled river stones with slings, tossed rocks, shot arrows, and threw hooks. The attacking Spanish managed to capture the small mesa but could not cross over to the main one because the gap was protected by walls.[73]

As the fighting dragged on, Vargas had reason to be discouraged. During the first day, Spanish forces sustained twenty-two wounded and estimated the Puebloans had fourteen or fifteen killed. Later, a force of two hundred Indians descended on a prisoner-snatch foray that was foiled; the tracks of many Indians coming to assist meant further reinforcements, and the defenders had enough food and water to outlast the attackers. New walls and heightening older structures promised to make life more difficult for the Spaniards, and the employment of a dozen scaling ladders proved fruitless because the angle was too steep and the ground, unsolid. The defenders countered any close-in moves by hurling large slabs of rock or using their slings and arrows to keep the attackers at bay. After two weeks, Vargas stopped the siege and went back to Santa Fe.[74]

In April, the Spanish attacked the people of Cochiti on a nearby mesa and in a three-pronged night attack, achieved complete surprise and captured the village. The Spanish used similar tactics at Guadalupe Mesa but obtained only partial surprise. The conflict ended inside the pueblo with seventy Indians dying in battle, five burned in their houses, seven leaping to their death off the mesa, and two executed after the fight. In summarizing the pueblo defensive strategy, the author makes the following points:

1.) Alliances with different Indian groups was evident in each of the battles.
2.) Piled river stones along the rim of the mesas and defensive walls at key points were used to deny enemy forces access to key terrain.

3.) "For the warriors, the mesa was a base to return to and defend if necessary, but war was waged primarily on the offensive. The series of engagements at the mesas demonstrate the basics of Pueblo strategy very clearly: war was carried to the enemy."

4.) To do this, the Indians used ambushes, surprise attacks, and psychological warfare (depriving the attackers of sleep, communicating through smoke signals, and utilizing deception).

5.) Fleeing, when defending no longer appeared possible, was a final move, so as to return and fight another day.[75]

Another example of a highly defendable site is given by the Zuni at their Dowa Yalanne (Corn Mountain), which they occupied from 1680 to 1692. Capable of housing over 1,000 people, the village was built on a rock formation three hundred meters high, with only one main trail to the top and a few smaller, easily defended trails with walls to deny access. There were also piles of stones serving as ammunition stockpiles; three dammed reservoirs to catch snow and rain water; and a steep trail about which Diego de Vargas commented, "the way up being so difficult and long, I was forced, on account of its bad places, to mount it on foot and, although it cost considerable effort, I succeeded. . ."[76] Cushing agrees, calling it "the giddy trail by which the heights were scaled [protected by] archers' booths and heaps of sling stones and munitions of heavy rock."[77]

Off the mesa, the Zuni poisoned the springs to deny water to the Spanish and weaken their force. The Indians also employed the supernatural powers of the Great Shell as directed by the Shell's keeper. He and an assistant prepared medicine as the Spaniards struggled up Corn Mountain. When the two priests were ready, painted and bedecked with ceremonial feathers, they made their way to the rim of the mesa with a small shell in their mouths that held special medicine. After telling the people that they were not afraid, "they blew the shells containing the medicine toward the enemy, who were immediately affected by it. The enemy at first appeared to be intoxicated. One would try to catch the other as he fell, and then both would stagger and soon fall. Nearly the whole army was destroyed. The survivors retreated."[78] The Zuni did not descend from the mesa until they had an agreement they could live by.

Taking well-constructed defensive positions can be costly in terms of men, time, and resources. The best way to capture a fortified village is through surprise so that the defenders cannot bring their power to bear. That is why Hopi literature concerning the demise of a site often stresses that it was taken by surprise. For instance, a race between Coyote Boy and a young man he deemed to be a witch took place. Coyote Boy beat his competitor, slashed his throat, and cut off his head, angering the dead man's relatives from Sikyatki, who were also witches. Even their village chief realized that these evil people must go—the *koyaanisqatsi* was too great. The leader went to the village of Qöötsaptuvela and presented a plan. During a communal harvest, while the men were in the fields, the warriors from Qöötsaptuvela would enter the village and set it on fire. The plan worked. "When everybody who was going to participate in the harvest party had descended to the field, they [the enemy] rushed the village. In no time they were inside. Quickly they pulled the ladders out from the houses where the women and children were. Having accomplished that, they set everything on fire. Some of the warriors had come with pitch they had gathered. This they smeared on the walls of the houses; as a result they quickly caught fire."[79] When the men in the fields saw the smoke, they ran back but had no weapons with them and were quickly dispatched. The village of Sikyatki became just a ruin.

Another example of the destruction of a Hopi town centers around a man, Pitsinsivostiyo, who lost his wife to a lover from the village of Hovi'itstuyqa. The jilted husband went to the Kisisipaya people to the southwest, enlisted their aid, and told them that he wanted them to raid, then destroy the village for him. They could keep the women and girls, the food, and anything else they wanted. They could also kill all the men and boys but had to allow *him* to be the one to kill his rival lover. Four days later, the night attack of the entirely encircled village took place while all the residents slept. Pitsinsivostiyo killed his rival with an arrow to the chest, gave a war whoop (the pre-arranged signal for the attack), and the enemy swarmed through the village, easily killing its occupants before they could even reach their weapons. "The Kisisipayas had an easy time murdering them all. After the slaughter they entered the houses and started plundering the people's valuables."[80] They rounded up the women and departed for their land, having destroyed the village that today lies in ruins.

While the destruction of the above two villages took place during prehistoric times, that is not the case with Awat'ovi, a pueblo whose existence extends back to 500 AD and was destroyed in the 1700s. The ruin has 1,300 rooms, 25 kivas, and 2 Catholic churches, with a foundation for a third. Its population at the time of destruction is estimated at around 800.[81] While accounts emphasize different aspects of the event and details vary even among Hopi villages, most agree that during the reconquest of the 1690s, the Spanish once again exerted their force at the villagers' expense. Many of the Hopis at Awot'ovi willingly accepted their presence.

Remembering what life had been like before the invaders were expelled, many Hopi villages resisted any type of re-institution of European culture including the efforts of the Catholic Church. The people living at Awat'ovi, however, allowed the church's presence back in, causing both internal friction and external censure from neighboring villages. Albert Yava provides an insider's view when he says, "Young people were not paying much attention to the religious traditions and were getting out of hand. There was constant trouble between the traditionalists and the Catholics, who were in the majority. People were getting hurt. The Catholics were ridiculing and interfering with the Hopi religious ceremonies. The kikmongwi [village leader] saw that everything was falling apart, but he couldn't stop it. He decided that the only thing that could be done was to destroy the village and wipe the slate clean."[82] That is what happened. Ta'palo, the village leader responsible for his people's welfare, became so distraught at what he saw happening that he visited other Hopi villages and enlisted the assistance of warriors from Oraibi, Walpi, and Mishongnovi to launch a surprise attack and kill all of the men and others ripe for destruction, then parceled out the women, children, and farm lands to the victors.

Ta'palo felt the only thing he could do to stop the wickedness was to have his people, as well as himself, killed. While some of the other Hopi leaders refused to participate, he was able to get enough warriors from the three villages to launch a surprise raid to end the debauchery. On the evening of the fourth day after all had agreed, the attackers moved near the village, hid amidst the boulders, and waited for a signal to attack after all were asleep. While waiting, "some sharpened the points of their arrows, others the blades of their stone axes. They made sure their gear was tight and strong. Dressing for battle, they painted their faces, putting red ocher along their eyes above the nose. From the nose down across both cheeks they drew lines with black hematite [black mineral powder]. Next, to be more powerful they tied white eagle plumes in their hair. Now they would be light of weight and would be able to run with great speed in pursuit of the enemy. By the same token, these plumes would ensure they would not tire easily."[83]

At first light, Ta'palo went by his kiva and signaled with his blanket for the attack to begin, then waited to be tossed into a kiva to be killed. Since this was the beginning of Wuwtsim, an important Hopi ceremony, the men and boys were sleeping in the kivas. The attackers went from kiva to kiva, pulling up the ladders so that there would be no escape, then lit finely shredded juniper bark and greasewood as kindling and tossed it into the ceremonial chambers, setting stacks of wood near the kiva doors aflame and pushing them in too. Finally, they took dry chili peppers hanging on the walls, crushed them, threw them in to add to the stinging smoke, and sealed the hatchway. The occupants had been caught totally by surprise, had no weapons, and soon died. The roof beams caught fire and collapsed on top of the bodies beneath. The raiders next went from house to house gathering the women and killing any men in hiding, while another group went to the mesa's edge to ensure no one escaped. Those caught were either shot or tossed over the cliff. All of the structures were then burned and the women herded off.

A small group of men and boys in hiding escaped. When the enemy left, they went through the smoldering ruins, obtained weapons, then went in pursuit of the captive women. They fought bravely but were all killed, their heads cut off and placed in a pile at a site known today as "Skull." Soon, a conflict arose amongst the victors as to who got to keep the women and girls. All three groups entered into the argument and finally decided to kill all female captives, since no one could agree. "No sooner had this been proposed than they started slaughtering the women and girls. They would just grab one and kill her any old way, either stabbing her or shooting her."[84] Others were mutilated as they begged for their lives and later left behind. This place is known today as "Death Mound." Some claimed to have rain-making power or special skills and so were spared. Eventually, the slaughter stopped, and the remaining prisoners were divided evenly amongst the three groups. The next day, a group of warriors returned to Awat'ovi to ensure that nothing remained of the village. Homes were torched and toppled, pots smashed, metates broken, and everything flammable set on fire. "The ruin was to stay the way it was. Being that way, they wanted no trace of it to be left. This had been the village leader's express wish. Ta'palo had, of course, lost his life together with the others."[85]

While much of the above is unpleasant, it is historically, ethnographically, and archaeologically documented.[86] Anasazi sites in southeastern Utah and neighboring states also have domestic sites that show the effects of warfare. Remains in Monument Valley, along the San Juan River, on Cedar Mesa, in Cottonwood Wash, and Alkali Ridge to name a few; a half dozen sites in La Plata, Sand Canyon, Castle Rock, and Mesa Verde in southwestern Colorado; as well as others in northwestern New Mexico and northeastern Arizona all show the concern and effects of warfare.[87] There is no missing the fact that whether offensive or defensive, warfare was an important consideration for the Anasazi, dictating how they lived, where they established their homes, and their daily activities.

Warfare as an expression of culture is fought in cultural terms, embodies cultural ideals, is technologically couched in cultural values, and is a function of time and place. The Anasazi were a gifted people who followed the examples provided by their gods while successfully living in a difficult landscape for hundreds and hundreds of years. But like all humans, problems arose, aggression followed, and whole communities were devastated. Abandonment of southeastern Utah, along with its sites, was the result. Today, all that is left to tell the Anasazi's story are the remains and material culture for the archaeologists to interpret, along with the teachings, ceremonies, and recorded statements from the elders who remembered. The rest is gone.

Chapter Endnotes

1. Steven A. LeBlanc, *Prehistoric Warfare in the American Southwest* (Salt Lake City: University of Utah, 1999).
2. Ibid., p. 195.
3. Donna M. Glowacki, *Living and Leaving: A Social History of Regional Depopulation in Thirteenth-Century Mesa Verde* (Tucson: University of Arizona, 2015), pp. 210–211.
4. Christy G. Turner, II and Jacqueline A. Turner, *Man Corn: Cannibalism and Violence in the Prehistoric American Southwest* (Salt Lake City: University of Utah, 1999).
5. For an extensive evaluation of what the Turners did and did not accomplish, see William H. Walker, "Witches, Practice, and the Context of Pueblo Cannibalism" in Deborah L. Nichols and Patricia L. Crown (editors), *Social Violence in the Prehistoric American Southwest* (Tucson: University of Arizona Press, 2008), pp. 143–183.
6. Deni J. Seymour, *A Fateful Day in 1698: The Remarkable Sobaipuri-O'odham Victory over the Apaches and Their Allies* (Salt Lake City: University of Utah Press, 2014).
7. Discussion of war and the powers and responsibilities for waging it are centered on the Hopi and Zuni in this chapter. Comparable institutions are found in other Puebloan groups. Elsie Clews Parson writes: "For the control of enemies, including witches, [there are] War society of Zuni and Scalp chiefs, male and female, and, of course, the societies that cure bewitchment, War chief and society of Hopi, War or Under chief and society of scalp takers of Keres, Jemez, and Hopi, Scalp chief of Tewa (San Juan) and women assistants or War society, War chief of the Cane and Scalp chief with men and women helpers of Isleta, and throughout the East and at Acoma and Laguna the annual War captains." Elsie Clews Parson, *Pueblo Indian Religion*, Vol. I (Lincoln: University of Nebraska Press, 1939, 1966), p. 115. See also pp. 124–126.
8. For a discussion of the etymology of the term *Anasazi* and the use of the word *Hisatsinom*, see Robert S. McPherson, *Viewing the Ancestors: Perceptions of the Anaasazi, Mokwi , and Hisatsinom* (Norman: University of Oklahoma Press, 2014), pp. 15–17.
9. Frank Hamilton Cushing, *Outlines of Zuni Creation Myths*, Thirteenth Annual Report of the Bureau of Ethnology, 1891-92 (Washington: Government Printing Office, 1896), pp. 375–376.
10. Ekkehart Malotki and Michael Lomatuway'ma, *Maasaw: Profile of a Hopi God* (Lincoln: University of Nebraska Press, 1987), pp. 155–156.
11. Ibid., pp. 156–159.
12. Ibid., p. 161.
13. Ibid., p. 164.
14. Elsie Clews Parson, *Pueblo Indian Religion*, p. 106.
15. For an overview of the role of the twins in various Puebloan groups, see Hamilton A. Tyler, *Pueblo Gods and Myths* (Norman: University of Oklahoma Press, 1964), pp. 209–220.
16. Matilda Coxe Stevenson, *The Zuni Indians*, Twenty-third Annual Report of the Bureau of American Ethnology, 1901-1902 (reprinted Glorieta, New Mexico: Rio Grande Press, 1970), pp. 580–581.
17. Ibid., pp. 593–594.
18. Ibid., pp. 587 and 590.
19. Ibid., p. 602.
20. Cushing, *Outlines of Zuni Creation Myths*, pp. 422–423.
21. Ernest Beaglehole, "Notes on Hopi Warfare," in *Memoirs Series of the American Anthropological Association*, 44 (Washington: Government Printing Office, 1935), pp. 17–24.
22. Ibid., p. 20.
23. Frank Raymond Secoy, *Changing Military Patterns on the Great Plains, 17th Century Through Early 19th Century* (Seattle: University of Washington Press, 1953), pp. 16–17.
24. Cushing, *Outlines of Zuni Creation Myths*, p. 358.
25. Barton Wright, *Pueblo Shields from the Fred Harvey Fine Arts Collection* (Flagstaff, AZ: Northland Press, 1976), pp. 2–12.

26. Frank Russell, *The Pima Indians* (Tucson: University of Arizona Press, 1908, 1975), p. 120.
27. Glen E. Rice and Steven A. LeBlanc (editors), *Deadly Landscapes: Case Studies in Prehistoric Southwestern Warfare* (Salt Lake City: University of Utah Press, 2001), p. 83.
28. Cushing, *Outlines of Zuni Creation Myths*, pp. 358–359.
29. Stevenson, *The Zuni Indians*, pp. 49–50.
30. LeBlanc, *Prehistoric Warfare*, pp. 112–113.
31. Clifton B. Kroeber and Bernard L. Fontana, *Massacre on the Gila: An Account of the Last Major Battle Between American Indians, with Reflections on the Origin of War* (Tucson: University of Arizona Press, 1986), p. 79.
32. Ibid., pp. 87–88.
33. Ibid., p. 83.
34. William H. Bailey, cited in James L. Haley, *Apaches: A History and Culture Portrait* (Norman: University of Oklahoma Press, 1981, 1997), p. 259.
35. Turner and Turner, *Man Corn*, p. 65.
36. Phil R. Geib and Winston B. Hurst, "Should Dates Trump Context? Evaluation of the Cave 7 Skeletal Assemblage Radiocarbon Dates," *Journal of Archaeological Science* 40 (2013), p. 2754.
37. Beaglehole, "Notes on Hopi Warfare," p. 23.
38. Turner and Turner, *Man Corn*, pp. 158, 254, 397, and 336. For Cowboy Wash, see Brian R. Billman, "An Outbreak of Violence and Raiding in the Central Mesa Verde Region in the 12th Century AD," in Nichols and Crown, *Social Violence*, pp. 41–68.
39. Ekkehart Malotki, *Hopitutuwutsi: Hopi Tales—A Bilingual Collection of Hopi Indian Stories* (Flagstaff: Museum of Northern Arizona, 1978), pp. 17–19.
40. Cushing, *Zuni: Selected Writings of Frank Hamilton Cushing* (Lincoln: University of Nebraska Press, 1979), p. 402.
41. Malotki, *Hopi Tales of Destruction* (Lincoln: University of Nebraska Press, 2002), p. 31.
42. Harold Courlander, *The Fourth World of the Hopi: The Epic Story of the Hopi Indians as Preserved in Their Legends and Traditions* (Albuquerque: University of New Mexico Press, 1971), pp. 123–124.
43. "Formerly at Acoma the Scalp-takers fed the Scalps wafer-bread and stew of rabbit or deer meat, and gave them water. Had the Scalps become hungry or thirsty, sickness or grasshopper plagues would have devastated the town. At Santo Domingo the Scalps are fed daily and given a smoke in a house in charge of a Flint society man. The San Felipe Town chief feeds the Scalps in his ceremonial house. The Nambe Scalps are kept in the house of the chief of the Winter People, but the San Juan Scalps are kept in the house of the woman war chief, whence they are brought out at an initiation into her society. At Hano, too, scalps were probably kept in the War chief's house, his maternal house; it was his child. (The Scalps are also called children at Santo Domingo. 'My niece' the Zuni Scalp chief calls the Scalp.) At Walpi the Scalps are kept in a cliff crevice, like the Hopi dead. Laguna Scalps were similarly kept in a cave. Isletan and Taos Scalps are kept in a kiva and offered pollen, meal, and red pigment, and Taos Scalps are painted red inside. A painted skull was found at Hawikuh. Two Hopi skulls marking the Hopi-Navaho boundary were daubed with red by passing Hopi or Navaho. . . .

"It is believed in Isleta that their Navaho Scalps talk and cry, sometimes very noisily. Taos Scalps give warning of an approaching enemy. Tewa Scalps are called Mist or Light Rain and foretell precipitation. People say, 'We are going to have a little rain, the Scalps are crying.' Zuni Scalps also foretell through omens 'how the world will be, how the days will be'; they are water and seed beings bestowing waters, seeds, wealth, longevity, power, and strong spirit. First Mesa Scalps were also water beings, since, in welcoming the returning war party, the cloud and rain sign was made on the trail by the Town chief and on it the women cast the scalps, all this three times before the final cast down the hatchway of Chief kiva. . . . Throughout Pueblo tales or myths, heads, not scalps, are referred to in killing or fighting episodes. Inferably scalp-taking is a later trait, an overlay on head-taking" (Parson, *Pueblo Indian Religion*, pp. 350–352).

44. Alexander M. Stephens, "Hopi Journal," Elsie Clews Parsons (editor), *Columbia University Contributions to Anthropology* 23 (1936), p. 98.
45. Ibid., p. 99.
46. Cushing, *Zuni*, pp. 154–155.
47. Ibid., p. 155.
48. Cushing, *Outlines of Zuni Creation Myths*, p. 424. For a longer version of this battle, see Stevenson, *The Zuni Indians*, pp. 36–39.
49. Ibid.
50. Ibid., pp. 425–426.
51. For example, Albert Yava provides a list of Hopi villages that were disrupted because of internal friction. "The people of Sikyatki had to go away because of evil things that had occurred, and because of enmity with Keuchaptevela, the old Walpi. The chief of Awat'ovi asked that his village be destroyed by the other villages because his people had lost respect for their spiritual traditions and had become undisciplined and ungovernable. The Snake Clan had to leave Tokonave because of friction with other people in the village. The chief of Pivanhonkapi had his village destroyed because, as in the case of Awat'ovi, the people had turned away from decent living. The Payupkis abandoned their village because of quarrels with nearby Tsikuvi. Oraibi was broken in two by dissension, so the Fire Clan and the Water Coyotes had to go away and build new villages" (Albert Yava, *Big Falling Snow: A Tewa-Hopi Indian's Life and Times and the History and Traditions of His People*, Harold Courlander (editor) (New York: Crown Publishers, Inc., 1978), pp. 37–38.
52. Ekkehart Malotki (editor), with Michael Lomatuway'ma, Lorena Lomatuway'ma, and Sidney Namingha, Jr. (as narrators), *Hopi Ruin Legends, Kiqötutuwutsi* (Lincoln: University of Nebraska Press, 1993), p. 341.
53. Yava, *Big Falling Snow*, p. 41.
54. Beaglehole, "Notes on Hopi Warfare," p. 22.
55. Yava, *Big Falling Snow*, p. 29. See also Courlander, *The Fourth World of the Hopi*, pp. 164–174.
56. Ibid., p. 33.
57. Ibid., p. 77.
58. Harry C. James, *Pages from Hopi History* (Tucson: University of Arizona Press, 1974), p. 25.
59. Ibid., pp. 26–27.
60. Yava, *Big Falling Snow*, p. 82.
61. Secoy, *Changing Military Patterns*, pp. 10–11.
62. Ibid., pp. 26 and 34.
63. Courlander, *The Fourth World of the Hopi*, pp. 186–187.
64. Ibid., pp. 188–190.
65. For a lengthy discussion of defensive archaeological sites, changes over time in sites and techniques, and arguments as to why these sites should be considered defensive, see Steven LeBlanc, *Prehistoric Warfare in the American Southwest* (Salt Lake City: University of Utah Press, 2007).
66. Cushing, *Outlines of Zuni Creation Myths*, p. 359.
67. Malotki, *Hopitutuwutsi: Hopi Tales*, p. xvii.
68. Parson, *Pueblo Indian Religion*, p. 30.
69. Courlander, *The Fourth World of the Hopi*, pp. 118–119.
70. Cushing, *Outlines of Zuni Creation Myths*, p. 350.
71. For additional information about ancient warfare in the Southwest beyond the Anasazi, see John R. Welch and Todd Bostwick (editors), *The Archaeology of Ancient Tactical Sites*, Arizona Archaeological Council Paper 32 (Tempe, Arizona: Arizona Archaeological Society, 2001).
72. Rick Hendricks, "Pueblo-Spanish Warfare in Seventeenth Century New Mexico: The Battles of Black Mesa, Kotyiti, and Astialakwa," in Robert W. Preucel (editor), *Archaeologies of the Pueblo Revolt: Identity, Meaning, and Renewal in the Pueblo World* (Albuquerque: University of New Mexico Press, 2002), p. 184.
73. Ibid., p. 187.

74. Ibid., pp. 187–188.
75. Ibid., p. 196.
76. T. J. Ferguson, "Dowa Yalanne: The Architecture of Zuni Resistance and Social Change during the Pueblo Revolt," in Preucel, *Archaeologies of the Pueblo Revolt*, p. 40.
77. Cushing, *Outlines of Zuni Creation Myths*, p. 331.
78. Stevenson, *The Zuni Indians*, p. 288.
79. Malotki, *Hopi Tales of Destruction*, p. 68.
80. Ibid., p. 119.
81. Malotki, *Hopi Tales of Destruction*, pp. 126–27.
82. Yava, *A Tewa-Hopi Indian's Life*, p. 91.
83. Malotki, *Hopi Tales of Destruction*, p. 186.
84. Ibid., p. 188.
85. Ibid., p. 189.
86. For different perspectives, see also Yava, *Big Falling Snow*, pp. 89–94; Courlander, *The Fourth World of the Hopi*, pp. 175–184; Turner and Turner, *Man Corn*, pp. 67–78; Peter Whiteley, "Re-imaging Awat'ovi," in Preucel, *Archaeologies of the Pueblo Revolt*, pp. 147–166; and Harold Courlander, *Hopi Voices, Recollections, Traditions, and Narratives of the Hopi Indians* (Albuquerque: University of New Mexico Press, 1982), pp. 55–60.
87. See *Man Corn* for a concise list of victims of warfare as of the turn of this century. Other studies include: Jonathan Haas and Winifred Creamer, *Stress and Warfare Among the Kayenta Anasazi of the Thirteenth Century AD,* Fieldiana Anthropology New Series 1450 (Chicago: Field Museum of Natural History, 1993); Glen E. Rice and Steven A. LeBlanc (editors), *Deadly Landscapes: Case Studies in Prehistoric Southwestern Warfare* (Salt Lake City: University of Utah Press, 2001); David Grant Noble, *The Mesa Verde World: Explorations in Ancestral Pueblo Archaeology* (Santa Fe: School of American Research Press, 2006); Brian R. Billman, "An Outbreak of Violence and Raiding in the Central Mesa Verde Region in the 12th Century AD," in Nichols and Crown, *Social Violence*; and Kristin A. Kuckelman, "Catalysts of the Thirteenth-Century Depopulation of Sand Canyon Pueblo and the Central Mesa Verde Region," in Timothy A. Kohler, Mark D. Varien, and Aaron M. Wright (editors), *Leaving Mesa Verde: Peril and Change in the Thirteenth-Century Southwest* (Tucson: University of Arizona Press, 2010).

CHAPTER TWO

Ute and Navajo Modes of Warfare
Culture and Environment as Determinants

The Anasazi departure from southeastern Utah and the greater San Juan River drainage created a vacuum of space eventually filled by two historic groups: the Utes and Navajos. These two very different tribes shared the same environment of the Colorado Plateau but lived very dissimilar lifestyles, spoke different languages, and were often at war with each other. Many of the following chapters are about specific events involving them and how each responded to a state of conflict. In this chapter, however, a broad approach is taken that examines general cultural principles of war-making. The Utes, following a brief introduction, will help the reader understand how this far-flung tribe adapted to the environment and developed tactics used to engage their enemy. The second part of this chapter will look at the role of traditional teachings in defining how the Navajo approached war. No Native American group has a more robust, vivid body of mythology than this people, whose war-making ability hearkens directly back to the stories from the creation of the world. Resulting practices are still in effect today.

As with the previous chapter on the Anasazi, there is an extensive literature on the Utes, but the primary focus here is on waging war.[1] The Utes covered a vast geographic area that included two-thirds of the states of Utah and Colorado, as well as the southern part of Wyoming and the northern part of New Mexico, along with a small portion of northeastern Arizona. Ute bands include Pahvant, Moanunt, Sanpits, Timpanogots, Uintah, and Seuvarits living in Utah; Yampa, Parianuche, Sabuagana, Tabeguache, and Muache in Colorado; with Capote in southern Colorado and northern New Mexico; and the Weeminuche split between southwestern Colorado and southeastern Utah. Today, the latter three groups are classified by anthropologists as Southern Utes and the rest as Northern Utes.

While there are small, specific differences between the two, for this discussion on warfare the categories of Northern and Southern Utes are merged. Although groups to the east availed themselves of the rich buffalo herds on the Plains and lived a more Plains Indian existence—a horse-riding, tepee-living, buffalo-hunting, warrior-oriented lifestyle—those to the west of these groups followed similar, but altered patterns. For instance, tepees made of buffalo hide to the east were made from deer and elk hide to the west. In some cases, Northern Ute sources are included here when looking at techniques of warfare, since only "slight differences exist between the groups [Northern and Southern Utes] in social and political organization, whereas almost no differences exist in ceremonial organization, and in measures of shamanism they are virtually identical."[2] In the same respect, the general-use areas mentioned above are not rigid in identifying most Ute bands, since all of them were highly mobile: a necessary aspect of their annual food quest. Many groups traveled hundreds and hundreds of miles each year in a cycle that took them to various seasonal hunting, fishing, and plant-collecting areas.

A final caveat is that there is no attempt here to examine the convoluted history of Ute alliances with other Native American groups or the Spanish and Euro-Americans. Later chapters will focus on the Southern Utes—specifically the Weeminuche and their close associate the San Juan band of Paiute—in greater detail by looking at the record from a more historical perspective. Here, a more cultural foundation is laid. Specialists still debate as to when these people arrived in the Four Corners region. The long-held conventional wisdom of archaeologists concerned with the Numic people suggests the possibility of a number of "waves" of migration. Most scholars agree that the initial starting point for this divisive splitting was in the area of Death Valley in southern California. Approximately 3,000 to 5,000 years ago, members of the large Uto-Aztecan language family started to subdivide into nine smaller groups. Numic speakers composed one of these divisions that include today's Utes and Paiutes. Fanning out from southern California, they moved in a northeasterly direction but remained on the edge of the Great Basin until about 1,000 years ago, when they entered rapidly into the Basin, then onto the Colorado Plateau.[3] Their language became increasingly diversified as groups split from each other, with one linguist suggesting that the Utes separated from the Southern Paiutes 400 years ago as they settled in the Four Corners region.[4]

Robert Euler, a noted Paiute historian, believes there were two migrations of Numic speakers into Nevada and Utah. The first one took place around the beginning of the Christian era, with the second taking place more than 1,000 years later, around 1150 AD (though others suggest the 1300s).[5] Some scholars argue that the Utes and Paiutes were not even in the region at this time. One explanation of migratory trends places Numic speakers in southwestern Utah some 440 years ago (about 1560 AD), in southeastern Utah and southwestern Colorado 370 years ago, moving along the Rio Grande 330 years ago, and out onto the Great Plains—their easternmost expansion—some 300 years ago.[6] Still others argue that they arrived in their present location 10,000 years ago and have remained there since.[7] This type of variance is to be expected when there are few material remains to be dated.[8]

For our purposes, the single most important cultural event is the introduction of the horse to the Utes during the historic period. In the previous chapter, Puebloan "ground" warfare provided an understanding of how Native Americans fought on foot. With horses magnifying some practices and eliminating others, lengthening the distance of travel, and increasing contact with both friend and foe, the Utes readily adapted to the changing circumstances. The Spanish introduced the horse to the Americas in the early 1500s; the Southern Utes, in constant contact with settlements at Taos and Espanola, New Mexico, were among the first to become fully mounted, with some scholars suggesting as early as 1640.[9] Other bands to the north and west did not have a real opportunity to adopt them until much later, the first documented instance being 1692.[10] When the Weeminuche were fully mounted on horses is open for debate. Some archaeologists believe that since they were the farthest Ute band to the west, this did not occur until the mid-to-late eighteenth century.[11] Until that time, dogs continued to pull small *travois* to carry loads. The shift to an equestrian lifestyle brought the Utes into the nineteenth century. This is not to suggest they became a part of the full-blown Plains Indian complex. As anthropologist Ann Smith points out, "The true picture is that of one people with a basically Basin culture, with a veneer of Plains culture in Colorado, which becomes thinner (and more recent) as you move from the Southern Ute bands to the White River and on over into Utah."[12] Still, the horse allowed larger groups to come together temporarily for seasonal economic and military purposes. On the other hand, forage for horses limited the time the Utes could remain together, especially as their herds expanded later in the nineteenth century.

Although the Plains may be where some of the Ute bands conducted business, collectively most of these people thought of themselves as "mountain" Indians. When one looks at their entire homeland, mountain ranges (with their resources) provided a critical part of the Ute economy. For many groups, deer were the "buffalo" of the mountain Indian; plants at higher elevations were in greater variety for specific uses; cooler temperatures gave a break from oppressive summer heat; and with winter camps in the lower elevations and summer camps in the higher, the land rested from resource depletion. From the aspect of warfare, mountains proved to be a formidable defense. They served as a protective bulwark against invaders, even for those living in the Great Basin or venturing onto the Plains. In Colorado, the Front Range of the Rocky Mountains, San Juan, and Sangre de Cristo ranges all became familiar refuges for Utes pursued by enemies, as did the Wasatch and Uintah ranges in Utah, to name a few. Monoliths such as Sleeping Ute Mountain in Colorado, Blue (Abajo) Mountain, the La Sal Mountains, Navajo Mountain, and Henry Mountain in Utah all comprised an important part of the network of mountains and canyons of the Colorado Plateau. Edward Dutchie, a White Mesa Ute, explained the significance of all the mountains to the Ute people. "They called themselves the mountain people or mountain Utes. The highest peaks were where they would go to out-run any tribe during the fighting days—head for the peaks and fight down from there. That's why the peaks are very important. On foot, white men could not run to the peaks like the Utes could."[13] In 1882, Colonel Richard I. Dodge wrote of the Utes, "All the powerful Plains tribes, though holding them in utter contempt on the Plains, have absolute terror of them in the mountains."[14]

Utes involved in ambushes, raids, and horse-stealing sought sanctuary in their familiar homeland where mountains and canyons created hardship and increased danger for pursuers. An example of what a good ally the mountains were is told by the Cheyenne. A party of twenty-eight warriors left the South Platte River on foot to steal horses in Ute country. After three days they arrived in South Park, Colorado, where they found fresh signs of a small Ute encampment close by. Snow began to fall and did not stop until the third day. The Cheyenne had no food, the snow was deep, and the prospect of stealing Ute horses had disappeared. They tried to break their way through the deep snow but tired and returned to camp. The men unraveled their rawhide lariats, cut limbs from a clump of cherry bushes, and fashioned snowshoes. Travel out of the mountains was arduous; for eighteen days they ate only rosebuds they found sticking out of the snow. Slowly their luck changed; a porcupine here, a couple of rabbits there, a wildcat, and two turkeys all provided limited sustenance. A windfall of nine turkeys on the twenty-first day gave them enough energy to locate a white man for assistance to return home. As for the Utes whom the Cheyenne had wanted to attack, they remained oblivious to the encroaching danger, protected in their mountain stronghold.[15]

The Cheyenne were not the only traditional enemy of the Utes. The Arapaho, Blackfoot, Navajo, Apache, and (at times) Comanche and Shoshone also raided the Utes for horses, captives, and war honors. The Utes exchanged Paiute women and children in a slave trade with the Spanish, Mexicans, and to a lesser extent, some Americans. That continued from the 1600s until its final gasps in the 1860s.[16] Winter camps were particularly secure, since the mountains to the east served as a barrier; friendly Shoshone-Bannocks occupied lands to the north of Utah; and to the west, small groups of weaker Paiute and Gosiute people presented no threat.[17] In each instance, the security of the Utes' relatively small bands depended on wise use of the terrain, an understanding of their enemies' capability, and the cultural values embodied in their own teachings.

Fig. 5—Introduction of the horse changed the conduct of life for the Utes. Warren A. Ferris, a veteran trapper intimately familiar with nineteenth-century Indian tribes on the Plains and in the Rocky Mountains, considered the Utes "by far the most expert horsemen in the mountains, [as the men] course down the steep sides in pursuit of deer and elk at full speed, over places where a white man would dismount and lead his horse." (Used by permission, Utah State Historical Society)

One of those important teachings involves the Shin-au-av brothers: Shin-au-av pa-vits was the elder, and Shin-au-av skaits was the younger.[18] Earlier in this narrative cycle, the younger became miffed at the elder's decision to have death as a permanent, no-return event. To show the folly in this decree, the younger killed the elder's son, then fled to their father, Tov-wots, to avoid the wrath of his brother. To protect the younger, the father gave him "a champion to fight his battles" and an antelope with many eyes that could detect an approaching enemy. The elder brother brooded over what had happened and wanted revenge on the younger brother who, with his people, was camped on the opposite side of the mountain from the elder with *his* following. On top rested the champion, wearing his protective stone shirt and depending on his vigilant antelope for early warning. One dawn, the elder set out for battle, "[making] his way among the rocks, creeping over the open spaces, determined to surprise the great champion." But the sentry detected the movement, and the fight began. The battle raged until noon, with the champion unscathed until he was able to slay the elder. "Then the conquerors went down in the valley; and when the people heard the tiding there was great rejoicing; and they sang the war song, and danced the war dance."[19]

The father warned the victors that the enemy would return and so insisted the champion and his antelope go back to the summit. The next day, the elder brother (who had obviously overcome the permanency of death) returned with his people and this time, instead of arrows, fought with spears. As before, he was killed, and his group was defeated. His opponents went to the valley rejoicing. The next day, similar events occurred; this time they fought with knives, and again they defeated the elder brother. All of this was exhausting for the antelope, who became so tired that they fell asleep and failed to warn the champion. The elder brother successfully killed the champion on top of the mountain because "there was no one to give warning. . . . Then the [elder brother] rallied his men and they poured over the side of the mountain, down into the camp of the [younger brother] and there was a terrible slaughter. Many were killed and many fled, and thereafter the younger brother never rallied to meet the elder in battle again."[20]

While this story could be interpreted as a metaphor concerning the divisions among Numic speakers—such as the Utes, Shoshone, Comanche, and Paiute—with their internecine conflict, there are also a number of points that illustrate how the Utes waged war generally. The advantage of the mountain both for observation and as a place to fight down from is underscored each time the father in the story places the champion and antelope on the summit. The valley, where life was easy, could become dangerous for the unwary. No matter how much stealth, cover, and concealment the elder brother and his people used, they were exposed and defeated. Vigilance, or lack thereof, and determination proved to be decisive elements in achieving victory. Not until the antelope rested, along with the champion, was the enemy successful. Dawn was the time for an attack; night was a time of rest and victory celebration. Ultimately, the entire reason for the conflict was revenge for the loss of the elder's son, resulting in whole communities entering a fray in which many died. The revenge noted here is characteristic of the tribal warfare waged by the Utes against neighboring groups for centuries.

The bows and arrows, spears, and knives used in this story were part of the Ute arsenal going back to prehistoric times. After the introduction of the horse, weapons became smaller and lighter for use on horseback. The self-bow and sinew-backed bow reinforced with mountain sheep horn and made of juniper, chokecherry, or service berry were between three and four feet in length. Individuals decorated their two-foot-long arrows according to a design they liked, there being no particular tribal identity. Arrow ownership, however, was important for individual claims in both hunting and warfare. Only Colorado Utes used spears and clubs, but both Southern and Northern Utes employed shields and knives.[21] Trade with friendly Spanish, Mexican, and Americans during the eighteenth and nineteenth centuries provided steel for arrow and lance points, knives, and (later) rifles. This was particularly true for the Utes, who usually maintained friendly relationships with these people, assisting them in fighting other tribes. Indeed, by the time the United States government was rounding up the Navajos, it was providing firearms—in some instances directly to their allies, the Utes. By the 1870s, between trade and battlefield capture, the Utes were well-armed with light repeating rifles, a complaint voiced by many a white man who stood on the receiving end. Fighting from horseback with this maneuverable weapon became an art, as warriors slipped to the side of their mounts, used the horses for a shield, and fired under the running steed's neck.

The Utes' approach to war was pragmatic. Even those who adopted parts of the Plains Indian culture did not adhere to the belief that battle was a place of social advancement. While they were known as brave fighters and skilled raiders, much of the ranked coup-counting found among other tribes—the Sioux, Cheyenne, Crow, etc.— was absent from Ute practices. Scalping by removing the hair just above the ears served as a trophy, looting the body of an enemy warrior was encouraged, and the selection of a war leader was based on ability and previous decision-making, but he was also subject to group censure if he made significant errors. Yet there was no attempt to obtain wealth or status that would have placed an individual above the members of the group. "The goal of Weeminuche raids was primarily the capture of horses, and secondarily the capture of prisoners who could be bartered to the Mexicans for horses. Warfare was not considered the vehicle for self-aggrandizement because there was no hierarchy of honors for which the Plains warriors strove, and because all loot of a war party was divided with other members of the band when raiders returned. The Weeminuche accepted that part of the Plains war complex which dealt with material results, and some of the tools with which to wage war. They rejected those ideological overtones which became the core of the business of the Plains tribes."[22]

Whether to trade, raid, hunt, or seek revenge, the Utes were concerned and organized for protection. Travelling on the Plains in search of buffalo meant that a camp moved through hostile territory, home to the Comanche, Arapaho, and others. Scouts surged forward while flank guards operated on both sides of the main column comprised of women, children, elders, and a few warriors providing close-in protection. In Canyon Country, this wide-ranging skirt of defense shrank dramatically in breadth but maintained the principle of security on all sides. If an attack occurred, the warriors moved toward the threat while the dependents moved to the rear away from the fighting and if possible, to the mountains to a rendezvous point or place where the warriors could establish an ambush. Ambushes in mountainous and canyoned terrain were particularly effective, especially when the Utes sent men behind those caught in a killing zone to steal their horses, ensuring an immobilized enemy while facilitating retreat for the ambushers.[23]

When establishing a campsite for a large group, the leader sent out scouts to take observation points on hills to see if an enemy approached. They maintained these positions, equipped with a small amount of food and water, and remained motionless until relieved by others who took their place. If one of the sentinels spotted an enemy, he would ride his horse back and forth, alerting the camp. Some of these guards may have been part of a Southern Ute warrior-training society called the Dogs, which was comprised of young men chosen to undergo training as warriors and hunters. Each morning, they ascended surrounding hills to detect the presence of any enemy and during movement, served as part of the rearguard. They wore a collar of slit wolf skin on their neck as a badge of honor and occasionally ate dog-meat stew, believed to give them the alertness and agility needed for their tasks.

Recruitment for this society was either through volunteering or by being kidnapped from their family. "There were times when the [society] entered camp to capture a pubescent boy who had just undergone the puberty hunting ceremonies. The novice was stripped and bluntly told that he must now become a hardened fighter. If the newcomer cried out, he was whipped. The entire aim of the Dog Company was to furnish the band with future protectors and valiant raiders, and in so doing it brooked no interference from camp youth."[24] On a smaller scale, individual families and groups also had the responsibility to train those young men not chosen to be in the society. The rigors of war and hunting remained the responsibility of all Ute males and so running, war games on horseback, contests of skill with bows and arrows and other weapons, and activities in heat and cold all toughened future warriors.

In addition to physical preparations and practices, there were also spiritual beliefs that added protection to an individual. Dreams were essential to much of Ute religion, specifying things from the past, as well as the future. They were the connecting link between the unseen and the physical world by which a person received supernatural power and direction. In a dream, an animal or bird taught of the medicine or spiritual force it held, or it foreshadowed an event that would soon take place. Bears and mountain lions were particularly strong spiritually, but badgers, eagles, wind, cyclones, lightning, the moon, and stars were also powerful.[25]

Just how effective this medicine was is attested to by many Utes who have seen this spiritual protection at work. Two examples follow. The first is of a raiding party who encountered an Arapaho camp in Wyoming. The Utes successfully stole many horses, but camp dogs alerted their owners, and the chase was on. Two of the raiders volunteered to stay behind as a delaying force while the others successfully escaped with their prize to the mountains. The two men fought hard, but the enemy killed their horses, and then the two men ran out of ammunition as the ranks of enemy forces continued to swell. One member of the fleeing Utes stayed behind to see what happened, and from the top of a mountain, he observed the following events: "They tried to kill [Archup's] father, but he and his friend were 'bullet proof' and they could not get them. Knives wouldn't go through their flesh, bullets couldn't kill them. The only way they got them was with rocks, and they pounded them to death. After they were dead, the enemy cut the two men up into little pieces. They were so angry because the Utes had killed so many Arapaho."[26]

Fig. 6—The Utes were known for being well-armed. These three men hold Model 1873 Winchester rifles, a favorite because of its fifteen-round magazine capacity, rapid-fire capability, and maneuverability on horseback. Its maximum effective range, however, was only about two hundred yards. The warrior on horseback poses with arrows in hand. (Used by permission, Utah State Historical Society)

The second example is from Buckskin Charlie, a Muache leader who was on the plains hunting buffalo with six other Utes. They were returning from a successful hunt, their pack animals loaded with meat, when two scouts reined in their galloping horses to warn of hostile Comanches approaching. It did not take long before a large assemblage of warriors "spread out in ten long rows" were upon them.[27] Releasing their packhorses, the Utes rode for three miles before joining a second group of ten men, only one of whom was armed with a rifle, since "this was before the time many Indians had guns." With no place to escape and jaded horses, the Utes had no choice but to stand and fight. Buckskin Charlie next took charge and delivered a war speech to encourage his comrades. After summarizing the difficult situation, he urged them to prepare to die, have brave hearts, and remember all the wrongs committed by the Comanches against the Utes. "When we are all killed but two, let those two stand side by side and fight. And when the Utes are all killed but one, let that last one die killing Comanches. If the Comanches kill your horse from under you, [then] stand on the ground and fight; if they break one of your legs, [then] stand on the other leg and fight; if they break both your legs, [then] lie on the ground and kill Comanches until you are too weak to put an arrow to your bow. Come, be brave, let us fight like Utes."[28]

The enemy formed their lines before the Utes and warned they would all soon be dead. The Utes responded with disdain. A first volley of arrows killed a Ute horse; the next killed a Ute man. Then "the fight was fast and hard and hot, and we fought for many hours, fighting until the sun was almost gone." Buckskin Charlie remembered that as casualties arose on the Comanche side, their ardor for war waned. They "turned and ran from us like cowards. We were brave men, we had good [medicine power], and so well did we fight that but one of us was killed, although more were hurt." Assistance from the unseen had carried the day. After burying their comrade and killing a horse over his grave, they rode to their camp in sorrow, swearing vengeance against any Comanche they might see in the future.

This overview of Ute war-making capability provides a basis for understanding the more detailed accounts that follow. Whether fleeing to the mountains or the sinuous canyon lands of southeastern Utah, ambushing pursuers from commanding terrain, protecting women and children from a hostile force, leading warriors outnumbered by the enemy, or evoking supernatural power for assistance, Utes were potent fighters. Central to these events were their knowledge of the land and their approach to war, which was filtered through cultural understanding. On home turf, they were formidable. Chapter Three looks at their fight against the Navajos in the 1850s and 1860s and shows just how feared the Utes became; subsequent chapters attest to their skill when opposing the white man. Ute warriors—whether on the ground or astride a horse—powerfully resisted enemy forces venturing onto their land.

The second half of this chapter looks at the Navajo, or Diné (translated as "The People"), another warrior group that had a very different orientation from that of the Utes. A note about sources is helpful in identifying the time period and events that provide good ethnographic information. In 1936, anthropologist W. W. Hill published *Navaho Warfare*, a nineteen-page monograph that has become the single-best treatise on the topic.[29] Unfortunately for the Navajo (but fortunately for today's reader), the Fearing Time and Long Walk period (1857-–1868) created an indelible scar on the tribal memory, making it one of two milepost events in their history (the other being the Livestock Reduction of the 1930s).

The next chapter will provide detailed accounts of what took place between the Utes and Navajos during this time in southeastern Utah. Here, a broader use of this excellent body of oral history gives a more general pattern of offensive and defensive practices and the beliefs that created them. Three books, in particular, provide graphic examples for this era: *Navajo Stories of the Long Walk Period* (a collection of forty individual accounts), *Wolfkiller*, and *Bighorse the Warrior* (the last two books being longer autobiographical renderings).[30]

There are many tribes in North America with extensive bodies of religious and cultural lore, but there are few that rival those of the Navajo. Daily life, from sunrise to sunset, centered on beliefs explained through complex cycles of stories that brought Navajos together, outlined ceremonial performances, healed the sick, protected people from harm, instructed proper behavior, and gave an understanding of a spiritual universe. Indeed, the most salient point of this traditional worldview is that paralleling the physical world, there is a spiritual domain that mutually interacts with those things visible and invisible. Thus, sickness may be caused by offending a power; survival in war is a matter of religious preparation and protection; future and past events, along with their outcomes, can be understood through divination; and an enemy can be defeated as much through supernatural means as physical effort.

The basis for most of the beliefs and practices associated with war-making and manhood in the past came from a lengthy mythology about two young men known as the twins: Monster Slayer (Naayéé' Neizghání) and Born For Water

(Tóbájíshchíní).[31] As with the Hopi and Zuni discussed in the previous chapter, these war heroes were born to supernatural parents—a mother, Changing Woman (Asdzáá nádleehé), and a father, Sun Bearer (Jóhonaa'éí)—at a time when the world was in its formative stage and inhabited with Navajo-eating monsters. The two boys, who had never met their father, were anxious to leave home, find their second parent, and receive assistance in making the world safe for their people. At first they needed to be strengthened and toughened for the journey ahead. This task fell to some of the holy people, who taught them through rigorous training what it would take to physically survive.

Upon leaving their mother, the boys also received protective amulets, prayers, and songs that guided them through spiritual dangers on their physical journey. As they traveled, evil monsters in different forms—Rocks That Crush, Slashing Reeds, Giant Cacti, and Boiling Sand Dunes—blocked their path and tried unsuccessfully to kill them. Spiritual power saved the twins each time. Finally, they reached Sun Bearer's home only to encounter more tests: first, to gain entrance into his dwelling and later, to prove that they were his sons. Most important of all of their powers came from the help of the Holy Wind (Níłch'i), a sacred being who guides, warns, protects, and teaches and is comparable in function to the Holy Ghost in Christian beliefs. The twins passed the tests; their father recognized them as his offspring and offered assistance. What did they want? The young men answered quickly that they needed weapons to destroy the monsters inhabiting the earth. At first reticent, Sun Bearer eventually gave them four types of arrows—zigzag lightning, sheet lightning, sunbeam, and rainbow—with instructions as to how to kill the evil they soon would face. The brothers returned to earth on a streak of lightning (in other accounts, a rainbow), ready to cleanse the world of its dangerous elements.

The twins were successful. They killed a wide variety of creatures—Big God the Giant, Horned Monster, Kicking Monster, Tracking Bear Monster, and many others—using the prayers, objects, and weapons they had acquired on their journey. By the time they had rid the earth of these evil beings, they had become accomplished warriors but also suffered from the ill effects of bloodshed, images of war, and spiritual trauma. Only after they disposed of their weapons and had a cleansing ceremony (now called the Enemyway (*Anaa'jí* or *Anaa'jí Ndáá*) did their swooning and illness from ghost sickness stop.[32] Then the twins could return to a life of peace, with war and carnage left behind.

This brief synopsis of a very long and detailed story is like a stalk of corn: a metaphor often used in Navajo culture. From it comes many other accounts and teachings that branch out to explain why young men are raised in preparation for war, what needs to be done before they depart, how they should conduct themselves to have the protection necessary to survive, and what needs to be undertaken after their return to remove combat's effects. In other words, this story presents a pattern for life that can be fulfilled in very concrete ways to receive the necessary assistance. Story and ceremony are its basis, but physical trials, as with the twins, are its counterpart.

As a young Navajo boy moves toward manhood, members of his family ensure he is trained properly. Extended running and rolling in snow to harden the body and inculcate alertness were common Navajo practices to prepare for hardship and provide strength. Samuel Holiday, a Navajo code talker during World War II, remembers what it was like as he received training from his mentor: "Ted Yellow was even stricter than my mother about getting up before dawn to run. The first week was half a mile, with the distances increasing each time. He had me run as hard as I could and yell to increase my stamina. When the first snow fell, my stepfather and I took our clothes off and ran away from the hogan to roll in the snow. He made sure the snow touched every part of my body. Finally he let me go and I ran as fast as I could for home, thinking I would not make it because of the cold. But once I got inside, my mother again warned me, saying, 'We make you run a race fast at long distances to strengthen your body and build endurance against hardship. You are preparing and protecting yourself.' "[33]

Too much sleep, comfort, and laziness could lead to death for a warrior and his people, so in the morning, boys aroused to the threat: "Wake up, be lively! If you are not up early, the enemy will come and kill you while you sleep. . . . [If slow to arise] the first thing that came along would kill them because their systems were filled with ugly things that they should have gotten rid of: they would be quick tempered, have weak minds, be unable to stand life's hardships, and therefore disgrace their families."[34]

As a boy entered manhood, there was a formal recognition ceremony provided by a relative or an older man who preferably had been a warrior. The mentor would perform a Blessingway ceremony for the initiate before they entered a sweat lodge to pray and sing songs of protection. Then the young man would start running with people accompanying him, taunting and testing his ability, just as the holy beings had done to the twins. Then the young man would run back to the sweat lodge to be counseled by a half dozen men. Each time one of the teachers finished his instruction, the young man emerged from the sweat lodge and was "molded" with objects associated with manhood and success in life: a horse bridle representing wealth, a bow and arrow representing protection, and an unblemished buckskin representing supernatural power and ceremonial knowledge. Next, an elder covered the young man with white cornmeal as the other men sang about the young man being a child of the holy people. Later, older women taught him about how a good man acts, after which participants gave gifts.

The weapons of a warrior were the same as those used by the twins. Bows and arrows, clubs, spears, knives, shields, and body armor each had their counterpart with that used by the holy people and were prepared under ritual conditions through songs and prayers that made the weapons invincible. A sinew-backed bow with a quiver of fifty arrows was the long-range weapon for most Navajo until well after the Long Walk. Unlike the Utes, who obtained the latest firearms easily, only a few Navajos owned low-grade *bii' na'jih* (literally "things that one puts inside"), or muzzle-loading muskets.

Arrows, however, were abundant. The stone or metal points and part of the shaft were dipped in one of three types of poison made of some combination of rattlesnake blood, the stingers of insects, yucca juice, and charcoal from a tree that had been struck by lightning.[35] A number of people attest to their effectiveness; one Navajo woman returning from captivity claimed the Utes had a real fear of being hit by poisoned arrows because their bodies, when struck, would swell and then die.[36] Bighorse, who lived in the Navajo Mountain area, commented that after an arrow was fletched with a split eagle feather, the designs next painted on added potency. "On one side you put a lightning with four zigzag points. This is for the enemy to be shot [representing the twin's arrows]. On the other side you just make a straight line going through. This is for the warrior. It's like a safe path. At the base, right next to the feather, you put four stripes, each one a different color: white, blue, yellow, black. They're for the warrior too—safety from all directions. Next you put mountain lion fat or bear fat on the arrow. This is to poison the person you shoot."[37]

Similar ritual attention was applied to other objects. The two-piece, six-foot lance also had a poisoned tip, two eagle feathers, and an arrow point for additional power. Warriors fashioned clubs in the tradition of the supernatural ones used by the twins. The eighteen-inch-diameter buckskin or double-buckskin shield also had suspended eagle feathers, sacred powder shaken from a red ground squirrel for invisibility, and painted designs of a bear's feet, Big Snake, a mountain lion, and other elements that brought protection. War shirts could be as thick as four layers of buckskin for those on foot and eight layers for those on horseback. Armor worn by the twins paralleled that worn by warriors, but theirs was made of flint so that arrowheads made of it were used in ceremonies for protection. That is why the Navajos teach that evil fears the presence of flint—because the power of the twins is present. Finally, a leather cap with eagle and owl feathers and abalone and white shell attached gives strength, power, and protection to the wearer.[38] From head to foot, a warrior ensured his safety through supernatural practices as outlined in the traditional teachings.

As the twins set out in search of their father, they met a number of holy beings who gave them help. One of the most important ones was Spider Woman, who invited them into her home. First, she taught the boys with her knowledge of life and then prepared something for them to eat. Putting cornmeal and other plants in bowls, she next dropped two precious beads—white shell and turquoise—into the mixture. The twins ate what was in their bowls, ingesting the two objects along with the food. Even today, the white bead is a symbol of internal protection, providing courage and other mental qualities necessary for the future. Turquoise protects the outside and is worn by Navajos as a means by which the holy people recognize and assist them. Another aid that can be swallowed during a Prayer Against Enemy (*Naayéé'ii Sódizin*) ceremony is a small eagle feather so that the participant will face fear and have his spirit live on.[39] In each instance, this eating of a medicinal object for protection is part of the ceremonial preparation a Navajo warrior undergoes before entering combat.

Next, Spider Woman gave each of the boys a life feather (*iina*) taken from a live eagle. These feathers were small, sometimes only down. In the past, they were obtained by digging a pit to camouflage a man inside who secured a live rabbit outside as bait for an eagle. When the bird attacked its prey, the man grabbed its legs and pulled it down into the hole as a captive. The desired feathers could then either be plucked and the bird released, or it could be smothered with corn pollen and a hood. Another way to secure live eagle feathers was to climb to a nest and pull a feather from a baby eagle.[40] According to Gladys Reichard, "The longer the bird struggled, the more potent were its parts in a ceremony. The feathers represent strength, speed and motion, deliverance; the pollen exposed to them stands for light and life, that is, the sheen of the feathers."[41]

Some life feathers were tied in a special knot before being placed in a corn-pollen pouch carried by the person seeking protection. Born For Water took eagle down to make prayer sticks, other holy people used the down to fletch arrows, and still others used the down for hair ornaments. "All the other gods received either tail feathers or down feathers from the eagles. Every sacred article was provided with some kind of eagle feather and the Navajo still use the sacred objects so trimmed to this day."[42] But it was Monster Slayer who was directly saved by his life feather when a giant monster bird (*Tsé ninááhálééh*) snatched him in her claws and flew to Shiprock Peak to dash the young warrior against it, seeking to turn him into food for her young below. Instead, he floated gently to the rock with his life feather and later defeated the monster bird.[43]

Fig. 7—Monster Slayer, one of the Navajo twins, is ready for war. Many of the supernatural powers these warriors used for protection were copied by Navajo men. The cap holds either an owl or eagle feather: predatory birds that see their prey from afar and strike with swiftness. Turquoise is a means by which the Holy People recognize an individual, and the "life feather" Monster Slayer grasps was given by Spider Woman for protection, while his traditional hair bun holds good thoughts and is a sign of manliness. The markings on his back, arms, and leg are his identifying symbol. (Picture by Charles Yanito)

When Navajo infants are born—both boys and girls—they receive a sacred name that is known only to them and close family members for ceremonial purposes. Often, these are associated with war, such as He Returns With The Warrior, He Went Out To War, She Meets The Enemy, or [She Is] Going to War.[44] Through this title, spiritual connections with the holy people are assured. During the blacking part of a war ceremony, the use of this name may either prepare an individual about to set out or purify a person returning. Animals, plants, and insects also have spiritual names that control power. If an individual is working against a person or group with witchcraft, the ceremonial name can also be used to sicken, curse, and kill. For that reason, few people are to have this inside knowledge of a person's spiritual identity.

The power of witchcraft as a force is seen in what happened to Abé Tsoh (Big Breast), who practiced sorcery known as *Tsosts'id Ha'oodzii* (Seven Words Will Kill An Enemy). Early one morning, she went to a water hole to fill her jug and became surrounded by the enemy (ethnic identity unclear). They encircled her with their horses, tore off her clothes, then discovered that she had two bags of witchcraft medicine. She sang her songs that directed the sorceress's power at them, then warned that by noon they would all be gone. The men shot and killed her, burned the witchcraft medicine, and joined a larger party of raiders. The Navajos, who had been watching this and other enemy activity, attacked the group, and by noon, three of the four men were dead and the other person's whereabouts unknown, thus fulfilling the sorceress's prophecy.[45] Just as the twins used words and songs to destroy their enemy, so did those participating in a war party. Clyde Kluckhohn, in his study of witchcraft, tells of an account given to him about a group of Navajos waiting one night to capture a flock of sheep guarded by Mexicans. The leader of the Navajos used witchcraft, shot a feather from a basket into the Mexican leader, and said, "If we hear a noise, we've got him."[46] The man gave out a yell and by the next morning was dead, causing the other Mexicans to flee. Thus, witchcraft, which is dependent primarily on songs, prayers, and words, can cause death and is just as real as the arrows and bullets fired for the same purpose.

The means by which prayers and thoughts are transmitted is through *Nítch'i*. This important essence participates with humans in two different ways. In Navajo thought, it is personified as an incorporeal personality who warns, guides, teaches, and protects an individual facing danger. Hill comments that the ceremonial aspect of war "was the most important part of any military undertaking" and that travel through enemy territory and the country itself "was potentially maleficent [so that] . . . a great amount of ritual was performed during the course of an offensive movement."[47] When a Navajo person moves beyond the limits of a safe, protected environment—such as the lands bounded by the four sacred mountains consecrated by the holy people—danger lurks. Crossing one of the four sacred rivers placed in the cardinal directions opens the door to foreign elements and trials that are primarily controlled by supernatural means. Once in enemy territory, precautions must be taken. This applies not only to actual combat but also concerns with witchcraft, strange powers, reduced ceremonial efficacy, and the unknown or unpredictable. The holy people know of these concerns and can assist, but they must be respected and given offerings in placating that which is harmful. They are contacted by prayer and song through the Holy Wind.

Traditional Native American enemies surrounded Navajo lands. Utes, Comanches, Apaches, Hopi, Zuni, and other Puebloan groups fought against them and willingly joined Spanish, Mexican, and (later) American forces. As with the Utes, Navajos were primarily concerned with raiding for horses and captives or in taking revenge for past wrongs. In order for them to wage war and have sufficient spiritual protection, there were several different ceremonial approaches—the Monster Slayerway, the Enemyway, and the *Yei Hastin* (*Yé'ii Hastiin*) Way—the primary difference between them being the songs and prayers offered. Monster Slayerway, the oldest based on the teachings, sprang directly from the practices of the twins. The leader of a war party was the one who knew the ceremonies and songs and could spiritually navigate his followers to a successful conclusion.

By the age of seventeen to twenty, a young man was ready to participate in war. If he wished to become a leader but had not yet had the necessary training, he would approach a medicine man who had this knowledge and accompany him into enemy territory, where they would build a sweat lodge in which instruction would begin. The novice would learn "the most important things pertaining to war, the secret names of the enemy, and the songs and prayers which were used before making an attack."[48] For four days, the instructor and student remained, learning the names and prayers: something that could not be done in friendly territory for fear that someone in the family or a relative would die, an epidemic would occur, or the enemy would attack. Once the information had been mastered, the young man was ready to organize and lead a war party.

Following the recruitment of warriors who wished to go against the enemy, the men spent anywhere from three to five days preparing. Songs and prayers first sung by Monster Slayer and now offered in a sweat lodge brought protection and success if performed properly. Offerings of pollen and *ntł'iz* (four types of sacred crushed stones and shells) ensured the assistance of the Sun and Wind People in providing protection to the travelers. Weapons and equipment were similarly blessed as the men gathered without women for their spiritual preparation. Many warriors wore a close-fitting cap, similar to those of everyday use except that just before engagement with the enemy, the wearer attached a special plume from either an eagle's or owl's tail feathers. "This protected the wearer just like the badge of Saint Christopher."[49] In addition to this, a warrior might wear a wrist amulet made of bear, mountain lion, eagle, and owl claws to provide strength and power, or a small medicine bundle with the "shake offs" from a bear, snake, thunder, and cyclone, along with a "live" eagle feather. These "shake offs" were made from pollen that had been placed on a creature or were from a place that was representative of these animals or elements. Once it had been put on the animal or its surrogate and the appropriate prayers had been said, the medicine man collected the pollen and put it in a medicine pouch to provide protection. All of these elements had strong supernatural powers (described in the teachings) that spoke of their ability to protect and make the warrior invincible.

There is no missing the parallels of offerings, the role of pollen, the power of the eagle, and the idea of carrying a medicine pouch as established by the twins' pattern. It was their power that was evoked through prayers that established the ability to defeat the enemy as mentioned in this prayer: "Step into the shoes of Monster Slayer. Step into the shoes of him whose lure is the extended bowstring. Step into the shoes of him who lures the enemy to death."[50]

Once the war party entered enemy territory, the leader began his chanting and prayers against the enemy, inviting others in the party to offer their own songs. They sang for the animals they had come to steal or the revenge they would exact. Strict rules of conduct; the seriousness of the undertaking; good weather conditions like wind and snow to cover tracks and muffle sound; and the ability to put all thoughts of home behind them were part of the mindset. There was even a secret "war talk" used only during hostilities:

> When the warriors entered the enemy's territory, the leader told the men to use certain words other than the usual ones for the animals and objects that they hoped to obtain. This was called "war talk" and "not talking plainly." The Navaho never practiced this "war talk" in their own territory because it was believed if they did that an attack from the enemy would follow. This

restriction lasted from one to three days of the journey. When the leader decided that the appropriate time had arrived, the party lined up in a row facing the enemy's country. At the coming of dawn, the leader began a song in which the rest joined. At a certain part of the song all turned toward their own homes and the taboo against "not talking plainly" was removed.

The leader told the men not to urinate in the brush. He also warned them that should they become separated and wish to communicate with each other, they were to use prearranged calls such as those of the coyote, wolf, whip-poor-will, or screech owl.[51]

This supernatural or spiritual aspect of war continued when the war leader, after his instructions to the group, sent two men from the camp to determine the outcome of future events by "listening." Navajos considered this the most reliable form of divination, although stargazing and hand trembling were also used. With "listening," the two men moved about one hundred yards from their group in the direction of the enemy to listen for noises, indicating success in their raid, such as the sounds of livestock, animals running, or a vision of some type that showed them obtaining their goal. On the other hand, if they "heard the cry of a crow, screech owl, hoot owl, wolf, coyote, or any other 'man eating' bird or animal; heard the footsteps or conversation of the enemy[;] or heard someone shout as if he were hurt (this is believed to predict the death of one of the members of the party), these were considered bad omens and the party would turn back."[52] Through *Nítch'i*, the Holy Wind, the future was known.

Two examples of receiving supernatural directions follow. George Littlesalt from Navajo Mountain tells of a man during the Long Walk period who used to divine the safe direction of travel for his people. He would go out alone at night and listen for warning sounds from the direction in which the enemy was located.[53] Mose Denejolie from Piñon, Arizona, provides more specifics:

> In those days when the Diné heard a real owl hoot at night, they believed the direction from which the owl was hooting was the safe direction to take. Often an unusual hooting for an owl could be heard. If the hooting was done by an enemy, they would flee away from the sound. When the "Bird that Whistles" [no clear identity given] made its noise—"ahoo, ahoo, ahoo"—the Diné would say the enemy must be approaching, and they would flee in the direction [this bird] was flying.

> Another direction indicator was the coyote. The direction from which a coyote howled was another safe direction to flee. The enemy would imitate the howl of a coyote, but the Diné easily could tell whether the howling was by a real coyote or by an enemy. . . . An owl was a safe path indicator when it hooted at night. The hawk, when it made its sound, was a bad or dangerous path indicator. So when the Diné heard the noise of a hawk, they would flee away from it. Also the crow. When it called "gaa, gaa, gaa" that was another sign of danger and the Diné would remain calm and not move around.[54]

As a war party approached their intended target, scouts moved ahead to detect enemy activity. Just before the attack, which was usually at dawn, the leader dressed in his war gear—including moccasins with Big Snake, a protective deity, painted on their soles—left the group. Alone, he sang songs, offered prayers, and called the enemy by their secret name to again ensure success. " 'The prayers are like this: he starts with the enemy's head and mentions all the different parts of his body right down to the ground, and ends his prayer in the ground. This is just the same as burying the man.' "[55] He then returned to his warriors, reported his efforts, and encouraged the men to prepare by painting designs of snakes for power, bear tracks for fierceness and bravery, and human hands to represent "a man." If the leader has performed his part of the ritual successfully and the warriors are prepared spiritually by following practices taught by the twins and other holy people when they first waged war, then "everyone knows and feels that they will be lucky."[56]

Soon, the attack commenced. Hill describes two types: a raid for Comanche horses, usually comprised of ten or less men, and an attack on Oraibi, which took up to 200 warriors. In the raid, the Navajos went on foot in search of horses. Embedded in the herd were Comanche guards; the Navajos sneaked into the village at night and cut loose a large string of horses they then stampeded. A chase commenced that lasted for three days, during which the Comanches fired their rifles whenever they got close. The Navajos took a zigzag route home, ran many of the horses to death, lost others during travel, ate some because they were so hungry, and eventually took turns driving the horses that were left while others slept, then caught up and took a turn pushing the herd. Their journey lasted a total of five days until they reached Fort Sumner. These men had learned of the challenge of raiding in foreign territory. Mirages in front and on their sides frightened them, hand tremblers and stargazers had to divine as to where water could

Fig. 8—Navajo war parties ranged far and wide, with some venturing into Mexico, out onto the Plains, and into the Great Basin. Traveling far from the four sacred mountains required intense ritual behavior and adherence to the songs and prayers that summoned the holy people to be there for protection. (Painting by Robert Becenti)

be found, and little food and rest made it all that much harder. Still, they returned safely and considered it a success.[57]

Several hundred Navajos attacked the pueblo of Oraibi to revenge past wrongs. The war party traveled to within a day's journey of their target and then camped, placing one man in their midst who spoke Ute well. He used the language constantly to fool any Hopis spying on them. The next day, as the Navajo arrived within a couple of miles of the village, Hopi warriors descended to greet them, realizing too late they were encircled by their enemy and in trouble. The slaughter began with some of the Hopis breaking out of the fight to return to their village atop the mesa. The Navajos ran off all the stock, fought and plundered within the pueblo until the leader told them to desist, and scalped the fallen. They returned to the Lukachukai Mountain area from whence they had come to hold an Enemyway ceremony and victory dance.[58]

A third type of offensive action ideally suited for canyon country was the ambush. This required an extensive knowledge of the terrain, control and planning of those involved in the ambush, and total surprise of the enemy. Small, informal ambushes characterized much of the fighting between Utes and Navajos, since both groups operated in a limited capacity to either avoid detection or spread out to find those in hiding. Wolfkiller provides a good example of this tit-for-tat warfare. He and a group of men were returning from a trading trip to their camp where the women, children, elders, and a few warriors had been in hiding. As they approached, they found a dead Ute horse with a Navajo arrow in its side and other indications of a fight. They arrived to find the camp decimated, many members dead or missing, and the tracks of the Utes' horses mixed with stolen livestock. Some of the old Navajo men began to pray for snow to slow the enemies' escape as each able-bodied man joined in pursuit. The snow came, but not before the Navajo rescue party spotted the Utes, many with a woman captive riding double. The Navajos moved ahead to a spot on the trail going down the mountain and put warriors on both sides. The snow caused the raiders to bundle in blankets so that when the ambush started, they were unprepared and unaware that they were in a kill zone. The Navajos opened fire but found it difficult to shoot at the Utes effectively because of the women riding behind. The raiders were totally surprised and had no idea of the size of the other force they were engaging, so they fled from the scene. The Navajos recaptured their sheep during a chase over several miles, while the Utes killed some of the older women and babies who slowed their progress. Eventually, however, they let all the rest of the captives go, except for those astride their mounts. The Navajos gathered what they could and returned to camp. Wolfkiller concluded with, "Now I knew what a Ute raid could be. If we had not surprised them, we would have lost all of our women and children, and they would have made raids on as many hogans as they could find."[59]

Even after a successful raid or ambush, the Navajos called upon the help of the holy beings for protection. As they left the scene of battle, the leader would draw four lines on the ground with a flint arrowhead. These marks represented the four types of arrows used by Monster Slayer, and so two of the lines were straight, symbolizing straight lightning and a rainbow, while above each of these was a line with four connected angles that stood for either zigzag lightning or a sunray. This drawing prevented the enemy from overtaking the raiding party. Spread Mustache used this technique to stop Comanches tracking him and his family. His grandson reported, "As the enemies were following, my late grandfather drew a line in front of them, and the Comanches just turned back. Afterward, below us here, just at the edge of the canyon, many of the Comanches were killed with arrows. The Navajos did not have guns. The rest of the Comanches departed to where they had come from."[60]

The Navajos were not nearly as formal and clearly defined when it came to defensive tactics. Part of the reason is found in the economic lifestyle they practiced. As hunters and gatherers and later, as stockmen and horticulturalists, the carrying capacity of the land encouraged dispersion. Limited grazing areas; the need to use both a summer and winter range for livestock; relatively small areas with enough good soil and plentiful water for crops; and a rugged terrain of desert, canyons, and mountains all facilitated a limited political organization of leadership with headmen at the top. The culture also encouraged a decentralized system of religious practice, camps comprised mostly of family and extended family (the "outfit"), a clan system that was widespread and did not function as a unified entity, and a strong sense of individual loyalty to and dependence on their own kin. When war occurred on a large scale, with a few exceptions, the general populace scattered and hid—at least until arrangements were made for a sizable force to counter the threat. Unlike the Hopi, Zuni, and Utes living in villages, the Navajo did not have a ready supply of men to call upon when in danger, but were dispersed.

When conflict arose, pre-arranged smoke signals and messengers, either on horseback or foot, were the primary means of notification to bring people together, but it could take a week or more to gather enough warriors for a full-scale attack.[61] The tremendous infusion of enemy forces into Navajo land during the Long Walk limited communication even more, encouraging people to scatter into the most inaccessible peripheral areas to avoid detection. Wolfkiller, living in southeastern Utah and northern Arizona at the time, gives a particularly good account of life on the run. As a young boy, he watched the women gathering seeds and grass for winter food, but the men could not hunt for fear of leaving their dependents unprotected. When winter arrived, they continued to live in the canyons but were constantly on the move, using only temporary shelters. "Then the heavy snow came and we were not so much afraid. Grandfather said we could build a hogan now, but we must build it among the rocks so that it could not be easily discovered. The rocks would serve as a chimney to carry the smoke up to the top of the mesa so anyone in the canyon would not be able to smell it."[62]

One of the problems with avoiding detection in Canyon Country was that not all good hiding places had enough exits to avoid capture or death. The ideal camp would have a number of covered and concealed routes that provided those fleeing with an opportunity to leave in the opposite direction of advancing enemy. Unless the position was unassailable by enemy forces, it could serve as a trap. Two examples show the trade-offs in hiding and defending. In January 1805, a Spanish expedition led by Lieutenant Antonio Narbona entered Canyon del Muerto, a branch of Canyon de Chelly, Arizona, in search of Navajos. A large group of men, women, and children had hidden in an alcove hundreds of feet above the canyon floor, accessible only by a narrow ledge. The Spanish detected them and opened fire from above and below, the bullets ricocheting off the alcove ceiling and walls, killing 115 inhabitants.[63] With no route of escape other than the narrow ledge that led into the site, what had been a refuge of safety turned into a death trap that is today called Massacre Cave.

Fast forward to 1863 and a rock formation called Navajo Fortress, just above the junction of Canyon del Muerto with Black Rock Canyon. This 700-foot-high monolith is almost separate from the connecting Black Rock Canyon and has extremely steep sandstone sides. When the Navajo living in this area heard about the approach of soldiers, they sent men fifteen miles away to cut long ponderosa pine poles in which they notched steps. Through this series of ladders that went from ledge to ledge, the Navajos created a system of access that could be raised and removed in time of danger. In the meantime, the women collected and dried food to bring on top of their citadel rock. Thirteen rock catch-basins held rainwater while improvised shelters protected the inhabitants, with one man suggesting there were eventually 300 people on top.[64] Without going into detail, the soldiers laid siege but never successfully forced the Navajos from their fortress. Food and water were the weak links in the Indians' defense, but those were also a problem for the soldiers, who left as supplies ran out and easier people to capture appeared. For the Navajos, this type of defensive success was rare.

Many Navajos fled to remote places like Navajo Mountain, which will be discussed in the next chapter. But underlying wherever they went were ceremonial practices to ensure they would not be taken captive. Bighorse said the people in hiding always ate quickly because they feared the enemy might be approaching. But even then, they took time to bless the pot in which their cornmeal mush had been cooked. "So before we eat, we have to make a circle around the top rim of the pot with charcoal. We put the path-line around clockwise, start at the East. And we make it all around, but we don't close the circle—just leave a small space, leave it open at the East. And then we make lines on the side of the pot. The first one goes from the ground up to the circle. The next one goes from the circle down to the ground, then up, then down, and so on. We just keep on going like that all around the side of the pot, clockwise. This is like lots of safe paths of escape. Up the mountain, down the canyon, or just anywhere to keep away from the enemy."[65]

Bighorse tells of medicine men praying for the return of captured Navajos: for the heart of their white captors to be softened, for the warriors protecting the people to be safe, and for the war to end. Things like the stirring sticks used by the women making mush, charcoal from the fire, corn pollen, and other objects all hold power that can be importuned for assistance.[66]

At the conclusion of a battle or at the end of a war, participants faced what is today called post-traumatic stress disorder, or PTSD. Navajo culture has a way of handling it. Returning to the story of the twins, the first enemy they sought to destroy was Yé'ii Tso (Big God), an offspring of Sun Bearer. After successfully killing him with Sun Bearer's help, the twins took his scalp and hung it in a tree to prove to the holy people that they indeed had the power to kill this giant. But shortly after they returned home and told their mother, Changing Woman, what they had done, the twins began to feel sick, overwhelmed with fainting spells and evil thoughts. She understood what needed to be performed and so prepared medicine made from lightning-struck plants and herbs. She sprinkled the men with it and then shot a spruce-and-pine arrow over them. The twins recovered from the harmful effects of the dead.[67] The power to combat what is sometimes called ghost sickness through the Enemyway (*Anaa'jí* or *Anaa'jí Ndáá*) ceremony has been passed on to the Earth Surface People from Monster Slayer and is still in use today.

If the spirit of the deceased is Navajo, then the Evilway ceremony is used to pray away the influence to the north, the place of the dead. On the other hand, if the bothering spirits are non-Navajo, then the Enemyway ceremony is used. This is a serious undertaking, since the purpose of this rite is not to chase away the enemy but to rid the patient of these spirits by killing them.[68] To ensure total healing, the ceremony may be repeated in longer or shorter forms four times over a number of years. Cleansing from the problem of ghost sickness is available for both men and women.

The use of the sweat lodge is the first line of defense, but if ill effects appear, then a ceremony becomes necessary. In the past, the Enemyway ceremony was most frequently used for men returning from war, but women who came in contact with a scalp or blood from the enemy by mistake could also be affected. If a man went into combat when his wife was pregnant, the unborn child later in life could be bothered by the enemy the father had killed. Also, if a man or woman had sexual intercourse with an enemy who later died, they could be afflicted by its ghost. Each nationality—Mexican, Anglo, Ute, Comanche, Hopi, etc.—has a sacred name that is used in the ceremony to sing against them. If a Navajo comes in contact with an object that has the blood of an enemy on it, sickness can result.[69]

Even the procuring of the enemy object—scalp, bone, clothing—for the ceremony must be done with caution. When a person travels to get an object of this nature for a ceremony, it is said "he goes on the warpath." Once it is obtained, it must be treated carefully by limiting exposure and contact with the person who has it. In the old days, it might be tied to a horse's tail or carried on a stick away from the procurer's body. It is then hurried to the place of the ceremony and hidden in a spot away from people until needed. To prevent contamination with the enemy's spirit, blackening (*jint'eesh*) with ash is done to a person to keep the evil away.

Preparation for and conduct of the Enemyway ceremony is filled with symbolic complexity that is only touched upon here.[70] The rich symbolism embedded within expresses deep cultural values concerning the dead and war. A preliminary blackening of a patient to prevent the enemy ghost from recognizing him—and which may exorcise the offending evil spirit—is performed to see if it has a positive effect. If it does, then preparation for a full Enemyway ceremony begins. A "scalper"—often an old man who has been involved in war—"goes on the warpath and brings home the scalp" using Bear and Snake songs (two powerful protectors) for his defense.[71] At the same time, two medicine men—one to prepare the rattle stick and another to receive it—select a date for the stick's preparation and the start of the ceremony. Each also makes a pot drum that, when played, beats the enemy ghosts into the ground. Blessingway singer Frank Mitchell says that decorating the stick is a remaking of the damaged spirit of the patient as a type of payment for the harm it has sustained. At the conclusion of the ceremony, this object is retired to a place it will not be disturbed but can peacefully return to its elements.[72] After the rattle stick is prepared, the patient or his representative takes it, mounts a horse, and rides with companions to the camp of the receiver, usually ten to twelve miles away. After the second medicine man in the receiver's camp has inspected it, he chooses an unmarried, reliable girl who then conducts a dance at which the men perform "sway singing." The next morning, friends and relatives of the stick receiver bring small presents—money, candy, food items, etc.—that represent the gifts given when enemies make peace and distribute them by tossing the presents out of the hogan's smoke hole. The patient, along with his group, then returns to the original camp.

Intensity of activity escalates. Dancing and exchanges continue, and at one point, preparations to "attack the enemy" become central. Just as Monster Slayer did following his return from war, the blackening of a patient and his wife (or surrogate) is performed to make them invisible to the ghost. The patient also receives a sacred name used only during rituals—if he has not already received one. This is kept secret.[73] He next puts on his left shoulder a yucca sash with a pouch attached that contains an object from the enemy and an arrowhead—proof of his ability to vanquish the foe. There are also yucca fiber bands tied with slip knots on his soles, ankles, knees, hips, backs of each shoulder, palms, ears, and the top of his head. A specially commissioned man (called the scalp shooter and strewer of ashes) selects a place distant from camp to place the enemy scalp or object. He then approaches it with the group observing and fires a rifle or arrows at the enemy.

Next, the patient and his wife symbolically (i.e., without touching the ash-covered object) act out thrusting a crow bill into the ashes. Having sprinkled the enemy object with the ashes, the scalp shooter intones, "It is dead. It is dead." As the group leaves the "attack" site and returns to the hogan for concluding ceremonial activities, the participants must be careful never to look back at the scalp.

As with so much in the Navajo universe, this final ceremony represents a spiritual conclusion to a physical problem. While every culture—to include the Ute, Zuni, and Hopi—have deep religious concerns and teachings about war, the Navajo take these same ideas and handle them in an intense ceremonial fashion that places them on an equal footing with the physical preparation. From the first affront to the last part of the Enemyway ceremony, protection and defeat of the adversary is handled spiritually. In the case of all four of the Native American tribes mentioned, fighting against an enemy was informed by the environment and taught through the traditional beliefs handed down by each generation from the beginning of time. Their mode of fighting is a direct expression of what is important in each of their ways of life. What follows next is a more detailed look at how this warfare unfolded in southeastern Utah.

Chapter Endnotes

1. Books particularly helpful about general Ute history are: Donald G. Callaway, Joel C. Janetski, and Omer C. Stewart, "Ute," in *Handbook of North American Indians, Volume 11: Great Basin* (Washington, DC: Smithsonian Institution, 1986); Virginia McConnell Simmons, *The Ute Indians of Utah, Colorado, and New Mexico* (Boulder: University Press of Colorado, 2000); William Wroth (editor), *Ute Indian Arts and Culture: From Prehistory to the New Millennium* (Colorado Springs, CO: Colorado Springs Fine Art Center, 2000); Omer C. Stewart, *Culture Element Distributions: Ute-Southern Paiute* (Berkley: University of California Press, 1942); James Jefferson, Robert W. Delaney, and Gregory C. Thompson, *The Southern Utes: A Tribal History* (Ignacio, CO: Southern Ute Tribe, 1972); and Anne M. Smith, *Ethnography of the Northern Utes (Papers in Anthropology No. 17)* (Albuquerque: University of New Mexico, 1974).
2. Callaway, Janetski, and Stewart, "Ute," p. 354.
3. Sydney M. Lamb, "Linguistic Prehistory in the Great Basin," *International Journal of American Linguistics*, Issue 24 no. 2 (Spring 1958), p. 99.
4. James A. Goss, "Culture-Historical Inference from Utaztekan Linguistic Evidence," paper presented at Plenary Symposium on Utaztekan Prehistory of the Society for American Archaeology and the Great Basin Anthropological Conference, May 1966, pp. 11 and 27.
5. Robert C. Euler, "Southern Paiute Archaeology," *American Antiquities* 29 (January 1964), p. 380; Alan D. Reed, "Ute Cultural Chronology," in *An Archaeology of the Eastern Ute: A Symposium,* ed. Paul R. Nickens, CCPA Occasional Papers1 (Denver: Colorado Council of Professional Archaeologists, 1988), 82; C. S. Fowler and D. D. Fowler, "The Southern Paiute: A.D. 1400-1776," *The Protohistoric Period in the North American Southwest, A.D. 1350—1700,* D. R. Wilcox and W. B. Masse, eds., Arizona State University Archaeological Research Papers Number 24, 129-162; see also Minette C. Church, Steven G. Baker, Bonnie J. Clark, Richard F. Carrillo, Jonathon C. Horn, Carl D. Spath, David R. Guilfoyle, and E. Steven Cassells, *Colorado History: A Context for Historical Archaeology* (Denver: Colorado Council of Professional Archaeologists, 2007), pp. 29–57; and Steven G. Baker, Jeffrey S. Dean, and Richard H. Towner, "Final Report for the Old Wood Calibration Project, Western Colorado," (Montrose, CO: Centuries Research, Inc.: May 1, 2008).
6. Goss, "Culture-Historical Inference," pp. 33–34.
7. Goss, "Traditional Cosmology, Ecology, and Language of the Ute Indians," in William Wroth (editor), *Ute Indian Arts and Culture: From Prehistory to the New Millennium* (Colorado Springs: Colorado Springs Fine Art Center, 2000): p. 29.
8. For a recent discussion of possible Ute early occupation in the Four Corners area, the unidentified people who archaeologists are calling part of the Canalla phase, and pre-contact history, see Minette C. Church, Steven G. Baker, Bonnie J. Clark, Richard F. Carrillo, Jonathan C. Horn, Carl D. Spath, David R. Guilfoyle, and E. Steven Cassells, *Colorado History: A Context for Historical Archaeology* (Denver: Colorado Council of Professional Archaeologists, 2007).
9. Harold Lindsay Amoss, Jr., "Ute Mountain Utes," doctoral dissertation (University of California, Northern Section, 1951), p. 66.
10. Frank Raymond Secoy, *Changing Military Patterns on the Great Plains,17th Century through Early 19th Century,* Monograph 21, The American Ethnological Society (Seattle: University of Washington Press, 1953, 1971), p. 28.
11. For a current in-depth discussion of the horse and the Utes, see Minette C. Church, Steven G. Baker, Bonnie J. Clark, Richard F. Carrillo, Jonathan C. Horn, Carl D. Spath, David R. Guilfoyle, and E. Steve Cassells, *Colorado History: A Context for Historical Archaeology* (Denver: Colorado Council of Professional Archaeologists, 2007), pp. 59–63.
12. Smith, *Ethnography of the Northern Utes*, p. 21.
13. Edward Dutchie, Sr., in an interview by Robert S. McPherson (manuscript in possession of author) (May 13, 1996).
14. Richard I. Dodge, *Our Wild Indians* (Hartford, CN: A. B. Worthington Press, 1882), p. 442.

15. George Bird Grinnell, *By Cheyenne Campfires* (Lincoln: University of Nebraska Press, 1926, 1962), pp. 64–69.

16. For a detailed examination of the slave trade in the Southwest, see Ned Blackhawk, *Violence Over the Land: Indians and Empires in the Early American West* (Cambridge: Harvard University Press, 2006); and Lynn R. Bailey, *The Indian Slave Trade in the Southwest* (Los Angeles: Westernlore Press, 1966).

17. Julian H. Steward, *Basin-Plateau Aboriginal Sociopolitical Groups*, Smithsonian Institution Bureau of American Ethnology, Bulletin 120 (Washington, DC: Government Printing Office, 1938), p. 238.

18. There are various spellings of the names Sinawav, Sinawav pavits, and Sinawav skaits as well as the other Ute names provide by John Wesley Powell. I have chosen to go with his original spellings. There are also a number of different versions of the stories and a mixing of characters. At the end of Powell's telling of this story, he wrote, "I will relate one as it is told essentially by tribes now widely separated. Sometimes Tov-wots is said to be the father of these two personages, though not always. Sometimes all these people are said to be brothers, at other times, cousins, and many other relationships are claimed, so that it seems impossible to unravel" (Don D. Fowler and Katherine S. Fowler, *Anthropology of the Numa: John Wesley Powell's Manuscripts on the Numic Peoples of Western North America, 1868-1880*, Smithsonian Contributions to Anthropology no. 14 (Washington, DC: Smithsonian Institution Press, 1971), p. 82.

19. Ibid., pp. 81–82.

20. Ibid., p. 82.

21. Smith, *Ethnography of the Northern Utes*, pp. 107–113; and Amoss, "Ute Mountain Utes," pp. 70–73.

22. Amoss, "Ute Mountain Utes," pp. 117–118.

23. Marvin K. Opler, *The Southern Ute of Colorado* (New York: D. Appleton Company, 1940), pp. 164–165.

24. Ibid., pp. 166–167.

25. Ibid., p. 142.

26. Smith, *Ethnography of the Northern Utes*, p. 248.

27. Verner Z. Reed, *The Southern Ute Indians of Colorado* (Dillon, Co: Vistabooks, 1893, 1991), p. 18.

28. Ibid., p. 19.

29. W. W. Hill, *Navaho Warfare*, Yale University Publications in Anthropology no. 5 (New Haven, CN: Yale University Press, 1936).

30. Broderick H. Johnson (editor), *Navajo Stories of the Long Walk Period* (Tsaile, AZ: Navajo Community College Press, 1973); Louisa Wade Wetherill and Harvey Leake (editors), *Wolfkiller: Wisdom from a Nineteenth-Century Shepherd* (Salt Lake City: Gibbs Smith, Publisher, 2007); and Tiana Bighorse and Noel Bennett (editor), *Bighorse the Warrior* (Tucson: University of Arizona Press, 1990).

31. There are a number of different versions of the story of the Navajo twins and their journey to their father. Among the most accessible are Don Mose, *The Legend of the Navajo Hero Twins* (Blanding, UT: San Juan School District Media Center, 2009); Paul G. Zolbrod, *Diné bahane': The Navajo Creation Story* (Albuquerque: University of New Mexico Press, 1984); Washington Matthews, *Navaho Legends* (Salt Lake City: University of Utah Press, 1897, 1994); Aileen O'Bryan, *Navaho Indian Myths* (New York: Dover Publications, 1956, 1993); and Berard Haile, *The Upward Moving and Emergence Way: The Gishin Biye Version* (Lincoln: University of Nebraska Press, 1981).

32. Berard Haile, *Origin Legend of the Navaho Enemy Way: Text and Translation*, Yale University Press Publications in Anthropology, no. 17 (New Haven, CN: Yale University Press, 1938).

33. Samuel Holiday and Robert S. McPherson, *Under the Eagle: Samuel Holiday, Navajo Code Talker* (Norman: University of Oklahoma Press, 2013), p. 39.

34. Hill, *Navaho Warfare*, p. 7.

35. Ibid., p. 10.
36. Johnson, *Navajo Stories of the Long Walk*, p. 145.
37. Bighorse, *Bighorse the Warrior*, p. 14.
38. Hill, *Navaho Warfare*, pp. 9–11.
39. Don Mose, in a discussion with the author (October 20, 2011).
40. For a description of this process and the accompanying myth, see Franc J. Newcomb, "Origin of the Navajo Eagle Chant," *Journal of American Folklore* 53 no. 207 (January-March 1940), pp. 50–77; and W. W. Hill and Dorothy W. Hill, "The Legend of the Navajo Eagle-Catching-Way," *New Mexico Anthropologist* 6/7 no. 2 (April-June 1943), pp. 31–36.
41. Gladys Reichard, *Navaho Religion: A Study of Symbolism* (Princeton, NJ: Princeton University Press, 1963), p. 533.
42. Newcomb, "Origin of the Navajo Eagle Chant," pp. 64 and 73.
43. Matthews, *Navaho Legends*, p. 129.
44. Franciscan Fathers, *An Ethnologic Dictionary of the Navaho Language* (Saint Michaels, AZ: Saint Michaels Press, 1910, 1968), pp. 119–21.
45. Chahadineli Benally, in Johnson, *Navajo Stories of the Long Walk*, pp. 256–259.
46. Kluckhohn, *Navajo Witchcraft*, p. 94, as cited in Ruth M. Underhill, *The Navajos* (Norman: University of Oklahoma Press, 1956), p. 76.
47. Hill, *Navaho Warfare*, p. 6.
48. Ibid., p. 8.
49. Ibid., p. 9.
50. Haile, *Legend of the Navaho Enemy Way*, p. 282.
51. Hill, *Navaho Warfare*, p. 12.
52. Ibid., p. 13.
53. George Littlesalt, in Johnson, *Navajo Stories of the Long Walk*, p. 166.
54. Mose Denejolie, in Johnson, *Navajo Stories of the Long Walk*, pp. 242–243.
55. Hill, *Navaho Warfare*, p. 14.
56. Ibid.
57. Hill, *Navaho Warfare*, pp. 4–5.
58. Ibid., pp. 5–6.
59. Wetherill and Leake, *Wolfkiller*, pp. 98–99.
60. Hill, *Navaho Warfare*, p. 16; and Ernest Nelson, in Johnson, *Navajo Stories of the Long Walk*, p. 171.
61. Bighorse, *Bighorse the Warrior*, p. 18.
62. Wetherill and Leake, *Wolfkiller*, p. 76.
63. Bill P. Acrey, *Navajo History to 1846: The Land and the People* (Shiprock, NM: Central Consolidated School District No. 22, 1996), pp. 110–111.
64. Teddy Draper, Sr., in Johnson, *Navajo Stories of the Long Walk*, pp. 45–49.
65. Bighorse, *Bighorse the Warrior*, p. 26.
66. Ibid., pp. 44–45.
67. Franciscan Fathers, *An Ethnologic Dictionary*, p. 366.
68. Harry Walters, in a discussion with the author (January 16, 2012).
69. Hill, *Navaho Warfare*, p. 18.
70. For two excellent detailed accounts, see Haile, *Origin Legend of the Navaho Enemy Way*; and Franciscan Fathers, *The Navajo War Dance* (Saint Michaels, AZ: Saint Michaels Press, 1946).
71. Franciscan Fathers, *The Navajo War Dance*, pp. 8–9. The information that follows about the Enemy Way is a condensation of information from this source, pp. 9–49.
72. Charlotte Johnson Frisbie and David P. McAllester (editors), *Navajo Blessingway Singer: The Autobiography of Frank Mitchell, 1881–1967* (Tucson: University of Arizona Press, 1980), p. 294.
73. Ibid., p. 295.

CHAPTER THREE

The Navajo and Ute War, 1855–1868
A Study in Culture and Conflict[1]

Ever since the Spanish entered the Southwest, there had been an intensification of warfare between Native American groups vying for trade relations to obtain everything from guns and horses to metal goods and cloth. Each tribe had to offer something the intruders wanted, which could take the form of anything from buffalo hides for the Plains tribes to agricultural products or blankets for the Puebloan peoples. One item on the top of the list for all, however, was slaves: a commodity that played upon already existing inter-tribal warfare. Each group could curry favor with the Spanish by raiding, capturing, and selling people, especially women and children, who provided labor at a time when most work was done by hand.[2] As fragile alliances formed first with the Spanish, then with the Mexicans, and eventually with the Anglo-Americans, Native American groups chose sides, entered the fray, shifted allegiance as necessary, and vied for power as part of their own self-preservation. The complexity of the situation among different warring factions could at times become dazzling.

At the risk of oversimplifying, for the most part, Utes and Navajos in the Four Corners region viewed each other as traditional enemies, although it will soon become apparent that there were exceptions. In general, Utes allied with the Spanish, Mexicans, and Anglo-Americans. By 1850, Navajo hostility toward the United States government, who had taken control of the Southwest through the Treaty of Guadalupe Hidalgo (1848), was becoming increasingly intense. The Americans sought an effective solution to capturing the will-o'-the-wisp Navajos, who raided and then disappeared into a territory that was mostly unknown. Who had more experience in ferreting them out of their lands than their traditional enemies, who had been doing it for years? In the Four Corners region, that meant the Utes, who at this point were having their own challenges with land loss, the Black Hawk War, and other external pressures.

The Southern Utes had an old friend in Christopher "Kit" Carson, who from 1853 to 1860 worked as their agent at the Taos agency. He became a trusted counselor to them, the military, and the white communities he had charge to protect. His facility with the Ute language and understanding of their culture built confidence in his judgment. In 1857, he estimated that the Capote band was comprised of 800–900 members, while the Muache had 600, but he gave no figure for the Weeminuche. The Navajo, he felt, numbered around 12,000.[3] Carson was fully aware of the Ute-Navajo friction and the military asset he had at his disposal. On July 24, 1863, he encountered Utes on the prowl and wrote, "Shortly after encamping I was joined by nineteen Ute warriors who had been operating against the Navajos on their own account. They report having met a party of Utes returning to their country having eleven captives and that there are two other parties now in this country. . . . I have hired five of this party as spies."[4] Carson and the Ute agent at this time, Albert H. Pfeiffer, promoted the use of their wards as "spies and guides" and soldiers against the Navajo. Their effectiveness on the northern frontier proved instrumental in destroying the offensive capability of the Navajo, who bestowed upon them the title "The Enemies You Continually Fight With."

By the summer of 1858, the Utes operated in large numbers in the heart of Navajo territory. Numerous reports filled military correspondence, such as "a large force of Utahs attacked the band of Cavilliard Mucho on the San Juan opposite (north) of the Carizzo Mountains, killing ten Navajos, capturing six women and children and the whole herd of (500) horses"; and "a party of Utahs, forty in number, crossed the Rio Colorado below the mouth of the San Juan into this country (Arizona) and came as far as the Canyon de Chelly and there killed Pelon, a chief of considerable property."[5] The government encouraged these forays, saying that the Utes "appear to have inspired the Navajos with a dread not to be gotten over."[6] In the words of General Dixon Miles, "Let loose on these [Navajo] Indians all the surrounding tribes and inhabitants, particularly the Utahs and Mexicans, the two they seem to dread the most."[7] The number of operations against the Navajos grew, netting large herds of livestock and captives for sale.

The Utes heartily approved of being auxiliaries to Anglo-American forces for two reasons. First, it fit their warrior ethos of providing protection for their people while taking the war to their enemies. "The best defense is a good offense" fit nicely into their desire to stop the incessant raiding of Navajo warriors. Second, this opportunity provided a chance for economic gain. As already mentioned, unlike many Plains tribes, who fought for honor and distinction, the Utes were more interested in what material windfall there might be. So when Colonel Thomas T. Fauntleroy, working with Carson, suggested that a band of 300–400 Utes augment the six to eight companies of Mexican volunteers and spearhead the thrust against the Navajo, there appeared to be real opportunity. Nothing would be more effective than to have them ferret out the enemy from the deep recesses of the Chuska/Tunicha Mountains, Canyon de Chelly, and areas as far west as the Little Colorado River. Indeed, field reports already indicated that camps in the Navajo Mountain region and the Carrizos were abandoned, the Navajos having pushed their large herds of livestock into the region south of the Tunicha Mountains.

Fauntleroy insisted that Carson guarantee the eagerness of the Utes, "the best riflemen in the world," to wage war. He continued,

> I desire that I may be allowed to employ them, as they do not require pay as soldiers, but only to be supplied for a short time with provisions, until they can get well into the Indian country. I cannot but recommend this plan as it will at once have the effect to get the cooperation of a most valuable force, and at the same time employ these restless people, who otherwise must foray upon our own settlements.[8]

This proved to be the perfect solution: let the Utes provide for their welfare at the expense of the Navajo while rendering a service that was difficult, at best, for the conventional military. Colonel Edward R. Canby appeared at Abiquiu to work out details with Agent Pfeiffer. Eighty Utes, serving as his guides and spies, marched into the area of Canyon de Chelly, while Pfeiffer took another 300 Indians and headed in the same general direction. Much of this fighting broke down into small unit actions, as the Utes forged ahead of the main body. The cumulative impression is that their primary goal was to obtain horses and captives as much as to defeat the Navajo.

Canby's summary of his campaign during October and November 1860 illustrates the Utes' effectiveness. He claimed his troops killed twenty-eight Navajos and captured 360 horses and 2,000 sheep. His Utes killed six Navajos and captured 600 horses and 5,000 sheep, almost double the soldiers' take.[9] Pfeiffer reported the same trend, saying that in a month's time, he had killed six Navajos, taken nineteen prisoners, and obtained 5,000 sheep and about 500 horses, the latter being captured by the Utes. The agent complained that once the Indians obtained the horses, they left him with twenty Mexicans to herd, with great difficulty, the prisoners and sheep to Abiquiu. Both white leaders resented the Utes leaving after getting what they wanted.[10] For the next five years, the war and this pattern of seizure of animals and captives continued.[11]

The effect of this raiding became apparent. Navajo leaders straggled in to various forts seeking mercy and to escape harassment. The Navajos agreed to return to their country, persuade others to stop fighting, and live peacefully as long as "the Utahs might be hindered from making any campaigns against them."[12] In spite of these overtures, the Utes continued the war for captives and booty. Though Civil War battles over slavery raged between the North and South during part of this same time period, the slave trade boomed in Rio Arriba, Abiquiu, and Taos. By January 1862, New Mexicans held captive a minimum of 600 women and children through a system described as "worse than African slavery." The number of unreported Indian slaves can only be guessed, but by 1865, General Carleton estimated that at least 3,000 were living in Mexican households.[13]

Navajos in southeastern Utah give clear testimony of what they experienced at the hands of the Utes during and after the "Fearing Time" that lasted from 1858 to 1868. Navajo and Ute relations, which had previously vacillated between uneasy friendship and overt hostility, now reached their zenith in full-scale war. In one sense, part of the blame for this friction may be placed on the traditional form of Navajo government. Agents at this time pointed out that fragmented band leadership had "no power to punish the bad men of the nation or prevent them from committing depredations when they are disposed to do so."[14] Often, these leaders were wealthy and paid an indemnity from their own herds. These rich men, or *ricos*, had the most to lose when total war occurred and so wanted to maintain a peaceful status quo. This was not true of the young men interested in building their herds and acquiring status.

Navajo oral tradition confirms this view. Approximately half of forty stories told by Navajo elders blame the start of hostilities on their people. The following are a few examples.

- "The reason for being taken to Fort Sumner was that the Diné were stealing from other tribes . . . and they were caught sometimes in stealing livestock."

- "It was because of the fighting between the Navajos and other Indians that our ancestors were taken to Fort Sumner."
- "They [ancestors] said it was our own fault that we were rounded up and taken to Fort Sumner. They said we used to kill Ute Indians, Pueblo Indians and Mexicans and bring their sheep back and that those actions caused the wars between us, the Army, and other Indian tribes."
- "Our late forefathers, those that were wise, begged their fellow Diné to stop going around stealing horses, sheep and cattle from the Mexicans; but the stealing went on. One of the men who was begging the Diné to quit stealing said, 'Don't be sorry when we get enemies like a road covered with ice—starvation, poverty, and cold. You will suffer; then you will understand.' "[15]

Martha Nez, living near Mexican Water, attributed the problem locally to Navajo men harassing Ute women who were picking sumac berries. The men killed some of the women, starting the conflict. "The uprising did not begin with the white people. It started with the Utes first."[16] Yellow Horse, a future Navajo leader, tells of traveling with friends to Mancos Creek, the "traditional boundary between Utes and Navajos."[17] There, they encountered an encampment of Utes, mostly women and children, whose husbands were hunting in the Gallina Mountains. The Navajos, seizing the opportunity, killed some of the men and women and stole the horses in retaliation for past wrongs. A Ute runner alerted the hunters, who chased the offending party toward the San Francisco Mountains before giving up and returning home. Many Navajos living along the San Juan River feared retaliation and left the area, heading for the Lukachukai Mountains and other secluded spots away from the enemies' domain. "Eventually the Utes won the battle because the refugees lost many people to starvation before spring arrived."[18]As for those who initiated the raid, they fled to the Fort Defiance area and were later taken to Fort Sumner. By then, Yellow Horse and his friends were starving and nearly naked.

Charlie Mitchell concurs, providing some delightful Navajo metaphors to explain what he experienced.[19]As he grew into young adulthood, his "arrows came into being" (i.e., he was old enough to own his arrows). Groups of young men, two or three at a time, sneaked off to steal horses, "which made them go wild." Others joined in, stealing and killing. The elders cautioned, "You should stop behaving so! Under no circumstances should you be behaving so. . . . My young

Fig. 9—Ute warriors following a trail in southwestern Colorado. Familiar with the land, excellent trackers, and implacable foes, they brought the fight to the heart of Navajo country and caused much of the northern part of their enemies' territory to be abandoned. The Utes sustained the pressure so effectively that they became known to the Navajos as "The Enemies You Continually Fight With." (Denver Public Library, Western History Collection, H. S. Poley, P-54)

men, my children, do not speak in that way! In peace we want to live. If ever on to us you should upset (the enemy), yes it is not easily remedied."[20]

The young men argued that with war came rain, and beautiful flowers resulted.[21] At first, the Utes "had respect for us," but after some were killed, "they rose up against us . . . and became pretty fierce." After attacking some Americans, "[Abraham] Lincoln became angry . . . [and] in accordance with his command, all of the different people—the Utes and the Pueblo Indians [etc.] . . . all of those who live around us were put down toward us. . . . And we being alone, all of the different tribes spilled over on us. From this side, from toward the north, the Utes came to trouble us."[22] Devastation and starvation followed.

George Little Salt remembers that some Navajos heard the piñon crop was plentiful in the La Sal Mountains and so "moved up there; and they picked the little nuts and lived with some Utes that they used to know before they went to the La Sals."[23] While harvesting the crop, other Utes appeared and chased the people, who escaped and fled to Oljato. Eventually, these people moved to Navajo

Mountain and joined a growing number of Navajos collecting in that area. There were frequent skirmishes against their enemy as each vied for advantage. His grandfather, Old Whiskers—a powerful medicine man who spoke Paiute—befriended some of the people who joined his group. It is interesting to note that although these Navajos fought some of the Utes, they also had both Ute and Paiute friends in the area.

John Holiday, a Blessingway singer from Monument Valley, provides a second explanation—beyond theft and raiding—as to why the Navajos suffered these trials. The following account, rich in detail, speaks as much about perception of supernatural events as what happened on the land. John's views go to the heart of Navajo understanding concerning cause-and-effect.

> Another reason for the captivity and eventual release of the Navajos from Fort Sumner was that an individual had been working against the people. This man had sacred powers to "talk," or pray, the Navajos deep into the ground. He lived at the edge of Rock Canyon, at Twin Stars [Sonsela Butte, Arizona] and a place called Green Cattail Flat. He encouraged the enemies against us who gathered at his place. There were many. Some medicine men went to the top of Navajo Mountain and performed crystal gazing [divination]. They saw this person coming in and out of his hogan, followed by a dog. "This is the man. The man who did this to the Navajos," they said. They did a ceremony then departed, next going to Promise Rock, about eight miles south of Gouldings [Monument Valley], by the windmill. That rock, or mesa, tapers at the end and is said to be a large snake or reptile. There is a small patch of sand, with some bushes on its mid-crown, where there is a hole-like spot. The men performed another ceremony there, singing to the person who caused all the friction. "If it is really him, he will not last but [will] perish before dawn," they said. These medicine men had sacred powers. It is said that the person died early that morning. This must have been during the summer, because the man was out hoeing his garden when his dog went past him from south to north, singing a song about Mountain Boy and saying, "Mountain Boy, you will die." The man who talked the Navajos into the ground, the one who sent the enemies, died.[24]

This account is steeped in cultural values. It emphasizes the power of prayer and how "good" is pitted against "evil" through the activities of opposing medicine men. This tit-for-tat retaliation in the spiritual realm is an underlying concept important in understanding Navajo worldview and how right and wrong can be controlled. The specific site names as to where events occurred give concrete reality to what is taught and make the land a mnemonic device for teaching and remembering values. The rock formation, said to be a snake, has protective powers (as does Navajo Mountain) that shield the practitioners while they perform the ceremony, much like Big Snake is a protector in Navajo mythology. Divination is the only way to see past actions set in motion against the People. The dog, according to traditional teachings, is a sensitive being who recognizes witchcraft and forewarns of harmful events. In Navajo culture, a family maintains a dog outside to keep evil away from the home. These sacred beliefs explain much about how physical events are brought about by spiritual means.

Fig. 10—John Holiday, Blessingway singer and a man knowledgeable about Navajo history of southeastern Utah, had family members who shared their experiences through oral history. Fundamental to understanding the Navajo view of the "Fearing Time" (1850s–1860s) is an understanding that the Holy People, spread throughout the landscape, provided physical assistance and supernatural protection that allowed the People to survive. (Photo by Stan Byrd)

John Holiday continued to speak of the effect that the roundup of Navajo people had on his family. He tells of his grandmother, Woman With The Four Horns (because of her sheep), living near present-day Richfield. As a newlywed, she and her husband were traveling to Rough Rock and had passed Kayenta when they saw a large dust cloud. Thinking it might be Navajos participating in an Enemyway ceremony, the couple remained in place until it was too late. A group of white men abruptly reined their horses in front of the husband and wife, while the leader drew his weapon. "He pulled a gun, and at that instant, my grandmother 'spoke to the gun' [prayed] and heard the click of the hammer, but no bullet [was] fired. Three times he pulled the trigger but nothing happened. Just then another horseman, a Mexican with a large sombrero, rode up and knocked the weapon out of the white man's hand. Then the gun fired."[25] The horsemen tied up the two Navajos, separated them, and split in different directions to continue their search for captives. The efficacy of prayer and the invoking of supernatural power mentioned in this experience was very much a part of the Navajos' understanding of what lay at the root of this conflict, as well as how to ameliorate subsequent problems.

There were groups that sought refuge at Navajo Mountain. Manuelito, a major war leader and one of the last to surrender and go to Fort Sumner, directed Bighorse to take his relatives and others and move behind Navajo Mountain for protection. Bighorse names thirty warriors who, with their families, would have comprised a sizable contingent of Navajos seeking safety in the canyons, along the San Juan and Colorado Rivers, and near the mountain.[26] Bighorse shares the experience of one of these men, Wounded Knee (Hastiin Bigodí), who received his name from a wound he sustained when he strayed too far from Navajo Mountain, was shot by soldiers, and was left for dead. Some Navajo warriors eventually found him and brought him back to camp.[27] Bighorse, in relating this event, emphasized the importance of prayer and the power of the holy beings.

The Navajos in hiding actively sought divine intervention through prayer for the people taken captive. Bighorse left no doubt as to its importance.

> The medicine man named Many Whiskers and another called Old Arrow go to the top of Navajo Mountain to pray to the Holy People. They pray that these captured Navajos [at Fort Sumner] will come back to their homeland safely, soon be free. At this time there are lots of medicine men. They pray every time before they eat—the whole family, all the time praying for the safe return. When they cook mush or any kind of food to eat, they use

> the stick, *ádístsiin*, that they stir it with. When they are finished, they take that stick out, with mush on it, and they pray with it too, for the safe return. And they can pray to the fire too. The charcoal that they use to cook with, they pray with it for their people to come home safely. They use corn pollen. And some of them use the corn that's ground. They do this every day and every night, before the sunrise and after the sunset—white corn before the sunrise and yellow corn after the sunset. And they pray for the warriors that are protecting them and for the white people who are holding all those people captive, pray to soften the white soldiers' hearts to let these people go free.[28]

Navajo Mountain, a sacred place, is believed to be the head of Earth Woman and the birthplace of Monster Slayer. During the Fearing Time, it acted as a shield for the people and prevented the enemy from gaining access to the territory. "The people and their medicine men had performed the sacred prayer of the protection boundary line that went from the San Juan River, north of Navajo Mountain, to the mouths of the canyons near Inscription House. The people dwelled behind this sacred line, therefore, they were never caught."[29] Navajos used this area, along with Rainbow Bridge, for rain-producing ceremonies and protection. Karl Luckert suggests that during the Long Walk period there was a major shift in religious thinking in which ceremonies became less focused on hunter rites and more focused on warrior rituals like Evilway. Blessingway and Protectionway ceremonies also became prominent.[30] Protectionway prayers passed down through generations exemplify the thoughts of those residing at Navajo Mountain: "I am spared! I am spared! Enemy has missed me! Enemy has missed me! Today it did not happen!"[31] A similar prayer intones, "I have survived for you!"

There were those who initially knew little about the raids and fighting. Wolfkiller, living in the Monument Valley-Kayenta area, recalled that he and his brother were herding sheep one day when they spied four successive columns of white smoke. Unsure what this meant, they asked their grandfather that evening, who after a second day of signaling, knew that it called for a council. After attending, he returned with confirmation of his suspicions. War with the Utes was upon them, caused by the theft of sheep and women by young warriors. The grandfather explained, "My children, it is as we feared. The spirit of war is trying to walk into our land, but we must try to stop it. . . . We have done nothing to cause this thing, but some of the people have made another raid, and our chief, at what they call Washington, has sent us word that we must leave our land and go with the soldiers to a place far to the east. . . . Now I think the people who have brought this on themselves should be taken, but we who do not want to have trouble should not be taken away from a land we know and are contented to live in."[32]

As the Utes invaded Navajo camps, the Diné spread to inaccessible recesses to avoid capture. Compare the lives of Wolfkiller with Hashkéninii: two men from different family groups who started out in the same Monument Valley-Kayenta area. Wolfkiller and his family, determined to stay in their country, did all they could to avoid detection. He left a chilling account of what it was like to live during the time. The feeling of helpless uncertainty, being ever vigilant, maintaining sentinels and scouts, moving constantly, surviving in winter weather without permanent shelter, building fires near large rocks that acted like a chimney to dissipate smoke, and continuously worrying about food all took a toll on the family's morale. Winter ended, and spring brought a new onslaught of enemy forays. Wolfkiller remembers a scout coming into camp announcing, "We are lost. The enemy has brought Utes to help them track us down, and they are coming nearer. They are cutting down the cornfields and killing the old people who cannot travel. They have taken many of the people out."[33]

The family moved farther into the canyons but to no avail. The soldiers approached while signal fires indicated that the group was surrounded and resistance was futile. The grandfather determined that surrender needed to be accomplished at night because, "The Utes would welcome the chance to kill as many of our people as they could if our people came while it was light."[34] The grandfather and two elders left the others behind and made their way to the soldiers' camp. Mounted Utes rode about, maintaining vigilance until long after dark. The Navajos were mainly concerned with avoiding any contact with them before reaching the soldiers, who they considered their source of safety. After a close call, the men infiltrated past the sentinels and made contact with a white man who spoke their language. They explained, "We would have come in to the soldiers' camp before, but we were afraid of the Utes. They have always been our enemies, and we knew that they would welcome the chance to kill as many of us as they could. . . . I asked him not to take any Utes to our camp. He said he knew he could trust us and would not send any Utes to our camp."[35] The party returned, gathered their belongings, and began their "long walk."

Hashkéninii enjoyed a different outcome. Like Wolfkiller, he was surprised one day when a rider came to his hogan and announced the dust they saw on the horizon belonged to the soldiers and that "there were some Ute scouts among the white soldiers and we were more afraid of them than the whites, as we had always been at war with them."[36] Scattering about the desert floor and nearby canyons to avoid detection, seventeen people reassembled at night and with a few possessions, headed north. Hashkéninii, mounted and armed with an old rifle, led the party and scouted for the enemy. Next, he turned west, traveling through a maze of canyons until he reached the south end of Navajo Mountain. His wife, her two sisters, and the rest of the group were exhausted, hungry, and footsore. The wife sat down and refused to go farther. The group selected a campsite, located a permanent source of water, began collecting seeds and nuts, killed an occasional rabbit, and prepared for winter. No sheep from their flock of twenty were to be eaten so that they would increase. Hashkéninii was a taskmaster, pushing his people through constant work to do what was needed to survive. His son recalled: "He drove everyone all day long and would never let us rest, knowing that we might starve." From this, Hashkéninii received his name, which translates as "Giving Out Anger" or "The Angry One."[37]

They remained at Navajo Mountain for six years, during which time only one Ute ever found them, and all he did was trade. Hashkéninii Biye' (Begay, The Son Of Giving Out Anger) did not realize until later that this person was Grayhair (aka Cabeza Blanca or White-Haired Ute), a scourge to Navajos in hiding. He is described as a bad man "who pretended to be our friend only in order to spy on us. When our flocks began to increase, he organized a group of young warriors and started for Navajo Mountain to kill us and also to get revenge on the people [Ute] who had thrown him out. At the south end of [Sleeping] Ute Mountain, he stopped to visit with some Utes, but he was so bad they killed him and his nephew. After that all the Utes moved away from Navajo Mountain and we had no more trouble."[38] By the time the government released the Navajos from Fort Sumner, Hashkéninii and his family were wealthy, with large herds of sheep and silver jewelry made from a vein of ore he had discovered.

Other Navajo groups collected in the Comb Ridge-Bears Ears area. Old Man Bob recalled, "There were no permanent homes because there were Utes raiding in this country in those days so we were afraid to stay in one place too long."[39] His mother told him that her family used to inhabit the area between the Dolores River (Colorado) and the Bears Ears long before the conflict began. Once the Utes started attacking, her family stayed more in the Bears Ears area, living in fear of Cabeza Blanca.

Old Ruins, born in 1871, shared his family story of his mother, Woman Who Walked Like She Was Crippled, and his father, also called Old Ruins, living north

Fig. 11— Hashkéninii, photographed in 1909, fled to Navajo Mountain during the Long Walk period. He successfully evaded capture and was there to greet the Navajos when they returned from Fort Sumner in the late 1860s. They had been incarcerated for four years. (Courtesy Utah State Historical Society)

of the Bears Ears. Crippled Woman's mother remained west of the Bears Ears and north of the San Juan River. A raid by the Utes pushed her group across the river before doubling back to the Bears Ears and joining a noted headman named K'aa Yélii.[40]

Not all Navajos were as fortunate. Woman Who Had Her House Burned was born at the Bears Ears, but with the start of hostilities, she ended up on Black Mesa, Arizona. The enemy, under the leadership of Cabeza Blanca, raided her camp, captured her, and sold her as a slave to a Mexican; she did not return home for two years, when the soldiers released the Navajos from Fort Sumner. "It was told by the Navajos that this leader [Cabeza Blanca] looked for Navajos who had sheep, horses, or young girls that he could capture and sell to other people such as the Mexicans."[41] Her great grandfather, Man Who Regained And Lost Horses, received his name when Utes and Mexicans stole his large horse herd. After he obtained more livestock, the Utes again took a large portion of them. Finally, his camp, comprised of many hogans located on Long Point near the Bears Ears, came under attack. Utes from the Dolores River area raided the settlement, killing him and others.[42]

As previously noted, there were exceptions, where some Navajo groups actually fled to the Utes during times of trouble. Take Cayetano, for instance. As early as 1805, this wealthy Navajo living in the Four Corners area had become an influential leader. His three sons were intimately involved with southeastern Utah and no doubt, the Weeminuche living there. Manuelito, born five miles south of the Bear Ears around 1820, grew to be one of the most prominent war leaders of the Navajo and was one of the last to surrender at Fort Sumner in 1866. K'aa Yélii (One With Arrow Quiver) was born for the Within-His-Cover People Clan (Bit'ahnii) near Shonto, Arizona. During the Long Walk period, at the age of thirty, he lived at the Bears Ears.

A third brother, Cayetanito, or K'aak'eh (Wounded), lived near Beautiful Mountain but also frequented the Montezuma Creek area.[43] Cayetano had close ties with some of the Utes living north of the San Juan, even though the river was said to serve as a boundary between the two tribes. During the 1850s, he planted crops in the vicinity of the San Juan River under the protection of the Capotes. Indeed, at one point, a Ute named Yeusache pursued a Navajo who had stolen some of Cayetano's livestock. This most likely refers to a report given by Charles H. Dimmock during Captain John N. Macomb's survey trip through southeastern Utah in 1859. He mentioned how a group of Ute warriors—among whom was Tamuche (a Capote) and Souvetah (or Sowiette)—"spent so many winters near the Elk Mountains that Colorado whites often referred to them as Elk Mountain Ute." The Navajo called Manuelito visited Macomb's camp.[44] Five days later, Tamuche returned, saying that a Ute named Nutria, assisted by some fellow tribesmen, had run off all of Cayetano's horses. A month later, some of Cayetano's Navajos stole two horses from Macomb's group "in retaliation for those taken from him by the Utes with us."[45]

Yet when the Capotes had eight horses stolen from them by Navajo raiders, two of Cayetano's sons-in-law, along with other Navajos, killed three Mexican herders and stole 10,000 sheep in revenge. A report of the incident stated, "The Navajos that committed this depredation are rich and influential men. . . . They live with the Capote Utahs . . . [and] have procured the return of the horses stolen from the Utahs who they say have promised to aid and assist them in defending themselves against all enemies."[46] Four months later, Cayetano appeared with Tamuche in Abiquiu to let the agent know that "on the branches of the Chama River some eighty miles from Abiquiu, all the Capote, Tabehuauche, and Mouache Ute Indians and the Navajos that are congregated within his agency are united."[47] Until some Mexicans killed him in January, 1860, Cayetano spent much of his time camped on the Animas and La Plata Rivers—Ute country—during a time when most Navajos fled south and west away from their vengeful enemy. Cayetanito (Little Cayetano) met a similar fate as his father three years later, also at the hands of the Mexicans.

Manuelito, one of the last *ricos* to surrender, by this time lived near the Little Colorado River. His success as war leader made him a symbol of Navajo resistance, which the military targeted. In February 1865, he received a visit from a Navajo he trusted, but ended the talk by insisting that "he intended to die where he was, that he was not stealing, that he could always be found . . . and did not intend to run away."[48] At that point, Manuelito's band, comprised of six *ricos*, had approximately 600 horses, 3,000 sheep, 30 warriors, and 100 old and young followers. Less than a month later following a Ute raid, another visitor found less than half the people, only fifty horses, and forty sheep. Manuelito said, "Here is all I have in the world. See what a trifling amount. You see how poor they are. My children are eating roots."[49]

Ten months later, a captive Navajo told the military that the Utes had dispersed Manuelito's group and that the war chief was living with his brother, surviving by hunting and eating buried corn he traded with the Hopis. Two months previous, Utes had attacked his band while he was absent. Cabeza Blanca killed most of the men, the Ute chief taking survivors and a large number of women and children with him to his own country. . . . A number were killed by the Utes on their way thither . . . [but] a treaty was made by the remnant of the band with the Utes, who told them . . . that we [military] intended to keep them in confinement, and that it was better for them to live in amity with them and in freedom.[50]

In spite of this peace, Manuelito turned himself in to the army. In September 1866, he surrendered at Fort Wingate, along with his twenty-three-member following.

K'aa Yélii, the third brother, faired somewhat better. He remained in the vicinity of Elk Ridge and the Bears Ears during this era and became the most powerful Navajo headman in southeastern Utah. Five or six hogans comprised his settlement located near a spring at what is today the Kigalia Ranger Station, named after him.[51] The people accepted him as their leader, adopting his policy of not provoking the enemy in order to avoid conflict. At the same time, he had an uncanny ability to escape raids and ambushes.

K'aa Yélii's sister, Woman Who Had Her House Burned, lived in his camp behind the Bears Ears with other Navajos at Place To Escape From The Enemy (Naznidzoodii), a canyon that facilitated disguised movement off Elk Ridge.[52] Her husband, Mexican Man, was born in the vicinity of the Bears Ears, where the couple stayed during the Fearing Time. Her maternal grandmother (no name) was not as fortunate. The Utes captured and sold her to Mexicans, who guarded her in a log cabin. She found a ladder inside and escaped, making her way to the mountains, where snow covered her tracks. She eventually reached the San Juan River, recognized Shiprock, followed the south side of the river to Douglas Mesa, then wended her way back to Naznidzoodii and K'aa Yélii's band.[53]

Cayetano and his three sons illustrate the complexity of Ute and Navajo relations at this time. From Cayetano's fleeing to and living with the Utes, to the decimation of Manuelito's band, to the studied avoidance of K'aa Yélii, there was a range of response. There appear to be two interrelated reasons. The first is the porous border created between Ute, Paiute, and Navajo expansion into the Four Corners region. As all three groups mingled at a distance from their tribal centers of gravity, each established their own use areas. Relations in trade, friendship, and marriage resulted. Items traded by the Utes included buckskins, buckskin clothing, elk hides, elk storage sacks, buffalo robes, saddlebags, horses, bandoleers, beaded bags, beaver skins, buffalo tail rattles, pitch for ceremonial whistles, and baskets. The Navajos traded woven blankets, silver, and agricultural products.[54] Navajo Mountain provided red-earth paint sold by Paiutes to the Utes.[55]

Paiutes also worked for wealthier Navajo families that had large herds of livestock that required tending. Navajo informants tell of using Paiutes to provide early warnings of danger. George Martin says that his father first met the Paiutes in the Bears Ears country, and they became his "watchers."[56] K'aa Yélii "had men posted to watch for the approach of enemy tribes" so that his group could flee.[57] Hashkéneinii practiced the same technique at his camp near Navajo Mountain. Others mention Paiutes hiding Navajos from Ute raiders, of intermarriage, and of sharing resources.[58]

These practices led to the second tie of kinship and inherent familial responsibilities. There were a number of times during these years of conflict when Navajos lived with Utes: a fact that can only be explained by family bonds that offered protection. Oral history suggests there were fairly peaceful relations between some members of the Ute and Navajo populace living in southeastern Utah and that it was the Utes living farther to the east who actually hunted for those in hiding.[59] At least in the Bears Ears and Navajo Mountain areas, there were strong ties amongst some of the San Juan Band Paiutes, local Weeminuche, and Navajos. Hashkéneinii, as an "outstanding" trader, visited many Utes and Paiutes living around the Bears Ears. He also had a number of Ute and Paiute wives.[60]

Surprisingly, the most dramatic proof of Ute, Paiute, and Navajo cooperation and protection occurred with one of the Navajos' worst enemies, Cabeza Blanca (a Weeminuche), who the Navajos describe as "a bad one, diseased, and very mean to his women." He was famous for ferreting out hidden Navajos, stealing the women, and killing the men. Many of his attacks occurred at night during a full moon or in bad weather while the Navajos were at home. He would rope the top of a forked stick hogan, pull it over with his horse, and shoot the occupants as they fled. The military is said to have agreed to his keeping anything he took, including horses, women, and children, which gave him strong motivation.[61] Not only did he track, capture, and kill many Navajos but he was also said to have weakened the effectiveness of Navajo prayers by taking a baby's heart, placing it in a crow's heart, then shooting it up a canyon cliff, where besieged Navajos were eventually defeated.[62]

One story tells of how the Navajos outsmarted Cabeza Blanca and his band.[63]Four Navajo warriors saw his war party entering a canyon and decided to prevent it from going any farther, even though they were heavily outnumbered.

Fig. 12—Ute warriors crossing the Piños River. While many were determined foes, some Utes appeared to have had friendly relations with Navajos, who remained in hiding. Both groups honored marriage and trade partnerships as important ties that bound certain tribal members. Still, conflict over boundaries and traditional rivalry generally characterized attitudes that persisted well into the twentieth century. (Denver Public Library, Western History Collection, H. S. Poley, P-57)

They built several large piles of wood for bonfires some distance apart. One man rode down and told the Utes they could not proceed because there were many warriors with bows and arrows and rifles waiting for them. The Utes did not believe him, so he gave the signal to the other men to light the bonfires. Suddenly, a great cloud of smoke went up, and he restated that there were many warriors ahead. The Utes decided not to take any chances and retreated.

There are mixed accounts of how Cabeza Blanca died. One asserts that the Navajos killed him through witchcraft chants, while another says his own people killed him over woman troubles.[64] Hashkéneinii's previously cited account is a third version. The military recorded its own version, linking Cabeza Blanca's death directly to southeastern Utah and friendships with Navajos living in this area. In September 1866, a group of "Pah Wymin," Capote, and Mexicans planned to go to the San Juan River to entice a band of Navajos to join them through pledges of friendship. Once the unsuspecting prey was lured to them, the group would kill the men and capture the rest. "It appears that Cabeza Blanca, a chief among the Wymin [Weeminuche] Utes, had some friends among the Navajos whom he wished to except from being killed to which the Capote Utes objected." [65]A fight ensued, and the Capotes killed Cabeza Blanca, then fled to Tierra Amarilla with two of Cabeza Blanca's sons in hot pursuit. The Weeminuche arrived at the settlement, killed three Mexican herders, wounded a woman, and captured some livestock before fleeing. "The Indians then left, joining as is supposed the Wymin and Pah Utes who had made friends with the Navajos in the meantime. The whole party of Wymin, Pah Utes, and Navajos then left that region and went to the neighborhood of Rio Dolores, Sierra del Latir (Mountain of the Throbbing, Beating (Ute Mountain)), and Sierra Orejas (Bears Ears) about one hundred miles from the settlements." Agent Pfeifer, the author of the letter, wished the "Wymin, Pah, and Capote Utes to bury the hatchet and be friends," then noted that "the Wymin numbered some 1200 or more; the Pah Utes some 1500; and the Navajos with them about 800 more, numbering in all 3500 [and] have been joined by the Green River Utes—driven from Utah by the troops or Mormons." As late as 1889, settlers in Aneth reported the presence of Cabeza Blanca's sons, who were acting as "mean and saucy as they can be."[66]

On June 1, 1868, the Navajos signed the peace treaty that released them from their incarceration at Fort Sumner and allowed them to return to their homeland to join those who remained. Many of the people had had vivid, livid memories of past wrongs with the Utes and emotional wounds that took a while to heal. As early as 1866, Navajos told the soldiers at Fort Sumner that "without protection from the Utahs who are our enemies, we would not care to go back."[67] Once returning became a reality, the Navajos indicated that they wanted to make a peace agreement similar to the one they had in the past so that they could trade and become "one people with them." On May 28, 1868, just before the treaty signing, General William Tecumseh Sherman warned the Navajos "that if you go to your own country, the Utes will be the nearest Indians to you; you must not trouble the Utes and the Utes must not trouble you. . . . You must not permit any of your young men to go to the Ute or Apache country to steal."[68]This advice was hardly necessary. Agent reports indicate that for the next few years, large Navajo populations avoided spreading close to the San Juan region. The friction of the previous war had burned an indelible scar into their memory—a scar that has continued to this day through their oral tradition. The Utes had earned their reputation from the Navajo: "The Enemies You Continually Fight With."

Chapter Endnotes

1. Portions of this chapter were previously published in Chapter Five of *As If the Land Owned Us: An Ethnohistory of the White Mesa Utes* (Salt Lake City: University of Utah Press, 2011).
2. For a good overview of slave raiding in the Southwest, see Ned Blackhawk, *Violence Over the Land: Indians and Empires in the Early American West* (Cambridge, MA: Harvard University Press, 2006); and Lynn R. Bailey, *Indian Slave Trade in the Southwest* (Los Angeles: Westernlore Press, 1966).
3. James L. Collins, "New Mexico Superintendency," *Report of the Commissioner of Indian Affairs* (Washington, DC: Government Printing Office, August 30, 1857), p. 273 [hereafter cited as *RCIA*].
4. Lawrence C. Kelly, *Navajo Roundup: Selected Correspondence of Kit Carson's Expedition Against the Navajo, 1863–1865* (Boulder, Colorado: Pruett Publishing, 1970), p. 28.
5. Samuel M. Yost to Collins, November 23, 1858; and John Garland to Lorenzo Thomas, January 31, 1858, in J. Lee Correll, *Through White Men's Eyes: A Contribution to Navajo History II* (Window Rock, AZ: Navajo Heritage Center, 1979), pp. 108 and 206 [hereafter cited as *TWME*].
6. William Brooks to assitant adjutant general, Records of the US Army Commander, Department of New Mexico, National Archives, Record Group 98, Washington, DC (July 15, 1858) [hereafter cited as Letters Received—Army].
7. Dixon Miles to William Nichols, Letters Received—Army (September 8, 1858).
8. Thomas T. Fauntleroy to Winfield Scott, Letters Received—Army (January 29, 1860).
9. Edward Canby to assistant adjutant general, Letters Received—Army (September 19 and November17, 1860).
10. Albert H. Pfeiffer to Canby, Letters Received—Army (October 16, 1860).
11. See L. R. Bailey, *The Long Walk: A History of the Navajo Wars, 1846–68* (Pasadena, CA: Westernlore Publications, 1978); Peter Iverson, *Diné: A History of the Navajos* (Albuquerque: University of New Mexico Press, 2002); Broderick H. Johnson (editor), *Navajo Stories of the Long Walk Period* (Tsaile, AZ: Navajo Community College Press, 1973); Kelly, *Navajo Roundup*; and Gerald Thompson, *The Army and the Navajo: The Bosque Redondo Reservation Experiment, 1863–1868* (Tucson: University of Arizona Press, 1982).
12. John Ward to Canby, Letters Received—Army (September 2, 1862); and Jose Francisco Chavez to Gorden Chapin, Letters Received—Army (September 8, 1862).
13. Testimony of James H. Carleton, Office of Indian Affairs, New Mexico Superintendency, "Letters Received," National Archives, Record Group 75, Washington, DC (July 3, 1865) [hereafter cited as Letters Received—N.M.].
14. James L. Collins, "New Mexico Superintendency," *Report of the Commissioner of Indian Affairs* (Washington, DC: Government Printing Office, August 30, 1857), p. 274 [hereafter cited as *RCIA*].
15. Florence Charley, p. 148; John Tom, p. 178; Dugal Tsosie Begay, p. 13; and Hascon Benally, p. 229 (all as cited in Johnson (editor), *Navajo Stories of the Long Walk Period*).
16. Martha Nez, in an interview by Baxter Benally and the author (August 10, 1988).
17. Yellow Horse, as cited in Will Evans, *Along Navajo Trails: Recollections of a Trader* (Logan: Utah State University Press, 2005), p. 65.
18. Ibid.
19. Charlie Mitchell, "A Navaho's Historical Reminiscences," in *Navaho Texts*, Edward Sapir (editor) (Iowa City: University of Iowa, 1942), pp. 337–97.
20. Ibid., p. 341.
21. The association between war, death, and rain is unclear. Although in Navajo philosophy, water is often associated with life, Monster Slayer, the most prominent Navajo war god, also controls lightning, which is connected to rain. Just as the Aztecs had Tláloc, the Mayans had Chac, the Totonacs had Tajín, and the Mixtecs had Cocijo as their rain gods, lightning and death were a part

of their modus operandi. Navajo bows and arrows had symbols associated with Monster Slayer and his lightning. In *Navaho Warfare*, W. W. Hill points out that following a successful raid, the leader of a war party, before leaving the objective, would draw four designs in the sand with a flint arrowhead. Zigzag lightning, straight lightning, sun ray, and rainbow arrows, all of which were used to kill the monsters inhabiting this earth at the time of creation, are symbolized by these four types. Lightning, arrows, and rain are connected (Yale University Publications in Anthropology, no. 5 (New Haven, CT: Yale University Press, 1936), p. 16.

22. Mitchell, "A Navaho's Historical Reminiscences," p. 345.

23. George Littlesalt, in *Navajo Stories of the Long Walk Period*, pp. 159–168.

24. John Holiday and Robert S. McPherson, *A Navajo Legacy: The Life and Teachings of John Holiday* (Norman: University of Oklahoma Press, 2005), p. 190.

25. Holiday and McPherson, *A Navajo Legacy*, pp. 177–78.

26. Tiana Bighorse, *Bighorse: The Warrior*, Noel Bennett (editor) (Tucson: The University of Arizona Press, 1990), pp. 40–41.

27. Ibid., pp. 42–43.

28. Ibid., pp. 44–45.

29. Joe Many Goats, in an interview with Marilyn Holiday and Robert S. McPherson (December 18, 1991).

30. Karl W. Luckert, *Navajo Mountain and Rainbow Bridge Religion* (Flagstaff: Museum of Northern Arizona, 1977), pp. 30–31.

31. Ibid., p. 6.

32. Wolfkiller, as cited in Louisa Wade Wetherill (recorder) and Harvey Leake (editor), *Wolfkiller: Wisdom from a Nineteenth-Century Navajo Shepherd* (Salt Lake City: Gibbs Smith, Publisher, 2007), p. 67.

33. Wetherill and Leake, *Wolfkiller*, p. 80.

34. Ibid., p. 81.

35. Ibid., p. 84.

36. Hashkéninii Begay, as cited in Charles Kelly, "Chief Hoskaninni," *Utah Historical Quarterly*, Volume 21 (Summer 1953), pp. 219–226.

37. Ibid., p. 221.

38. Hashkéninii Begay, as cited by Charles Kelly, "Notes," Charles Kelly Papers, Special Collections, J. Willard Marriott Library, University of Utah, Salt Lake City, Utah.

39. Old Man Bob testimony, in Doris Duke #734 (January 27, 1961). All Doris Duke materials cited are in the Special Collections, Marriott Library, University of Utah, Salt Lake City, Utah.

40. Old Ruins (Kit'siili) testimony, in Doris Duke #704 (January 18, 1961).

41. Eddie Nakai, in Doris Duke #23 (January 21, 1961).

42. Ibid.

43. White Sheep testimonies, in Doris Duke #687A and #687B (March 15, 1953 and January 6, 1961); and Frank McNitt, *Navajo Wars, Military Campaigns, Slave Raids, and Reprisals* (Albuquerque, NM: University of New Mexico Press, 1990), p. 80.

44. Charles Dimmock, as cited in Steven K. Madsen, *Exploring Desert Stone: John N. Macomb's 1859 Expedition to the Canyonlands of the Colorado* (Logan: Utah State University Press, 2010), pp. 67 and 155–156.

45. Ibid., p. 89.

46. Henry Dodge to Meriwether, *TWME* (April 19, 1856), pp. 32–34.

47. Lorenzo Labadi to Meriwether, *TWME* (August 7, 1856), p. 50.

48. Asa Carey to assistant adjutant general, Letters Received—Army (May 10, 1864); and Joseph H. Eaton to Benjamin C. Cutler, Letters Received—Army (February 8, 1865).

49. Carleton to no addressee, February 15, 1865, *War of the Rebellion*, Series I, Volume 48, Part I (Washington, DC: Government Printing Office, 1866), pp. 864–865; and John Ayers to Cutler, Letters Received—Army (March 20, 1865).

50. Edmund Butler to assistant adjutant general, Letters Received—Army (January 18, 1866).
51. Paul Goodman, in Doris Duke #689 (January 6, 1961).
52. Warrior Woman (Desbaa') testimony, in Doris Duke #703 (January 18, 1961).
53. Ibid.
54. W. W. Hill, "Navaho Trading and Trading Ritual: A Study of Cultural Dynamics," *Southwestern Journal of Anthropology*, Volume 4 (Fall 1948), pp. 377 and 380.
55. Mabel Dry testimony, in Doris Duke #110 (July 25, 1967).
56. George Martin, Sr., in Doris Duke #913 (March 22, 1961).
57. Paul Jones, in Doris Duke #712 (January 19, 1961).
58. Maggie Holgate, in an interview with Gary Shumway, Doris Duke #956 (June 13, 1968).
59. For a discussion of friendly relations with the local Utes and Paiutes living in the Bears Ears area, see testimony of Billy Holiday, in Doris Duke #668 (July 21, 1961); George Martin, Sr., in Doris Duke #913 (March 22, 1961); Cecil Parrish, in Doris Duke #667 (January 6, 1961); Paul Goodman, in Doris Duke #689 (January 6, 1961); Pat Shortfinger, in Doris Duke #694 (January 11, 1961); and Anderson Cantsee (Ute), in Doris Duke #739 (January 28, 1961).
60. Billy Holiday testimony.
61. John Smith, *Navajo Stories of the Long Walk Period*, p. 137; and Charles Kelly, "Interview notes with Hoskanini Begay," Charles Kelly Papers, Special Collections, Marriott Library, University of Utah, Salt Lake City, Utah.
62. Fred Descheene, as cited in *Navajo Stories of the Long Walk Period*, p. 210.
63. Howard W. Gorman, as cited in *Navajo Stories of the Long Walk Period*, p. 28.
64. Ibid.
65. Major Albert Pfeiffer to A. K. Graves, Letters Received—N.M. (December 10, 1866).
66. William Davidson to Southern Ute Agent, Letters Received—N.M. (April 11, 1889).
67. Navajo council with miltary, *TWME* (February or March, 1866), p. 139.
68. William T. Sherman in council, *TWME* (May 28, 1868), p. 133.

CHAPTER FOUR

Fighting on Hill and Dale
Cowboys, Cavalry, Utes, and Terrain Considerations, 1875–1885[1]

During the 1870s and 1880s, the Four Corners region opened to an intense period of exploration and settlement by both Native American and white people interested in its resources. For the white man, mining, cattle grazing, farming, and other industries held possibilities. For the Navajo, new lands to graze their sheep, hunt deer, grow gardens, and sell their wares gave reason for expansion. In both instances, this came at the expense of the Utes, who had roamed, hunted, and gathered in a large territory generally unknown to others. With the friction from the Long Walk period now over, a variety of people turned their eyes toward a land that seemed relatively open. First on the white man's agenda was to have the region officially removed from Ute control, then mapped for distribution. The process started with miners in southwestern Colorado, who sought to remove Indian ownership and obtain precious metals. Part of the Ute domain came under this initial assault, which was soon followed by cattle interests in pursuit of grass. For the Indians living in southeastern Utah, the reverberations from this act took longer to reach than those living to the east, where loss was immediate. It was just a matter of time, however, before they felt the impact. George W. Manypenny, a former Commissioner of Indian Affairs and contemporary advocate for the Utes, put it this way: "With the surrender of the portion of the Ute reservation obtained by the Brunot agreement [1874], the Indians had a right to, and did expect that, they would be relieved from any further inroads; that having given up the mining territory, they would be protected in what was termed the agricultural lands. But this was a delusion. The grazing country was just as much coveted as the mineral, and the 'ranchmen' intruded to prospect for good locations . . ."[2] The Utes were anything but happy about what was beginning to unfold.

Little wonder that when elements of the 1875 Ferdinand V. Hayden survey party appeared in southeastern Utah, they were unwelcome. They had spent the two previous years in Colorado as part of a national effort to survey unmapped territory. Now they needed to complete the unfinished portion of southwestern Colorado, a small adjoining strip in northern New Mexico, and a portion of southeastern Utah. Hayden divided his force into seven elements: four of whom had specific geographical areas to work in; a fifth to handle general triangulations; a sixth to collect photographs of scenery and Anasazi ruins; and a seventh to transport supplies. The southwestern division, under geologist W. H. Holmes, covered an area of 6,500 square miles, which included part of the San Juan River; the La Plata, Mancos, and Dolores Rivers; and McElmo and Montezuma Creeks, all of which fell in the domain of Ute territory. Smaller teams—one led by topographer Henry Gannett, another by James T. Gardner (in charge of triangulation), and a third, the photographic team under the direction of William H. Jackson—also explored and recorded parts of the same area.[3]

The surveyors realized the Indians' sensitivity to what they were doing. The year before, the Utes denied access to one survey party, believing they were working on reservation boundaries. On August 4, Gannett's party joined forces with Gardner's since both were heading for the La Sal Mountains and felt that one larger group was safer than two smaller ones. Prior to their departure, Ouray warned "that the Indians in the Sierra La Sal Mountains . . . were likely to steal stock if they got a good chance. He said that a group of seven men would be safe in the region, but they must watch their animals carefully, and if one man was caught out alone he might not be safe. In short, these Sierra La Sal Indians were represented to me as sneak thieves, who would bear much watching."[4] When the combined party left their base camp on the Dolores River, there were thirteen men: seven armed with rifles and the rest with revolvers. They saw no signs of Indians until they reached the base of the mountains, estimating that nine lodges were camped on the Utah-Colorado line. Six more joined them two days later. By then, the geographers had climbed the highest peak, Mount Peale, twice and completed their topographic sketches and triangulations before setting off for Blue Mountain.

On August 15, the men broke camp, having christened the highest peak in the range Mount Peale (12,721 ft.) after Albert C., a member of the party. They departed for the Abajo range (known locally as Blue Mountain) approximately forty miles straight-line distance south. An interim destination was "Cold Spring" at the top of Peters Hill, marked on a map produced by a previous mapping party led by Captain John N. Macomb in 1859.[5] They traveled over Indian trails much of the time, reaching the southern drainage running off the La Sals where they surprised an Indian boy and old man irrigating several small patches of corn. Both fled, but their presence encouraged party members to believe they had seen other Indians. Concerned there might be an unfriendly encounter, the white men left the area.

Late afternoon found the party in the hot, sagebrush-covered Dry Valley with Gannett a half mile behind the main group taking topographical notes and Gardner ahead, searching for water. Some Utes approached Gannett making signs of peace, shook his hand, then accompanied him to the larger group, where a second party reined in, whooping amidst a cloud of dust. Members of Gardner's group recognized three of the warriors as men they had encountered hunting twenty miles east of the Dolores; the Indians had similar recollections. The Utes produced a paper showing that they were from the White River Agency and declared themselves to be Yampa. They urged the survey party to camp with them at a muddy watering hole and not proceed to the spring at the top of what is today known as Peters Hill. The water from the runoff was not potable, however, and the terrain was open to attack. Next, they wished to trade for powder and tobacco, but there was none to spare. All this time, the white men noted how the Indians were evaluating their weapons and generally eyeing the group. With a friendly "adios," the groups shook hands and parted.[6]

As soon as the rearguard cleared the brow of a nearby hill, the Utes reached the top and opened fire from behind. At first the surveyors thought it was not aimed at them, but when other shots followed, the men flew into action. Some raced to the rear of the train and wanted to charge, but Gardner declined. Given the tired mules, the Indians' fresh mounts, and the protective hill they fired from, the white men decided to break contact but dispatched a small group to a nearby knoll to cover the main party's southern advance across Dry Valley. The warriors maintained a running engagement, directing fire from a number of hills while keeping a 500-yard distance. Evening approached, the animals were exhausted, the men tired and hungry, and there was no chance of reaching water before dark. Finding a spot in the flat sea of sage out of range from firing points on surrounding hills and the South Point plateau, the party formed a defensive perimeter of packs and *aparejos* (pack saddles) and "corralled," or tethered, the livestock on both sides of the defense. Gardner and two other men moved 300 yards from

Fig. 13—A portion of the Ferdinand V. Hayden survey party photographed at Parrott City, Colorado, a few days after their fight with the Utes. One of the leaders of the survey described what happened to four of the men pictured here when he noted, "They had just reached my camp after having been attacked by the Paiutes and had lost everything but their riding animals. They arrived a sad and hungry lot." (Hayden Party Photo File, Folder 3, American Heritage Center, University of Wyoming)

this position to a ravine where they could prevent the Indians from infiltrating close enough to put effective fire on the defenders. Part of this strategy was based on men carrying "needle rifles" with a maximum effective range of 650 yards.[7] The Utes were armed with muzzle-loaders and a sprinkling of Winchester rifles, neither of which had a distance of more than 250 yards. Thus, the night defense and the following day's movement were based on maintaining a large gap between the two forces, keeping Indian fire from the distant hills ineffective.

As the defense took shape, the Utes maintained a steady volume of fire which either fell fifty yards short of the target or whizzed wildly overhead. At one point, a shot hit the bell mare, Polly, and was close enough to send Gannett, Ben Northington, and Peale diving for the enclosure, Peale getting his foot entangled on the way, pitching him in an inglorious sprawl behind the barricade.[8] Their weapons—"seven breech-loading rifles, more or less good, and four large revolvers, which it was quite obvious were no use against those long range-loving cowards"—were supplied with "ammunition [which] was neither very abundant nor very good."[9] Two canteens of muddy water and some crusts of bread left over from breakfast provided a hasty supper. A schedule to replace the picket at midnight and a watch within the barricade freed some to sleep before their turn to guard arrived.

A full moon rose, making the landscape as "bright and light as day."[10] The Utes began infiltrating through the sagebrush, while each of the opposing sides fired at muzzle flashes. Those who returned fire would shoot, then roll three times to avoid being pinpointed. Concealing themselves effectively in the sagebrush and crawling closer reduced the disparity in firepower, making the Utes' weapons more effective. For five hours the sporadic exchange continued. Lack of water, food, and sleep took its toll; Gardner, who at midnight was relieved of picket duty, realized something had to be done. Knowing he had a slow-moving, eighteen-mule pack train and tired mounts, that he was open to ambush from surrounding hills as soon as the party left its barricade, and that the Indians held part of the ridge that led up the valley and canyon to the top of Peters Hill and the spring, he decided to find an alternative route onto the plateau to the surveyors'-south.

Gardner ordered the animals saddled, packed, and formed into a column protected by four riflemen skirmishing in pairs to the front and three to the rear to deny any high ground for sharp-shooting Utes before the party passed out of rifle range. At first light the group abandoned their position amidst war whoops. Besides seeking a slope that allowed them to gain the plateau, they desperately needed water. For five hours the men rode "around the whole of the open [Dry] Valley," exchanging fire while trying but failing to beat the Indians to commanding terrain.[11] Wishing to avoid the trail that headed up the canyon on Peters Hill for fear of ambush, the party sought tentative breaks in the escarpment that allowed them to reach high ground. An old warrior positioned on a high rock to the rear signaled the party's every move with a red cloth, directing the reaction of the Utes below. Whenever a rifleman from the survey group dismounted to take a shot, the targets dispersed, maintaining a healthy distance. Cuthbert Mills of the *New York Times* paints a vivid picture of what the fighting was like:

> And now commenced a game of long shots, which if we had not been so anxious about getting out of this natural trap, would have been quite amus-

ing. Some of the Indians rode to our rear, a fellow on a powerful gray horse kept to our right, and [Clarence] Kelsey, Ben Northington, and I fell back as rear guard. The enemy commenced banging away at us, and the gray horseman was especially active in wasting his ammunition. This was endured for some time, and then Ben, losing patience exclaimed: "Dash me but I'll try a shot at that fellow, though I am short of ammunition," and dismounting he did so then shook his head. The shot was a wide one. . . . At this time they were paying their attention to us from the left. There were three there—two close together, the third a little way behind. I aimed at him, and, as the gun cracked, our fellows gave a shout of derisive laughter. The bullet struck up dust just at the horse's heels, and the rider gave the animal such a sudden stroke with his whip that it jumped and fell headlong over the sagebrush. When it scrambled up the Indian was still in his seat. He had never lost it.[12]

The exhausted mules walked slowly, spurning the spur as the sun parched man and beast. The valor of the survey party was not enough to carry the plan that seemed checkmated with every attempt. Signs of faltering among some members appeared. Gardner took a straw vote after explaining the options. Did the men want to go back the way they had come, proceeding up the canyon while fighting all the way, or did they want to continue to search for another route? Most agreed to do whatever the group wanted, but the majority with definite opinions wished to press forward to Peters Spring. Gardner agreed, and although he might lose some men in the effort, it appeared to be their best chance.

Following a feint to the west, his party headed for the eastern side of Peters Canyon, where piñon and juniper trees provided cover and concealment over the foothills leading to a small plateau, then talus slope, and finally, rimrock at the top of South Canyon Point. It was the only practical choice, as the Utes, mounted on fast horses, raced to the west side and assumed positions in the rocks, approximately 300 to 400 yards from where the party would begin its ascent. Gardner and another man first provided covering fire from a hill on the east side of the canyon, then Gardner moved higher to provide continued support while his companion returned to guide the train. Those Indians not ensconced in the rocks traveled up the canyon, then skirted down the east side below the rimrock. The white men urged the heavily laden pack mules and tired mounts over the slope, using the terrain and vegetation for concealment. Effectively hidden, the Indians provided "nothing but whiz, bang, whiz, bang, whiz, bang," as their targets labored uphill.[13] At this point, Gardner wondered if there might be some type of break in the rock formation that would grant access to the plateau above—"one chance among a million, but the odds were better than going through the canyon."[14]

As man and animal plodded up the slope and onto the narrow flat, they found a pool of alkaline clay water almost the consistency of paste that they drank to slake their thirst. Aware that the Indians were intending to head them off, Gardner pushed the party forward, traveling on the plateau at the base of the talus slope. Five packs fell off or had to be readjusted due to the difficult travel, giving more time for the Indians to assume new vantage points in preventing escape. Suddenly, the Utes opened fire from the high ground, perhaps sixty yards away, just below the rimrock. "Jim," the white mule, made a fine target and was the first to be killed, two others eventually suffering a similar fate with another lost in the trees and three more being wounded. The firing grew intense. Each member of the party took up a position behind a tree or rock, reporting that the Indians' fire was accurate, with clipped branches or chips of rock falling close about. As for the Utes, they were perfectly concealed.

In the meantime, Gardner had been able to get around an angle of the slope, where he spied a narrow deer path that led upward and possibly through an indentation in the rimrock. He and packer Shep Madera traversed the steep incline to see if there might be a trail. Their first thought was to relieve the pressure on the men below, but a ledge masked their view of the enemy. One unlucky Ute fifty yards away, however, fired and then exposed himself to see his effect—only to have Madera bring him down. Cheers from below reported the result. Robert Adams next joined the pair as they traversed part of the slope, locating the exact route of the concealed deer trail, which took them to the edge of the plateau.

Elated at the stroke of luck that had befallen them, the three rejoined the party to report. There was no doubt that the mules could never make the ascent under fire while loaded with all the equipment. After a few minutes of deliberation, Gardner "order[ed] to 'cut loose' with feelings which actually brought out tears. Had there been time, everything would have been piled up and burned; as it was they went to work with knives and cut everything from the backs of the mules in such a way that scarcely a whole rope, an unbroken package, an unsmashed can or box, or anything cutable or breakable was left."[15] Ammunition, four days of rations, a frying pan and pot, and their field notes and scientific work were all the camp equipment the group took with them, while each man secured a coat for warmth and a sleeping blanket. They destroyed the rest, then went up the slope, herding or leading the livestock. "A miracle, almost, now occurred"—an unopposed ascent.[16]

Men and animals clambered to the top, left the protection of a small piñon and juniper forest rimming the canyon, and began their flight over a sagebrush-covered plateau. Destination: Mancos River, then La Plata River and the supply camp. It was 1:30 p.m. on August 16, and the heat was intense. Water remained uppermost on everyone's mind, second only to the Indians' signal shot notifying their comrades they were aware that the whites had given them the slip. The Utes' efforts a couple of hours later to head off the whites and keep them from water failed. Gardner believed that his enemy guessed the surveyors were heading to the Dolores River and so rode ahead, but the white men took a trail that snaked its way to the southeast in the general direction of the Mancos River. Five hours later, the party found a spring, rested, watered, and ate a supper of bread, ham, and tea. Then they plunged on. Two hours later, they stumbled upon a Ute encampment, with the Indians pursuing them to a hill "ki-yi-yiing," then moving forward while saying "amigo" and asking who these travelers were and where were they going. The groups parted as friends, the surveyors continued for another two hours before camping.[17]

Two more days of constant travel brought them to springs at Hovenweep where they rested. The next day, they arrived at McElmo Canyon, then traveled near Sleeping Ute Mountain, the Mancos River, and finally, just before dark, to Merritt's ranch, where they made pea soup from the produce of Merritt's garden. They also learned that Holmes' party had camped five miles ahead, as they were wending their way to the supply base at Parrott City. The next day, August 20, both groups arrived. Gardner's men were bedraggled. Peale wrote, "A more haggard-looking party could scarcely be found. Out of about sixty consecutive hours we had been in the saddle forty-eight, with about five hours' sleep and nothing to eat save a few scraps of bread and ham."[18] Gardner added, "The fight was incessant from 5 o'clock p.m. on the 15th, till the afternoon of the 16th, except three hours in the night. Out of thirty-two animals we brought off twenty-eight. Three of these are wounded, but not badly. Not a man was wounded and none are sick. The work is not much interfered with, for the western part of the topography, in the dangerous country, was about complete."[19] The leader went on to praise his entire group.

Other participants gave additional reasons for success: 1.) "[O]ur men were armed with long-range needle guns"; 2.) Gardner's cool courage in leading and his topographical knowledge of the area; and 3.) lack of boldness of the Indians.[20]

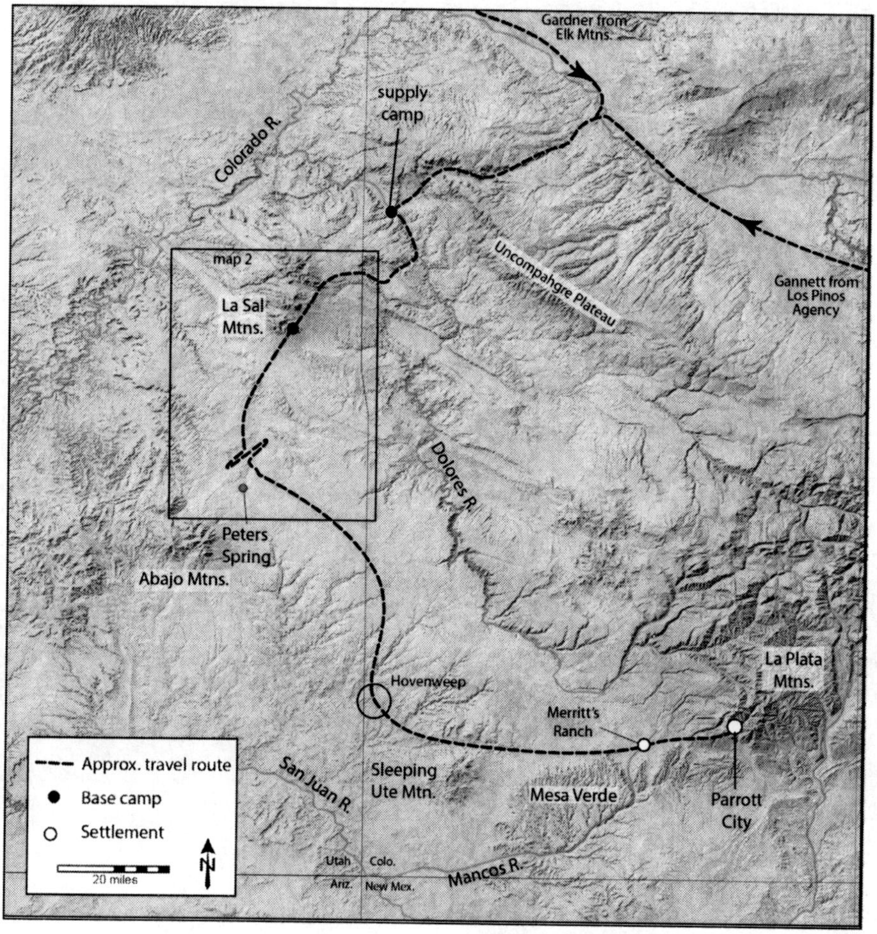

Fig. 14 —Hayden survey route and location of skirmish in southeastern Utah. (Maps by Winston B. Hurst)

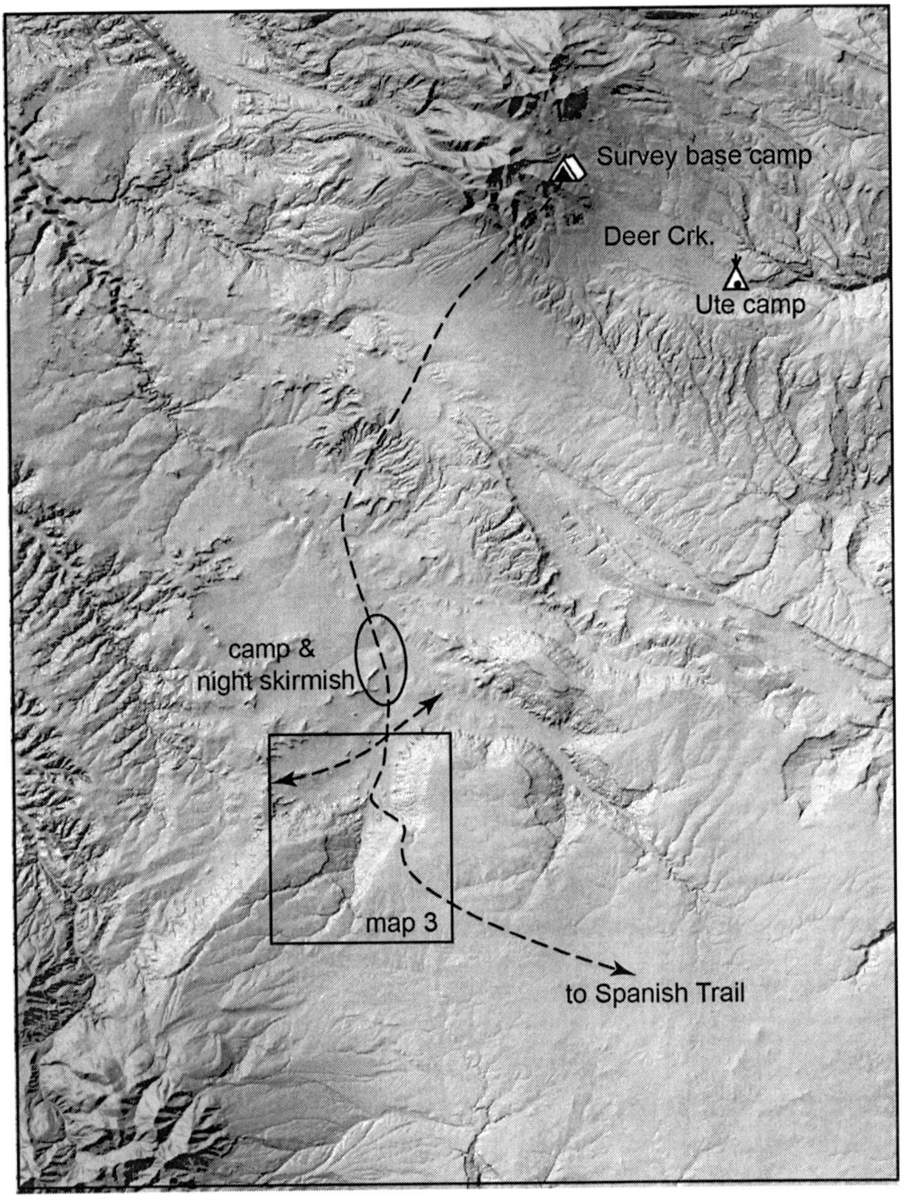

Fig. 15a—Hayden survey route and location of skirmish in southeastern Utah. (Maps by Winston B. Hurst)

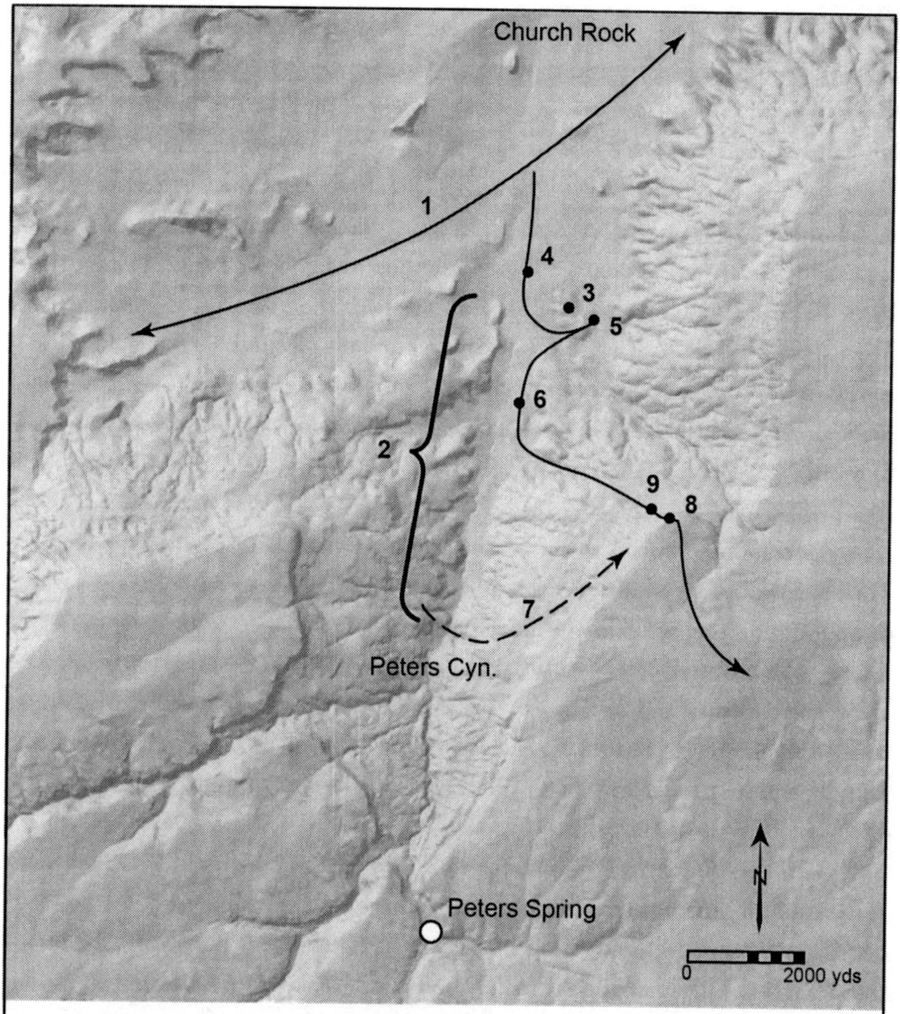

1. Five-hour running skirmish in failed search for alternate route onto mesa
2. Ute ambush position on high ground west side of wash
3. Gardner & Adams ahead of main pack train find cover on wooded hill
4. Main pack train forced to within 300 yds of Ute rifles to get across arroyo
5. Main pack train finds cover behind Gardner's hill
6. Party makes run for spring, using trees for cover, abandons run for spring, avoids ambush by heading upslope toward break in caprock
7. Utes reposition via bench to intercept surveyors, firing from caprock talus
8. Gardner, Adams and Madera find trail, kill or wound one Ute in talus
9. Surveyors dump gear, escape up trail onto mesa

Fig. 15b —Hayden survey route and location of skirmish in southeastern Utah. (Maps by Winston B. Hurst)

This small skirmish, while an excellent example of problems fighting in Canyon Country, had far more political reverberations in Washington than in Colorado and Utah. On a practical level, however, mapping of the area made it known and hence available for entrepreneurs. Take for example, three brothers—Dick, George, and Billy May—who settled as cattlemen in the Big Bend country of Colorado in 1877. They prospered, utilizing the open range between Mancos, Colorado, and the Blue and La Sal Mountains in Utah. The mining camps of Rico, Telluride, and Silverton welcomed their beef and encouraged expansion of the business.[21] Two years later, other businessmen—John Thurman and J. H. Alderson—went into partnership on a large herd of high-quality horses and pastured them on the Utah-Colorado border near present-day Dove Creek, where they built a cabin. The men opened for business, selling their stock to local buyers.[22]

Among these buyers were Dick May and Byron Smith, who appeared at Thurman's cabin on May 1, 1881, to purchase horses, presumably for the spring cattle roundup that was just starting. On their way, they met some cowboys who warned of a group of Utes "on the prod" and told May and Smith to turn back. What the two men did not realize is that a few days before, Thurman had discovered the same Indians trying to catch some of his prize stock. He beat them soundly and sent them angrily on their way. How events unfolded next and who discovered the results are left to conjecture.[23]

There is no doubt, however, as to the outcome. The Utes killed Dick May at the cabin following a hard fight. Around his body lay a quantity of expended cartridges, outside were two dead horses, and the cabin was burned.[24] The Indians also killed Thurman approximately half a mile away from his home and stole an estimated $1,000 from the bodies, 100 horses, 900 pounds of flour, 5 rifles, 3 pistols, a shotgun, 75 pounds of ammunition, and assorted other goods.[25] According to an Indian account received during an interrogation after the Pinhook fight, four Utes met May at the cabin. He came to the door, grabbed one Indian and threw him down on the ground, then walked over and shot two of their horses. The Utes became angry, killed the two men, then left.[26]

Word of the incident soon reached the settlement at Big Bend, approximately forty-five miles away. Along with several other men, Dick May's brothers, George and Billy, left on May 3 to determine what had happened and to retrieve the bodies. After a thorough search of the area and the discovery of Thurman's corpse on Cedar Point in Colorado, the group buried him where he fell but took May's remains back to Dolores. Byron Smith was never found.[27]

The Utes involved in the incident traveled about but eventually reached Blue Mountain, where they stole horses from Joshua B. "Spud" Hudson and other ranchers along the way. "Spud," a Colorado cattleman hailing from the Purgatoire (universally called Picketwire) River country of southeastern Colorado, was angry. His camp, called the Double Cabins, was located about six miles north of present-day Monticello and became an important landmark in the events that followed. But not only Hudson's stock was lost; others in the vicinity were missing animals, as well as having had their cabins raided. On May 14, several ranchers again encountered Indians taking stock, and after some shooting during which perhaps one Indian died, the men returned to their towns to form a posse.[28] They soon joined forces and went in search of the culprits; the Utes by this time had procured a herd estimated at 350 stolen horses, plus their own animals. They had also "wantonly killed hundreds of cattle belonging to the stockmen of this vicinity."[29]

Hudson formed an initial posse of twelve men, but after finding the Indians' deserted camp at Dodge Spring and realizing their numbers, the Blue Mountain posse spent a few more days recruiting help and doubling their force to twenty-five. They then followed the Utes' trail to the southern end of Blue Mountain.[30] Along the way, the cowboys found tired ponies and an occasional goat from the Indians' herd but feared pressing the chase because of possible ambush in the canyons.[31]

At the same time, another small army, this one from Colorado, was underway. While some of these volunteers came from the livestock communities of Mancos and Dolores, the majority hailed from the mining town of Rico, with a population of 1,500 people. Their stated intention was to protect the cattlemen and recover stolen animals as the spring roundup played across the ranges of southeastern Utah. Their real intent, however, was to fight Indians. They had formed at Dolores on May 31 and had selected their leaders: Bill Dawson as captain, with Billy May as second-in-command.[32] The papers reported that "a company of about sixty-five men, well-armed, left Big Bend (Dolores) for the Blue Mountains to try and gather up stock. . . . And should the Ute Indians molest them, they are determined to fight for their rights."[33] On June 1, they set out for what they hoped would be a quick victory.

Colonel Henry Page, agent for the Southern Utes, commented about the wisdom of any group undertaking such a mission. He may or may not have been aware of Dawson's men presently en route to Utah when the *Dolores News* printed his remarks on June 4, but he certainly was accurate. Page pointed out that this particular group of Indians, "who make their home in the Sierra La Sal and Blue Mountains[,] are a fearless and wayward set."[34] More importantly, he identified who comprised this group of Indians.

> The Pah-Utes, as they are termed, are a powerful party of renegades from the four Ute tribes—the Uintahs, White Rivers, Uncompahgres, and Southern or Ignacio Utes. They are comprised mainly of the younger bucks of these tribes and number about 100 families. They make their home in the Sierra La Sal and Blue Mountains, and are a fearless and wayward set. No organization exists among them. They are practically free-lancers, although in cases of emergency, where some leadership is essential, they recognize that power in two of their members. If war should be opened on these renegades, the Government would find their conquest difficult. . . . [Their] country is rough and inaccessible to troops throughout. . . . Hence it will be seen that a small and moderate band of Indians could keep at bay an immense army.[35]

Dawson's force was neither an immense army, trained as soldiers, nor knowledgeable about the terrain. Future events proved Page's wisdom correct.

The posse traveled over the rolling sagebrush country along the Colorado-Utah border, arriving at Hudson's Double Cabins on June 3. There, they met yet another group: members of Company C, 13th Infantry, under the command of Captain Benjamin H. Rogers from Fort Lewis, Colorado. The soldiers had arrived four days before with orders to scout the region for Indians while protecting any whites in the area collecting cattle. They reconnoitered the area along the eastern edge of Blue Mountain and reported the Hudson and O'Donnell cabins deserted, indicating the Blue Mountain posse had already left. As soon as Dawson's men arrived, they sent out scouts to determine the Indians' location, the soldiers apparently unaware that they were attempting to find the Indian camp for a future attack. By the time the soldiers were out of food and ready to return to Big Bend and (eventually) Fort Lewis, however, they realized that this band of men was doing much more than just looking for cattle. There is some suggestion that the soldiers and the cowboys were at odds with each other, the former feeling the latter should stay out of the Indian-fighting business.[36]

It is reasonable to assume that shortly after the military left, Hudson's Blue Mountain posse and Dawson's men from Colorado joined forces. For seven more days, the entire group remained in the saddle. The Utes separated into small bands, taking different routes, then rendezvousing at pre-designated sites, making tracking even more difficult in this terrain.[37] The posse scoured the area of Comb Wash, Blue Mountain, Indian Creek, and parts of Dry Valley: all favorite Ute camping sites.[38] The men traveled through Hart's Draw to Hatch Rock, where Hudson had his winter camp. Horses belonging to members of the Blue Mountain group were fatigued, having been out for more than three weeks. One man described them as "leg-weary and foot-sore."[39] Consequently, once scouts cut into the Indians' trail crossing Dry Valley and headed toward the La Sals, the Colorado cowboys left in pursuit, but Hudson's group remained behind, arriving after the fight had ended. The land had exacted a toll on his force as it traveled through the canyons and over the mountains. Dawson's group was also dwindling for various reasons. For instance, Billy May and seven others returned to Colorado because they did not agree with the existing leadership, while another eight men went on a separate scouting expedition and ended up at the Double Cabins. By the time the fight started, there were only thirty-eight in the field.[40]

Fig. 16—These Colorado cowboys, photographed in the field in 1887, proved to be one of the Utes' greatest enemies. The strong animosity felt between the two factions frequently erupted into warfare. Several of the men in this picture participated in both the 1881 and 1884 fights in southeastern Utah. (Courtesy San Juan County Historical Commission)

As the Colorado cowboys continued on the trail, they encountered tired stock, water holes used by the Indians, and increasingly fresher signs. A full lunar eclipse on the evening of June 12 was an auspicious occasion in both camps. According to A. (Albert) M. Rogers, whose account is the only one to mention this, two of the cowboys spotted the Utes' camp, reported its location, and urged forming a plan of attack. There were those who argued that the eclipse should be used as a powerful sign for the Indians to give up the murderers of May and Thurman, as well as the captured livestock. The majority of the men, however, wanted a fight. The disagreement was strong enough that when Dawson, speaking to those not in favor of a fight said, "Boys! Strike for your country and your homes," twenty-two of them left the next morning.[41] This could be referring to Billy May and his group, although the time sequence, numbers, and events seem somewhat askew and embellished.

The next day, the remaining cowboys followed the Indians undetected. That night, an exceptionally bright comet became visible in the evening sky, presenting another opportunity to play upon Ute beliefs. It was again voted down. Rogers said that he had been told "by Indians who were in the fight, that they had no heart to fight the white men after the Great Spirit had darkened the full moon and burned up a star, and that if we had demanded the surrender of the guilty Indians and the return of the stolen stock, they would have given them up without resistance; but we wanted an Indian fight and we got it."[42]

On the morning of June 15, Dawson's men struck. They found the Indians' horse herd (said to have numbered 1,500) as well as 800 goats. The Utes, resting in the area of today's Wilcox Flat/Warner Lake on the La Sal Mountains, were just breaking camp. Some of them spotted the cowboys on a mesa approximately three-quarters of a mile away and sounded the alarm. The men prepared to fight, while the women hastily packed what they could and started toward the north end of the La Sals.[43]

According to Rogers, the cowboys swept down one long hill and up another to the Indians' camp, capturing a sizeable portion of the Utes' livestock, as well as nine women who were guarding it. Dawson decided to leave thirteen men behind to retain the prize before giving chase to the fleeing enemy. Those who stayed settled in and eventually began playing "seven up" and "coon can"—two types of card games—with some of the younger women. Other cowboys slept while some guarded. The older Ute women, however, quietly and peacefully prepared an escape. At the signal, all the women fled to their horses and drove the Indians' herd before them, along with the mounts of the cowboys. "The discomfited heroes [cowboys] sadly shouldered their saddles and wended their way to Moab, eighteen miles distant."[44] In reality, this group probably attempted to rejoin Dawson's pursuing force and became disoriented by the terrain.

Exactly how much credence can be given this story, told only by Rogers, a member of a later rescue party, can be argued. That there was an eclipse and bright comet can be proven. Nothing has ever been said, however, about this group of cowboys straggling into Moab. And for Dawson to deplete his fighting force by half on the verge of battle seems unwise. Eyewitness accounts vary as to the number of men involved in the ensuing fracas, but there were probably between fifteen and eighteen who actually participated in the major firefight of the first day. The other half became separated and ineffective, but little has ever been offered as explanation for their not going with the attacking force. It seems highly probable that these were the men who remained with the Ute livestock and only later attempted to take part in the battle. They failed because of lack of communication and knowledge of the land.

The pursuing cowboys estimated that the Indian band numbered about 100: 65 men and 35 women, children, and old people. These figures are the reverse (30 men, 60 others) of what Platte Lyman reported near Bluff.[45] Whatever the composition, the white men gave chase through the Indian camp, with its assorted unpacked goods scattered about the clearing. They continued the pursuit, moving across Bald Mesa and hoping to intercept the Utes before getting away. Dawson needed to develop the situation before committing the entire force to an ambush and so moved down the trail, leaving the rest behind and ending any coordination and planning between the two groups.

The Ute men fought a rearguard action, slowing the advance of the cowboys while the women and others herded the remaining stock ahead. The posse pursued for a number of miles, fighting cat-and-mouse through the trees, rocks, and brush along a well-established Ute trail. The group halted when it reached Mason Spring at the head of Little Castle Valley, which descends to the north end of the mountains and the Colorado River beyond. Dawson selected six men, one of whom was Jordan Bean, and sent them forward to fix the enemy. According to Bean, their instructions were to "overtake the Indians and make a stand on them, and he [Dawson] would bring the rest as fast as possible."[46] Risky business for sure, but the leader was slow to commit his entire force to an ambush.

The point element traveled warily down the trail, passing over Bald Mesa toward Pinhook Draw and Harpole Mesa. It was ideal terrain for a defender. From Mason Spring and Draw, there are two possible routes into Little Castle

Valley. The first is the steep, V-sided Porcupine Draw, a straight canyon approximately one-and-a-half miles long but under two-tenths of a mile wide, opening directly into Castle Valley. Its southwestern wall is the twelve-mile-long Porcupine Rim; the northeastern side is a sharp-spine ridge covered with huge boulders and large rocks. The far side of this ridge descends into the larger U-shaped canyon known as Pinhook Draw. This valley forms a wide sloping bowl, approximately one-half mile across and three miles long. With almost vertical walls to the east and northeast and with Harpole Mesa to the north, these features pinch into a "hook" that narrows to a quarter mile before opening into Castle Valley. Both Pinhook and Porcupine Draws are cut by intermittent streambeds that are thick with scrub oak, while oaks, piñons, and junipers also grow on their slopes.

The six men moved cautiously down the trail, detecting the flash of a red blanket and an Indian pony in the oak and rocks on the slopes to their side. As they descended, the Utes opened fire, and as planned, Dawson moved the rest of his force forward to develop the situation. The Indians held the high ground on both sides and poured murderous shots from the hillsides onto the valley floor below. Command and control of the cowboys fell apart. Most sought shelter in the brush or in the streambed and hillocks in the valley before returning fire. All accounts agree that Dave Willis was the first killed, as he stood in the open and blasted at targets in the scrub oak.

The men in the lead rode for the protection of an arroyo. Thinking they were safe from the bullets sweeping the battlefield, they discovered too late that the Indians had enfilading fire from various angles down into the winding ditch. Mancos Jim, a Ute participant, later recalled the bravery on both sides. He said:

> Dave Willis never took shelter but stood out in bold relief and fought till he fell dead. The other boys tried to protect themselves by getting into a shallow arroyo or washout, but they were surrounded and when the Indians charged from one side, hanging onto the ponies, yelling and shooting, the white boys would raise to fire. The Indians in ambush in another direction [would] shoot them down.
>
> The white boys were extravagant with their ammunition, which they exhausted about dusk after fighting all day, and the Indians then rode around the washout in a circle, shooting into the living and lifeless bodies till there was no sign of life in the bloody pit.[47]

With the main force an estimated 100 to 150 yards distant from those in the arroyo, Dawson knew he could not provide effective supporting fire. Tim

Jenkins, a slightly built member of the posse, rode to the men in the ditch and urged them to retreat from almost certain death. Indian marksmen maintained a steady fire until Jenkins regained the main body, but none of the trapped men followed, paralyzed by fear.[48] Six eventually died in this general area, some of them being wounded before killed, as suggested by the bandages found on their bodies.

The Utes, "armed with Winchester rifles," maintained pressure on the beleaguered cowboys.[49] This point is made by a number of the participants. The cowboys felt that their enemy was far better armed—supposedly with .44-caliber Winchesters and plenty of ammunition. Probably some of this weaponry was booty from the Thurman cabin. The white men, on the other hand, had a "'duke's' mixture of old buffalo guns, Sharps rifles, and a few Winchesters, [as well as] old-fashioned black powder guns with a short range and a slow velocity of bullets [that] made distance shooting a guess."[50] This last statement is only partly accurate. The Sharps rifle had approximately three times the range (600 yards vs. 200 yards) and a heavier bullet (500 grain vs. 200 grain) when compared to the Winchester. But the single-shot Sharps could not compare to the fifteen-shot lever-action Winchester, especially appreciated by the Utes for in-close fighting. On the Pinhook battlefield, most of the Indians' positions were well within range of their weapons.

One story from the battle tells of a large warrior who climbed on top of a boulder and directed the fire of his men to critical points of the battlefield. Many of the cowboys shot at him but were ineffective.[51] Perhaps this was the same person who the newspapers falsely reported as a "Mexican seen with the Indians, apparently commanding different squads of Indians. On the second day, the Mexican rode to the summit of a knoll, patted his Winchester and six-shooters and cried aloud, 'Shoot you cowardly sons-of-bitches,' and the boys fired but failed to get him."[52]

There were other frustrations in the fight. Jordan Bean tells of how he and Harden Tarter entered the fray and then,

> it was every man for himself. . . . We soon found some big rocks, lay down there and were shooting at some Indians above us on the mountainside. We were doing fine until one Injun seemed to be a pretty good shot for he got me in the left temple. I had my head thrown back so far—the hill was steep—the bullet didn't go in very far but grazed my skull and knocked me out.[53]

Later that afternoon, Bean regained consciousness, unaware of what else had transpired. None of his companions were in sight; he learned later that his friend, Tarter, was dead. As Bean looked about, he spotted a large Indian standing on a rock. Bean, fearing that the Ute had seen him, dropped down and crawled into a thicket of scrub oak and remained silent. A horse, standing nearby, attracted the Indians' attention, and two warriors walked over. They talked about the blood on the ground, and one man started toward the brush that concealed Bean and made a low whistling noise but never found him.

Under the cover of darkness, the wounded cowboy made his way back to a spring he had used that morning. His overwhelming thirst drove him to drink too much, which made him even sicker. But with additional rest and some controlled drinking, he began to feel better. In the morning with the resumption of activities, Bean spotted members of the posse moving out to the battlefield again. They were surprised to see him, believing he was dead, but moved him back to their camp and rendered aid.[54]

Once the cowboys had extricated themselves from the battlefield and returned to Mason Spring, they counted their numbers. At that point, before Jordan Bean arrived but after the trapped survivors had left the intermittent streambed and hillocks, there were nine men missing. Depending upon whether or not Dawson had actually detailed thirteen of his men to guard the Ute herd, this figure could represent as much as half of the force engaged in the fight. As the sun set, a cloud of dust approaching up Porcupine Rim provided another answer. The missing group of cowboys appeared with a new appreciation of the terrain they had encountered. They had heard the firing in Castle Valley starting around noon. Hoping to come in behind the Utes, they had traveled a good distance along the Rim, searching for a route down the 1,400-foot escarpment to the valley floor below. They had found none. Realizing their mistake, they had returned to the head of the draw but had been ineffective for the entire battle. In Dawson's words, "We have had hell here all day and we don't know how many men have been killed. It's just too bad you were not here with us. More than likely we could have routed the Indians out of their trap."[55]

There were also the wounded to take care of. Harden Eskridge received a bullet below the ankle that shattered many of the small bones in his foot. During the fight, he wore "a large, gaudy Chihuahua hat . . . that was riddled with bullets so that it cannot be worn and his hair was nearly all cut off with scalp wounds from grazing bullets."[56] James Hall received a shoulder wound, injured ribs, and a leg wound that began above the knee and exited through his calf. Miraculously, he healed without any permanent damage. In the morning, Jordan Bean arrived with a wound in the temple, most likely caused by a ricochet.[57] After receiving immediate first aid, these men remained with the posse for the next two days.

In the meantime, Dawson spent the first night hoping to continue the battle in the morning and at least determine the location of his missing men. With the second half of his group present, he would reenter Pinhook Draw with around twenty-five of the original Colorado posse. The combined force of Moab and Colorado men headed down to the battlefield to learn about the fate of those missing. The fighting of the previous day had ranged around Pinhook Draw and Harpole Mesa. The searchers found the first body out in an open area near an old trail that passed over Harpole Mesa. As they gathered around the body, who was most likely Dave Willis, the Indians on the side of the mesa opened fire and commenced the second day of fighting. The white men retreated uphill toward Bald Mesa, taking cover in an aspen grove on its side. An old Ute woman came through the brush, apparently unaware of the disposition of the cowboys, and was killed.

Dawson took stock of his situation and realized how desperately he needed additional help. He did not believe sufficient assistance could be garnered from Moab, eighteen miles away, so he turned to the next closest source: Rico. In midmorning of June 16 (the second day), D. G. Taylor began the 150-mile ride. According to Bean, sixteen settlers from Moab, on their way to investigate the Indians' activity on the mountain, saw the rider and fired shots, but missed.[58] Taylor completed the journey in five days, arriving on the afternoon of June 21. The next day, a portion of the rescue party left Rico, camped at Dolores that night, and was joined by the remainder of volunteers in the morning. The group elected Worden Grigsby as its leader and set out for Utah. On June 24, they arrived in the vicinity of the La Sal Mountains, but by this time their initial group of forty had dwindled to twenty-four.[59] They also were far too late to help against the Utes.

The Colorado cowboys had other concerns. Dawson worried about the three wounded men and the small detachment of two guards left to protect them in camp. A group started back but received fire from the Utes, who now were between them and their destination. The cowboys retreated to the aspen grove again, and after a few more hours of fighting, the Indians broke contact and began moving to Dolores and the Ute reservation. The Colorado and Moab men returned to their camp, ending the second day of fighting.[60]

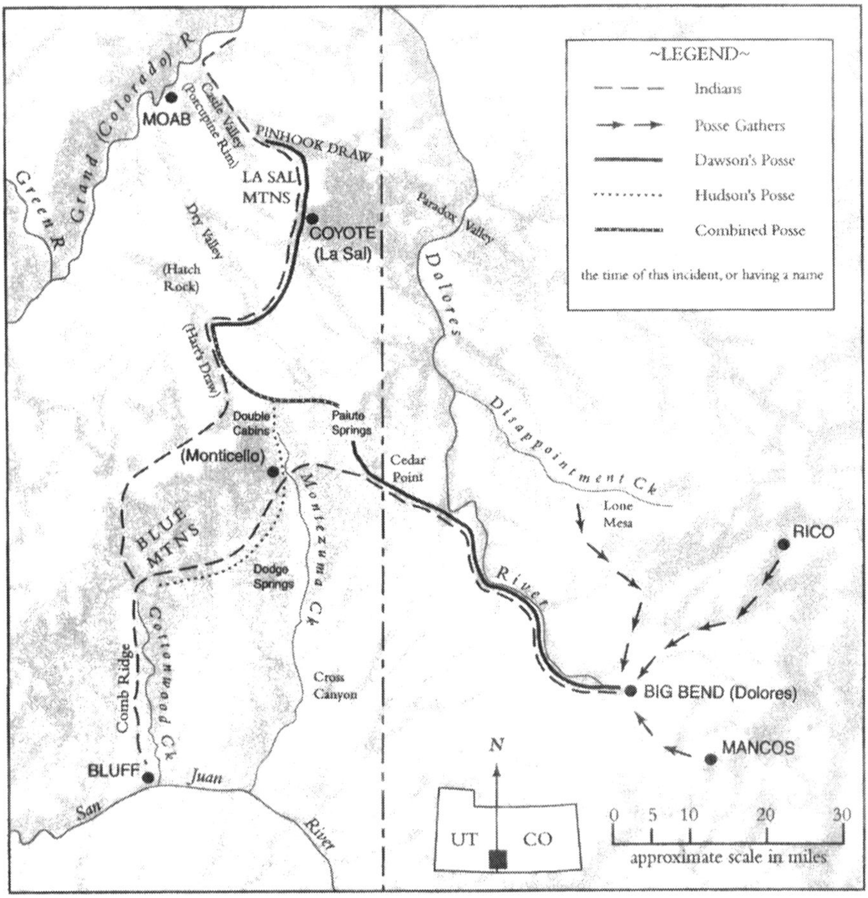

Fig. 17—Map of the Pinhook Draw Fight (Map by Connie Bartos, provided by Utah State Historical Society)

That evening, the cowboys decided they had had enough. The contingent traveled to the lower end of Pack Creek (near the settlement of Moab) to rest and obtain assistance for the wounded. The three injured men descended on horseback to a point out of the mountains, where a spring-cushioned wagon could be used for the rest of the trip.[61] Four days after the fight, a group of men returned to the battlefield to bury the dead. The land lay silent, the Indians and the sounds of battle long since faded. By then, the corpses were badly decomposed, and some accounts tell of how the heads had been smashed, as if with a rock. Another version states that all the bodies were riddled with arrows and rifle shots.[62] No other mutilation had occurred. The burial detail interred the dead, but the body of T.

C. Taylor remained missing, bringing the final count to ten men killed.[63] The following day, the entire group started for Colorado.

In the meantime, Worden Grigsby and the twenty-four men of the rescue party completed the trip from Rico in two and a half days, arriving at Coyote, southwest of the La Sals, on June 24. Although they did not encounter the main body of the returning posse, they did meet two of the participants, who related past events. They spent the next day at Coyote, then traveled to the site, noting how much of the terrain lent itself to ambush. Unsure of exactly how the fight had unfolded, they pieced together events from the equipment and dead animals encountered along the way. That night, they camped on a mesa overlooking the battlefield, then started back the next day. Grigsby's group met the returning posse which was camped at Hudson's Double Cabins, and four troops of Buffalo Soldiers of the 9th Cavalry. Their commander, Captain Henry Carroll, had elements from three different posts—Fort Bayard, Fort Cummings, and Fort Seldon—all in southern New Mexico. The next morning, the two groups parted company. The Colorado men returned by way of Paiute Springs, Cross Canyon, Big Bend of the Dolores, then separated and rode to Rico, Mancos, and Durango. The soldiers continued on their way in search of the Utes but followed a cold trail. Many of the Indians had traveled to Dolores and the safety of the Ute reservation. The military returned to Fort Lewis on July 24, empty-handed after their 200-mile jaunt.[64] Observers were convinced that the Indians hid behind the sanctity of the reservation and government control (read: "interference") to the detriment of the settlers.

The Ute side of the Pinhook Draw Battle is available in only fragmentary pieces. One definite participant was Mancos Jim, who not only discussed the incident but was in possession of Dave Willis's rifle. In conversation with a local trader in 1886, Jim said that he had lost "eighteen of his best and four average Indians in that fight."[65] This figure is in complete agreement with the estimates made by white participants, although only three bodies were actually found near the battlefield. Still, the number seems far too high, given estimates of male participants, the reported dead, and the fact that the Indians deemed the battle a victory. Various accounts suggest that among those killed was one of the sons of Cabeza Blanca and "Oco-co-mo-want, the chief or principal man of the renegade band," which could possibly be the same person.[66]

Poco Narraguinep, more commonly known as Polk, took pride in telling white men about his part in the fracas. He claimed three individual kills, and according to local historian Albert R. Lyman, "his years of insolent safety since that time have no doubt convinced him that it was a good business."[67] During a skirmish on Blue Mountain before the Pinhook fight, some civilians captured Polk's horse with things on it from the O'Donnell cabin, identifying him with the group that had passed through and ransacked both it and Hudson's Double Cabins. His father, Narraguinep, boasted to a number of white men at Dolores that the Utes would attack Fort Lewis and " 'clean it up.' That the Utes knew the killing of Thurman and May was to take place is shown by their telling several men the day before the massacre 'not to go beyond the Great Bend, as somebody would heap kill white people out there pretty soon.' "[68]

It was only a matter of time before smoldering resentment between cowboys and Indians erupted into another conflict. The affair started simply enough. On July 3, 1884, a substantial group of cowboys had assembled in an early summer roundup at the foot of Blue Mountain.[69] Three combined outfits belonging to William "Billy" H. Wilson, Charles "Race Horse" Johnson, and the Carlisles were camped on the South Fork of Montezuma Creek (known today as Verdure Creek).[70] The one-armed Texan, Billy Wilson, had previously lost his appendage in a fight with Comanches, but he and Johnson now owned ranches in the Dolores area and grazed their herds on Blue Mountain.[71] The Carlisles also controlled part of this range, and all shared the roundup efforts, separating stock for the respective owners.

A group of Utes, some of whom had off-reservation passes signed by Agent Patten, were in the area to hunt. They camped below the cowboys and surprisingly enough given past events, were invited to visit and eat with their white neighbors. During the interchange, the cowboys noticed the Indians had three horses belonging to Johnson and another to cowboy, "Spud" Hudson, whose involvement in the Pinhook incident was well-known. Four men went to the Indian camp to reclaim the livestock but met resistance. As the cowboys attempted to cut out the horses from the Indian herd, a medicine man named Brook drove the horses back. Hank Sharp attempted to get a rope on one of the horses, while according to white accounts, Brook drew his knife and stabbed two or three times at his antagonist, giving Sharp a slight slice on the neck. Whether it was more of an attempt to cut the rope as opposed to killing the cowboy, no one will ever know, but there was enough provocation in the cowboy's mind to shoot the Ute in the mouth, with the bullet passing out of his neck.[72] Brook lived, but he was not the only person to be wounded that day.

The Utes took up positions near their camp and started firing, while the women and children fled. The four cowboys retreated to their camp, sounded the alarm, and joined the others in gathering horses in the corral, hitching four large mules to a wagon to haul gear and preparing to lead a hasty retreat. By this time, the Indians had surrounded them and were firing at the hustling men. Joseph H. Nielson, a Mormon from Bluff who was working with the cowboys at the time, grabbed Billy Wilson's two sons, ages eight and ten, and headed for a nearby gully. There, they lay until the fighting ended. "Only a heavy hand on the neck of each curious lad kept his head from popping up each time a shot was fired."[73] These boys later made a twenty-nine-hour ride—without food or rest—back to Durango with the remainder of the cowboys. Nielson took a separate route at night, fleeing down Montezuma Canyon to the San Juan River and back to Bluff, fearing his involvement might antagonize the Utes against the settlers there.[74]

In the meantime, the cowboys started up the hill from Verdure on what was then called the Bluff Road. Apparently, they abandoned two wagons and some equipment at their camp, while the third wagon only reached a place known as the Salt Lick (later named the Roundup Ground) two or three miles southwest of Verdure before it, too, was lost. The Utes allowed the slow-moving vehicle, surrounded by the men and many of their horses, to get within range. They hid in the clumps of oak brush that dotted the surrounding landscape, then opened fire. Four mules died, the Utes captured the horse herd (estimated at between 100 and 150 animals), and two men—a cook called Cook and Adolf Lusk, who was in charge of the herd—were wounded in the foot and thigh, respectively. Some of the cowboys lost their only horse and had to ride double.

The situation turned desperate. With only seven rifles and the rest six-shooters and "most of them out of cartridges, having shot them away at deer for fun," the cowboys were in no position to resist.[75] The Utes, on the other hand, "wore new shirts and had new Winchesters and revolvers, bought in Durango with the money paid them as an annuity at Ignacio, the Southern Ute Agency, by Agent Patten."[76] It was time for the white men to withdraw. They made their way to the towns of southwestern Colorado, much exhausted and chagrined that they had once again been bested. The Utes picked through their booty, gathered their newly acquired horse herd, and began a leisurely move to the rough country west of Blue Mountain, a proven refuge during times of conflict. They left behind the remains of the burned wagon, "the old iron from which was scattered in the Roundup Ground for years after."[77]

Word spread quickly but with varying reaction. The Mormons in Bluff were concerned about the possibility of escalating violence. Platte D. Lyman wrote in his diary, "During the past week a difficulty occurred between cowmen and Indians on the South Montezuma during which 2 Indians were killed and 2 white men wounded. This may yet lead to considerable trouble."[78] To the people of Colorado, this incident was one more example of Indian depredation and a threat to their financial investments. Their estimated 17,000 cattle were part of a $2 million investment in the livestock industry, which was now "at the mercy of the Indians."[79] Circumstances were ripe for another showdown. This time, however, the military took charge.

Captain Henry P. Perrine, with F Troop, 6th Cavalry, left Fort Lewis with forty-nine men on July 6—the day after receiving the news. On the way, he stopped at Dolores and asked for volunteers to help get the horses back. Sources surrounding this conflict are fairly abundant, including accounts from Harold Carlisle, the military, and the *Dolores News*. But the most complete rendering of events was by a Colorado cowboy named Sam Todd.[80] According to the newspapers, "eighty cowboys armed to the teeth and swearing vengeance against the Utes" departed for the battle.[81] Military accounts are more modest and say there were forty-five who joined the expedition, while Sam Todd agrees more with the newspapers, estimating ninety.[82] At least part of the cowboy force rendezvoused with the main body at Cross Canyon and selected Rube Lockett from Dolores as their leader.[83]

On July 7, Second Lieutenant B. K. West also left Fort Lewis with a detachment of thirty-five men of B Troop, 6th Cavalry to assist Captain Perrine. The latter reached the scene of the earlier fight on July 10, with West joining him three days later, bringing the final count of white participants to no less than 130, with the possibility of as many as 175.[84] The Utes were probably at not even half that strength, and many of those were non-combatants. A contemporary estimates their "force from 75 to 100 strong under Narraguinip and Mariano."[85] Being encumbered with women, children, and all their belongings, the Indians were at a distinct military disadvantage.

On the other hand, Perrine created a logistical problem with such a large force. Not only did he have to bring supplies for his own men, but according to Todd, he told the civilian volunteers not to bring any food because his sixteen pack mules would carry plenty for everyone. While no one knew how long the expedition would take, the two weeks it required strained the supply resources of such a large group. Water, an even more precious commodity in the high desert environment, proved most critical.

The same day that Perrine's force arrived at the battlefield, Sergeant Christian Soffke and his soldiers from B Company, 22nd Infantry, on an unrelated mission to Henry Mitchell's post, arrested five Utes who had been involved in the Verdure fight. He took their arms and horses, placing them in custody because "several settlers on this river threaten to kill them on sight," and he felt he could protect them until they returned to the Southern Ute Reservation.[86] Two days later, Red Jacket, leading forty men, threatened an attack if the sergeant did not release his prisoners to his custody, promising to bring them to Agent Patten within five days. Red Jacket, Topine (Tahpuni', or Drowsy), Johnny Benow, and Narraguinep, who was supposedly leading the main group, were among those demanding the prisoners' freedom. All four of the men were notorious for their part in previous conflicts. Once the sergeant learned that Captain Perrine's force was headed in another direction and there was no hope of assistance, he freed his prisoners.[87]

Patten, in the meantime, had sent Ignacio and other Southern Ute leaders to the western end of the reservation to ascertain if any of their people had been involved in the conflicts or if it had just been the band of renegade "Paiutes." The agent wrote with satisfaction that he was convinced that his charges were innocent, and as far as they were concerned, if these "Paiutes . . . all got killed, it will be a good thing."[88] Patten's desire to exonerate "his" Indians reflects more his desire to remain clean of accusation than total reality. No doubt there were many Southern/Ute Mountain Utes who claimed no affiliation with the fleeing Indians, but there is also no doubt that others had strong links and were members of the Utah group. Still, many Utes professed innocence. Perhaps part of their denial sprang from a letter supposedly received from the US Department of the Interior by a man in Durango named George W. Kephart. In it, the letter authorized "settlers to shoot any Indian seen attempting to join the renegades from the reservation."[89]

When Captain Perrine arrived at the scene of the fight, he found nine dead horses, eight others wounded beyond use, and Billy Wilson's dead mules. The trail of the Utes was easy to follow, as it skirted around the southern edge of Blue Mountain. Bloody bark poultices used to dress wounds were left at various campsites. Harold Carlisle, who apparently was not accompanying the military but was intimately connected to the events, described what the soldiers found: "the band had traveled slowly, making about ten miles a day, camping in more than one place for two days, playing cards, barking trees, and even making race tracks on the heads of Cottonwood and Indian Creeks, to test the metal [sic] of the stolen stock, and tending their wounded, as was shown by the rags littered about in their camping places."[90] Finally, the sheer number of horses—stolen or otherwise—as

Fig. 18—Mancos Jim, or Winchester, was perhaps the best-known of the "Paiutes," defending his land against white encroachment. He participated in the Pinhook Draw and Soldier Crossing fights and was well-known on both sides for his bravery and leadership. (Courtesy San Juan County Historical Commission)

well as the goats the Utes herded along as a mobile source of food, left an indelible trail easily followed.

Today, this path is not as readily discerned. According to Albert R. Lyman, it was called the Big Trail or Old Trail and was a well-known thoroughfare that led westward into a maze of canyons, slickrock, and widely separated sources of water and campsites.[91] Based on Todd's description of where the Utes went, a best-guess mapping of the trail would start in Verdure, cross upper Recapture Wash and Johnson Creek, then proceed to the Round Mountain-Mormon Pasture area on the divide between the San Juan River and Indian Creek drainages via a trail across what is now known as Bayles Ranch. From the Round Mountain area, they traveled south along Elk Ridge through the Big and Little Notches and to the Bears Ears area on south Elk Ridge. At the springs or ponds near the northern end of the Bears Ears, the Utes rested. They then moved northwest about ten miles to the vicinity of a small land formation now called the Pushout, thence off Elk

Ridge to the north bench of Cheesebox Canyon and on to White Canyon, where the fight occurred. Once the military expedition left the springs at the base of the Bears Ears and the aspens and ponderosa pines of Elk Ridge for the piñon and juniper canyon country below, it was terra incognita. Todd states that if the trail did not pass by water, the men would look for birds to find it, a risky proposition at best.

As the pursuers sat astride their horses on the western rim of Elk Ridge, they spied two pillars of smoke about a half mile below and two Indians riding their ponies down the steep slope to the valley. Sam Todd believed these were signal fires to warn the main group. Harold Carlisle goes even further, suggesting that these two Indians were actually Southern Utes sent by Agent Patten to bring in any of his charges involved in the incident. Now they were serving as a rear guard and had ridden seventy-five miles at a rapid pace to warn the renegades. Patten and Ignacio denied any knowledge of these two men supposedly working in their employ. While Carlisle's thought appears to be mere conjecture, it does portray the feelings of distrust toward the US Indian Service in general and Agent Patten in particular.

A large cloud of dust ten miles away revealed the Indians' encampment, and through binoculars, the military could see them preparing to move. The steep, rough, mile-long descent off Elk Ridge took much longer than the cowboys and cavalry had anticipated.[92] By the time they reached the Indians' camp, their prey was long gone, as was the water they hoped to find. The Utes had availed themselves of rain water trapped in a sandstone basin and before departing, had watered all their stock. Todd explains, "From the tracks the goat herd had been watered last, and they had taken it all. (The goat herd they always took with them on the war trail, as they could out-travel a horse and they had them to eat while they were too busy to hunt.)"[93]

The lack of water proved crucial. It was one o'clock on a hot July 14th afternoon, and temperatures in that country easily rose to well over 100°F. The soldiers had filled their canteens that morning but were now out of water. The cowboys had even less and according to Todd, complained less, even though the soldiers did not share what they had. The horses suffered from lack of water even more, being described as "wet with sweat after the first ten miles."[94] Although the heavy, six-foot-tall Todd had brought a second mount and changed horses every five miles, the rough canyon country took its toll on horse flesh. To compound the problem, there was no breeze to disperse the dust. As the gap between pursuer and pursued closed, the soldiers and cowboys rode in suspended dust clouds "like ashes" left by the fleeing Indians.

The chase wore on. The Utes separated into three bands. Closest to the advancing white men was a group of six or seven warriors serving as a rear guard to fight a delaying action. Two miles ahead rode the main body of warriors, and another four miles ahead of them were some men, with the women and children driving livestock and hauling equipment. Occasionally, a tired Indian pony stood in the trail, so played out that it would not step aside until whipped with a quirt—one more indicator that encouraged the pursuers.

Captain Perrine felt his prey was in his hand and at any moment he would close with the enemy. He followed relentlessly. Todd reports, "We thought we could surely catch them before sundown and kept at a hard gallop. . . . While we couldn't see them, we thought we were right at them and would catch them in a few minutes. So it kept up all that afternoon."[95] One account tells of how an occasional shot or two from the Utes' trail element also slowed the soldiers down.[96]

Even with the passing of sunset, the pursuit continued. Not until total darkness made tracking impossible over slickrock did the exhausted pursuers get a rest. "We tumbled off, layed [sic] down with the bridle reins in our hands, and lay [sic] there until the moon came up. [We then] took the trail again, a tired, thirsty, hungry outfit, [with] our horses suffering for water more than we were."[97]

The pursuers followed the Utes across the inner gulch of White Canyon at the location named on modern maps as Soldier Crossing. From there, the chase turned northwest, following the southwest bench of White Canyon along what Carlisle identified as the trail leading from Bluff City to the Colorado River on today's Utah State Route 95. The road passes along the bench between the inner gorge of White Canyon on the right and the massive 1,500-foot cliff-capped escarpment of Wingate Mesa on the left. Daylight found the pursuers between these geographical features, hot on the Indians' path.

The trail soon left the White Canyon bench and climbed westward to the high, narrow mesa dividing White Canyon from Red Canyon. There, the Utes positioned themselves for an ambush at what has since been called Piute Pass, a narrow declivity through the caprock overlooking a steep, exposed talus slope. Todd continues:

> When full daylight came we were at the foot of this wall and the trail led to a narrow break in it, barely wide enough for one horse to go into. We halted, of course, to investigate. We knew we were close to them because for the last three miles we had found a number of give-out horses wet with

> sweat, and some of the last ones were still panting. And while we were talking, we heard a goat bleat just on top, and it was plain to us boys that we were in a trap. The Captain, however, said no, there was no trap and we must climb that mesa, but considering the necessity for water, we would halt and send a detail to hunt for a rain water tank.[98]

The command was now unsure what action to take. Joe Wormington, a civilian packer and scout for the military, volunteered to climb to the gap and see if he could determine the Indians' location. A young cowboy named James "Rowdy" Higgins anxiously joined him. He had lost his mother and father to Indian warfare in Nevada as a child and often expressed his eagerness for revenge. Although members of the party warned of the possibility of a trap, every indication being that the Utes were waiting on top, the two men disregarded the cautions and started up the hill. When they approached within seventy-five feet of the gap, the Utes opened fire. Higgins fell wounded but had enough strength to crawl into the protection of a large boulder. Wormington, though wounded, picked himself up and tried running straight down the slope. Struck by a second volley, he tumbled head over heels before coming to rest with his feet and legs propped against a large rock, his head and shoulders downslope. His face was not visible to those below, but they could hear him moan and say something inaudible. He never moved again.[99]

Below was pandemonium. The Utes' attention now focused on the swirling tangle of men and horses. They fired round after round, tearing up the ground but hitting only Todd's horse. Bunched together in the confusion, the mass of men made an easy target. Todd, in retrospect, found it difficult to explain how so many shots could miss so many people, unless the Indians were just shooting at the clump of men without picking out specific targets.[100] Some of the cowboys and soldiers were in such a panic that they fled without their horses, "the crowd tearing down the hill to a bunch of cedars for shelter."[101] They left seven saddled mounts behind, a dangerous practice given their situation. Others were more determined and took the time to lead their animals over the rough, rocky terrain to protective cover. Extra horses, the pack train, and now the soldiers' mounts were all safeguarded in the rear, while the cowboys and cavalry maintained fire on the gap and its surrounding area.

The Indians still had the upper hand. Lying flat on the rocks above, they were invisible to those below. The steadiness of aim they had lacked at the beginning of the fight was now replaced with accurate range estimation and a freedom to shoot "close at whatever they could see, so that a hat held up on a stick was sure to get a hole in it."[102]

Captain Perrine now faced three major problems. The first was the two wounded men on the hill. According to a later newspaper account, he tried without success to find volunteers who would follow him up the exposed slope to retrieve the wounded.[103] Around nine o'clock that morning, with the sun baking the landscape, Wormington stopped his groaning and breathed his last. The soldiers turned their binoculars on Higgins as he gasped for air. His pale face and labored breathing were the only signs of life, but by noon, he was dead too. Mancos Jim took advantage of the situation to amuse his people and taunt the soldiers below. He would jump up on the rock face, dance around, and holler, "Oh my God, boys, come and help me" or "Oh my God, boys, a drink of water," mimicking the cries of the wounded the Indians could hear so clearly because of their close proximity.[104] No doubt this was met with a shower of lead but without effect. A short while later, Mancos Jim repeated his performance. Thus, the day wore on.

Perrine's second problem was water. After a day and a half of heavy exertion and fear in blistering heat, the situation had turned desperate. No one in the party knew the country well enough to locate any of the several small springs that lay hidden within a few miles of their position, and there were no birds in the area to lead them to water. The nearest sure source was the one left behind at the foot of the Bears Ears, and that was twenty miles straight-line distance in a land where nothing is straight-line and most of which was uphill. All the men could talk about was water.

As the shadows lengthened in the canyon, Captain Perrine faced his third concern. He knew the Indians enjoyed an intimate knowledge of the land, while he did not. If his troops were to be flanked and perhaps driven from the rocks and trees at the foot of the trail, the situation could degenerate into a chaotic rout, especially if it took place at night. To prevent this from happening and with the idea of retrieving their fallen comrades, the soldiers agreed to sight their rifles in on the gap during the day so that at night they could maintain a steady fire that would deny the Utes' use of the pass. Under this covering fire and protected by darkness, four of the cowboys, including Todd, would move up the slope and retrieve the two bodies. Following that, it was retreat.

As the four cowboy volunteers quietly crawled over the trail on the bare, rock-strewn hill, Todd heard a noise. He turned to his companions to find they were gone and that seven Indians were coming up behind him along the path,

Probable route of pursuit off the Pushout looking south.
1. the Pushout rim; 2. trail descends hogback ridge crest to saddle, traverses the lower north slope of the ridge, then breaks out southwest onto the Cheesebox Canyon bench; 3. charred juniper stumps next to trail, possibly the trees burned by the Ute rear guard.

General view of Piute Pass battle site looking south.
1. Ute Position at pass. 2. Probable U. S. Position in talus slope and grassy bench area.
3. Probable location of Wormington & Higgins bodies; 4. cached .50-70 caliber unfired rounds;
5. modern bladed road; 6. trail route from the Pushout via the Cheesebox/White Canyon bench.
Dotted lines indicate inferred trail routes.

Fig. 19 & 20—Maps by Winston B. Hurst

each leading one of the saddled horses left behind earlier that day. He dropped off the side of the trail and laid flat, the Utes clearly silhouetted against the night sky. Alone, he slithered toward Higgin's body, only to find the Indians stripping it. Moving to Wormington's location, he found more Utes going through the same process. There was also a dog sniffing around that started to growl. Todd knew that he could "do no good" and that if detected, could fire only a few shots before the muzzle flash gave away his position, and all was over. He slowly picked his way back down the hill.

When he returned to the perimeter, he learned that his companions had heard the horses coming, feared calling ahead thus giving away their position, and so had moved off the trail and laid low. Oblivious to the danger, Todd had made his way blithely *up* the trail. His companions had returned to safety, assuming that he would also recognize the danger and come back down. All during this time, the force maintained a steady volume of fire on Piute Pass. How the Indians had managed to get through it was a mystery.

To the captain, this was bad news. The Utes had apparently descended by another route to collect the horses, thus signaling the very high risk of a flanking attack. If they gained control of the trail to his rear and stood between him and water, all could perish. He ordered everything hastily packed and prepared for movement so that by ten o'clock, the column, frazzled and parched from two days of stress, got underway. Fear was still a factor. Four hours into the retreat, a man named Joe McGrew became deathly sick, most likely from dehydration and exhaustion. As Todd called for assistance, McGrew fell from his horse and had to be carried to the side of the trail. The sergeant of the troop asked what was wrong, then told the men to tie the sick cowboy onto his saddle and continue, explaining, "[We] can't delay the whole command or a part of it here in a hostile country," to which Todd replied, "Sergeant, we have quit and are no longer under command."[105]An hour's rest put McGrew and his companions back on their horses, and by eight in the morning, they had re-joined the retreating column as it climbed back up on Elk Ridge.

The Utes, at this point, were headed in the opposite direction. According to Albert R. Lyman, based on reports of Bluff cattlemen, at least some of the Indians followed the Old Trail across Red Canyon, thence across North Gulch (now Moki Canyon) via a large sand slide[106] to the Pagahrit, a natural body of water in Lake Canyon.[107] There, they camped for a time, celebrating their victory and leaving behind their abandoned *wickiups* and a scattering of dead and wounded cattle belonging to the Bluff Mormons before eventually making their way southward across the San Juan River to the isolation of Navajo Mountain.[108]

Three hours after the military rode on top of Elk Ridge, they reached the spring at the base of the Bears Ears, where they "drank and drank. As soon as the men had drunk all they wanted, they began to tumble over and go to sleep."[109] A lone sentry, who was himself groggy, had the responsibility of keeping watch. Around two o'clock, Todd awakened him by letting him know that Mancos Jim was coming. Suddenly, a half-asleep soldier sprang to life and had to be reassured that it was a false alarm. The men now discovered that the packs containing all of the provisions had somehow been lost. All that was available were two jars of pickles donated by Captain Perrine. His willingness to share was admirable, but given the fact that no one had eaten in two or three days, his offer did not go too far. As for Todd, he was not "pickle hungry."

The cavalcade next moved to Johnson Creek at the foot of Blue Mountain, where they located five stray cattle belonging to "Racehorse" Johnson. The men killed two steers, skinned them, and cut the meat off in slabs, "every fellow having a stick with a chunk of meat roasting on it . . . . In less than an hour after the animal was dead, it was eaten up."[110] The party camped there that evening, and then some moved on toward Colorado, while Perrine's cavalry headed south to Mitchell's trading post to assist in peacekeeping efforts there. The captain dispatched Lieutenant West's B Troop back to Fort Lewis, while he and F Troop established a summer encampment on the San Juan.[111]

The spring of 1885, while quieter in Utah, was not without its issues. Underlying much of the conflict remained the question of food. The Southern Utes were starving. Their agent noted that he issued only one pound of beef and three-and-a-half pounds of flour each week for every man, woman, and child.[112] A few months later, Colonel Peter T. Swaine, Commander of the 22nd Infantry, Fort Lewis, did his own math and calculated there were 983 Southern Utes on the reservation who, for the past year, had received a per-capita daily allowance of less than a half pound of beef and about a quarter of a pound of flour.[113] Little wonder that the Indians left their reservation in search of food.

There was just such a party comprised of at least six men, four women, and a child camped at Beaver Creek near the Dolores River on June 19. According to the Ute version told by Chief Jack House in 1940 and a statement given by Ignacio six months after the occurrence, this hunting party of twenty-five to thirty people had traveled from Sleeping Ute Mountain and camped on the west side of Beaver Creek, approximately twenty-two miles north of Dolores.[114] Both cowboy and Indian accounts agree that there were several tepees set up on a grassy flat, which the white men surrounded at night to await the dawn. There is also mention of a "sentinel tepee" located on a prominence overlooking the camp to provide early warning.

At sunrise, thirteen cowboys "at last carried out their threats to shoot Utes on sight."[115] Holding the high ground and hidden by boulders, they waited for the sentinel to come out of his tepee. When he did, they first killed him and then poured shots downslope, where the awakened Indians sought cover and returned fire. One woman came out holding an infant over her head to show that it was a peaceful hunting camp with women and children present. By the time the cowboys finished, they reported one woman standing in the open, screaming hysterically, while others had escaped down the canyon. After the smoke cleared, four men, two women, and a child lay dead (in some accounts only three men died), with the rest fleeing.[116]

Following the cowboys' departure, the woman went through the remains and found a young man shot through the legs, an old woman wounded in the leg, and a baby who was unharmed. The party started back to Ute Mountain, but the travel was too painful for both the wounded man and woman. He found shelter in an oak grove and camouflaged himself with leaves, then awaited help. The baby started whimpering, so the terror-stricken women, fearing they were being pursued, covered its mouth and accidentally smothered it. A short distance down the canyon they were traveling in, they hid the infant's body for future burial, traveled a ways, then concealed the old woman in the oak brush. The younger woman traveled by night for three days before returning to Ute Mountain and her people.

Once news arrived, reaction was instant. Utes set fire to rancher John Genther's home in Montezuma Valley, then killed him and wounded his wife as they fled the burning building. Not one of their five children was injured. One of the three infantry companies (thirty men) already deployed in Mancos Valley went immediately to the scene, where they joined two troops (sixty men) of cavalry. With the distinct possibility that the Indians who committed the outrage had already fled to the reservation, Major David Perry of the 6th Cavalry proceeded to Blue Mountain to "protect cattle interests" so that "the spark of war may not have an opportunity to kindle the hearts of the young bucks," while at the same time giving "confidence to citizens."[117] Ignacio, other Ute leaders, Agent Christian Stollsteimer, and two cavalry companies went to the massacre site. The position of the unburied bodies indicated that they had been attacked while asleep.[118]

Word of the massacre spread throughout the Four Corners. Navajo Agent John H. Bowman complained of Utes trespassing in the Carrizo Mountains and other reservation lands. He reported ten tepees occupied by old men, women, and children who were "Utes and Piutes" from Utah. The younger men and women had left them there for protection while they avenged the deaths of the six killed in Colorado, having already killed three white people. They "were prepared to fight and would send their women and children across the [San Juan] River on the mountain as soon as trouble commences."[119] He requested that the Ute agent control the "renegades, cut throats and thieves" because they were in Navajo territory "for no good purpose and their influence is bad upon our people."

The planned disposition of troops worked. Colonel Swaine wrote with surprised relief that he had prevented the Indians from wiping out all of the scattered settlers and rampaging on the "warpath." As for the cowboys who openly boasted they would kill any Indians encountered and who welcomed "a disastrous and bloody war," the colonel believed they had "little regard for the fate of the innocent settler" or the "lives of inoffensive Indians whom they so cowardly assassinate."[120] With so many men already in the field providing protection and taking preventive measures, Swaine had to balance his operational arm with the possibility of a Ute uprising that could besiege both the agency and the fort. He also feared that units traveling about could become so splintered by different tasks that they could be "whipped by detail." Fortunately, none of these concerns materialized.

This decade of violence, 1875–1885, holds many lessons about waging war in Canyon Country. The importance of knowing the terrain is among the most crucial. Tactics (ambushes), logistics (water and resupply), cultures (finding and fixing the enemy), and weaponry (employment of weapons) all figured into the success or failure encountered on each side. The Utes followed the practices outlined in Chapter Two, including avoiding large-scale warfare, using ambushes and raids, providing an early warning system, obtaining goods as opposed to war honors, and fleeing to the high ground. The military, as a professional force, followed its standard operating procedure: a topic that will be discussed in Chapter Six. The cowboys, on the other hand, provide an excellent example of raw courage and determination but lacked the organization, knowledge of the enemy, and an intimate understanding of the land to be effective. Whether getting rimrocked, running out of water, being ambushed, or remaining united, there were just a lot of issues that needed to be addressed before waging war with the Utes.

Chapter Endnotes

1. Portions of this chapter were previously published in Chapters Six, Seven, and Eight of *As If the Land Owned Us: An Ethnohistory of the White Mesa Utes* (Salt Lake City: University of Utah Press, 2011).
2. George W. Manypenny, *Our Indian Wards* (New York: Da Capo Press, 1972), pp. 418–419.
3. Ferdinand V. Hayden, *Ninth Annual Report of the United States Geological and Geographical Survey of the Territories Embracing Colorado and Parts of Adjacent Territories: Being a Report of Progress of the Exploration for the Year 1875* (Washington, DC: Government Printing Office, 1877), pp. 1–6.
4. James T. Gardner, "Ute Warriors," *Rocky Mountain News*, Issue 4 (September 5, 1875). Unless otherwise noted, no newspaper accounts will have page numbers cited because they are retyped manuscripts from the F. V. Hayden Collection, Special Collections, American Heritage Center, University of Wyoming, Laramie, Wyoming.
5. See John N. Macomb, *Report of the Exploring Expedition . . . in 1859* (Washington, DC: Government Printing Office, 1876).
6. Mills, "The Hayden Survey," F. V. Hayden Collection (September 9, 1875).
7. The Dreyse needle gun received its name from its long firing pin that struck a percussion cap, igniting the black powder charge and sending a .61 acorn-shaped round at a muzzle velocity of 1,000 feet per second. This breech-loading, bolt-action rifle increased the rate of fire over muzzle-loading weapons in a five-to-one superiority, leading eventually to a standardized cartridge. This rifle was used in both the Austro-Prussian and Franco-Prussian wars. By 1871, the Prussian military had replaced it with improved weaponry, but surplus needle guns made their way to the United States. From "Franco-Prussian War: Dreyse Needle Gun," http://militaryhistory.about.com/od/smallarms/p/needlegun.htm?p=1.
8. Peale, "Diary," F. V. Hayden Collection, Special Collections, American Heritage Center, University of Wyoming, Laramie, Wyoming, p. 16.
9. Mills, "The Hayden Survey" (September 9, 1875).
10. David Grey (Aldrich), "The Hayden Survey," *The Daily Inter-Ocean*, F. V. Hayden Collection, Special Collections, American Heritage Center, University of Wyoming, Laramie, Wyoming (September 8, 1875).
11. Gardner, "Ute Warriors," *Rocky Mountain News*, F. V. Hayden Collection, Special Collections, American Heritage Center, University of Wyoming, Laramie, Wyoming (September 5, 1875).
12. Mills, "The Hayden Survey" (September 9, 1875).
13. Ibid.
14. Grey, "The Hayden Survey" (September 8, 1875).
15. Mills, "The Hayden Survey" (September 9, 1875).
16. Grey, "The Hayden Survey" (September 8, 1875).
17. Peale, "Diary," p. 17.
18. Peale, "Chain and Level—The Hayden Geological Survey," *The Philadelphia Press*, F. V. Hayden Collection, Special Collections, American Heritage Center, University of Wyoming, Laramie, Wyoming (September 9, 1875).
19. Gardner, "Ute Warriors" (September 5, 1875).
20. Grey, "The Hayden Survey" (September 8, 1875).
21. A. W. Dillon, "Early History of Montezuma County," in *Dolores Star* (September 4, 1908), p. 1.
22. Mancos Minutes, La Plata County, Colorado, Special Collections, Marriott Library, University of Utah, Salt Lake City, Utah (September 25, 1881). Members of the Mancos and Dolores communities wrote this important document on September 25, 1881, which was signed by many of the participants in the Pinhook Draw fight. Consequently, its information appears highly accurate, not being subject to vague recollection.
23. Events surrounding the Pinhook Draw fight have been discussed in a variety of sources, includ-

ing interviews, letters, newspaper articles, reminiscences, second- and third-hand accounts, and secondary sources—many of which are conflicting. Materials gathered shortly after the fight from participants who later shared their story are used here. Not all the conflicting information has been resolved, nor have all questions been answered. In a number of instances, what follows is the most logical explanation of what occurred based on primary sources, a walk of the battlefield, and the attitude of the times. Evaluation of some of the more prominent sources is given in future endnotes.
24. Wilson Rockwell, *The Utes, A Forgotten People* (Denver, CO: Sage Books, 1956), pp. 220–221. This author validates his version of the May and Thurman killings from interviews and letters from the 1930s. Most of the testimony was given a long time after the event but seems plausible.
25. "Interesting Indian Intelligence," *Dolores News* (May 14, 1881), p. 1.
26. Agent W. H. Berry to commissioner of Indian affairs, Special Collections, Marriott Library, University of Utah, Salt Lake City, Utah (July 18, 1881).
27. Rockwell, *The Utes*, p. 221. Although Indians subsequently claimed that Smith had been killed (and an unidentified body was found several years later), he could have escaped. An article published in the *Dolores News* on May 25, 1883, tells of how Smith, who was in jail in Santa Fe, had been talking about his escape from Indians near the Utah-Colorado border.
28. Jordan Bean, "Jordan Bean's Story and the Castle Valley Indian Fight," *Colorado Magazine* 20 (July 1943), p. 19; and Mancos Minutes.
29. *Dolores News* (May 28, 1881), p. 2; Cornelia A. Perkins, Marian Nielson, and Lenora Jones, *Saga of San Juan* (Salt Lake City: Mercury Publishing Company, 1968), p. 238; and "Mancos Minutes."
30. Conflicting accounts written at the time or shortly after raise questions about accuracy. To see how far astray some of these stories can be from actual events, read C. N. Cox, "Late Indian Troubles in the San Juan Country," *Colorado Magazine*, Issue 17 no. 6 (June 1940), pp. 30–34.
31. Perkins, *Saga*, p. 238; Faun M. Tanner, *The Far Country, Moab and La Sal* (Salt Lake City: Olympus Publishing Company, 1976), pp. 119–120; and Frank Silvey, *History and Settlement of Northern San Juan County, Utah* (Moab: Times-Independent, 1990), pp. 13–14. Silvey is an oft-quoted source on the Pinhook battle, and though he was not a participant, his brother Jack was part of the rescue party from Rico. Some of Silvey's version is unsubstantiated by other documents or eyewitness accounts.
32. Bean, "Jordan Bean's Story," p. 20.
33. "A 'Quien Sabe' Case," *Dolores News* (June 11, 1881), p. 2.
34. "The Stronghold of the Paiutes," *Dolores News* (June 4, 1881), p. 1.
35. Ibid.
36. "Operational Returns," Fort Lewis, microfische #M617, National Archives, Washington, DC (October 1878–August 1891); "War on the Border," *Denver Tribune* (June 25, 1881), p. 2; Silvey, *History*, p, 19; Bean, "Jordan Bean's Story," pp. 19–20; and "The Fight with the Utes," *Denver Republican* (June 29, 1881), p. 1.
37. Jones Adams, "In the Stronghold of the Pi-Utes," *Overland Monthly*, Issue 22 no. 132 (December 1893), p. 586.
38. Jordan Bean, "Jordan Bean" (unpublished account in possession of author) (May 14, 1941). Bean recorded his memories in several articles and interviews, most of which were written sixty years after the fight. In spite of the lapse in time, his statements have proven to be quite accurate and verifiable using other sources.
39. Perkins, *Saga of San Juan*, p. 240; Silvey, *History*, p. 20.
40. "The Fights with the Utes," *Denver Republican* (June 29, 1881), p. 1; A. M. Rogers, "A True Narrative of an Indian Fight," *Echo of the Cliff Dwellers*, La Sal National Forest Publication, microfilm #40, Utah State Historical Society, Salt Lake City, Utah (April 1912). Many of Roger's minute details are accurate (i.e., the eclipse and the comet), but he injudiciously wrote his story as though he were a participant in the battle when, in fact, he has been verified as a member of the Rico rescue party. He gleaned much of his material from other sources and the participants, as well as his first-hand experience.

41. Ibid.
42. Ibid., p. 46.
43. Ibid, p. 42; "Second Anniversary," *Dolores News* (June 16, 1883), p. 3.
44. Rogers, "A True Narrative," pp. 41–42.
45. "Second Anniversary," *Dolores News* (June 16, 1883), p. 3.
46. Bean, "Jordan Bean's Story," p. 20.
47. Untitled, *The Idea* (Durango newspaper) (June 16, 1886), p. 1.
48. Rockwell, *The Utes*, p. 222.
49. "The Indian Battle," *Denver Tribune* (July 9, 1881), p. 3. This appears to be a very accurate source, having been written within three weeks of the battle and whose contents were "acknowledged as reliable by the survivors who have returned and furnished the facts for the following." It is also interesting that it corresponds closely to what Mancos Jim, a Ute participant, claimed five years later.
50. Silvey, *History*, p. 17.
51. Ibid.
52. "War! With the Indians," *Dolores News* (June 25, 1881), p. 1.
53. Bean, "Jordan Bean's Story," p. 20.
54. Ibid., pp. 20–21.
55. Silvey, *History*, p. 19.
56. "War!," *Dolores News* (June 25, 1881), p. 1.
57. "Second Anniversary," *Dolores News* (June 16, 1883), p. 3.
58. The actual number was probably closer to ten men from Moab. This is based on what Joseph Burkholder, a member of this group, stated in an interview with Faun Tanner (see endnote 53).
59. "Return of Rico's Reinforcements," *Dolores News* (July 9, 1881), p. 2.
60. Ibid.
61. Bean, "Jordan Bean," p. 3; and Eliza Burr (Moab resident) (statement in possession of author) (November 30, 1948).
62. Ibid.; and Adams, "In the Stronghold of the Pi-Utes," p. 590.
63. "The Indian Battle," *Denver Tribune* (July 9, 1881), p. 3.
64. Operational Returns, 9th Cavalry, Calendar of Letters Received, FLC (1881).
65. Untitled, *The Idea* (June 16, 1886), p. 1.
66. Jones, p. 591; and Thomas Magraw to R. S. Mackenzie, Record Group 94, Letters Received—Adjutant General's Office, National Archives, Washington, DC (June 25, 1881).
67. Lyman, "History," pp. 22–23.
68. Lieutenant Colonel R. Crofton to Colonel Henry Page, Record Group 75, Bureau of Indian Affairs, Consolidated Ute Agency, Federal Records Center, Denver, Colorado (June 9, 1881).
69. See Robert S. McPherson and Winston Hurst, "The Fight at Soldier Crossing, 1884: Military Considerations in Canyon Country," *Utah Historical Quarterly*, Issue 70 no. 3 (Summer 2002), pp. 258–281.
70. James Monroe Redd clarifies exactly where the two groups were located: "The cowboys were camped on the top of the hill just above Verdure where the dugway goes up. It's a pretty good road now. It used to be a narrow dirt road. The Utes were camped down in Verdure where the Barton home is now" (from James Monroe Redd, Jr., in an interview with Michael Hurst, CRC-J4, Charles Redd Center for Western Studies, Brigham Young University, Provo, Utah (February 15, 1973), p. 9.
71. Don D. Walker, "Cowboys, Indians, and Cavalry," *Utah Historical Quarterly*, Issue 34 no. 3 (Summer 1966), pp. 254–262. This article is an annotated letter written by Harold Carlisle eleven days after the fight and published in the *Denver Republican* on July 29. Rich in detail and contemporary when written, this is an important primary document.
72. Walker, "Cowboys, Indians, and Cavalry," p. 257; Cornelia Adams Perkins, Marian Gardner Nielson, and Lenora Butt Jones, *Saga of San Juan* (Salt Lake City: Mercury Publishing Company, 1968), p. 242; and H. L. Mitchell to Warren Patten, Consol. Ute Agency (July 8, 1884).

73. Adams, et al, *Saga*, p. 242.
74. "A Serious Conflict," *Dolores News* (July 12, 1884), p. 3; and Albert R. Lyman, "History of San Juan County, 1879-1917," Special Collections, Harold B. Lee Library, Brigham Young University, Provo, Utah, p. 40.
75. Lyman, "History of San Juan," p. 41; Sam Todd, "A Pioneer Experience," Utah State Historical Society Library, Salt Lake City, Utah, p. 1; and "A Serious Conflict," p. 3.
76. "A Serious Conflict," p. 3.
77. Albert R. Lyman, *The Outlaw of Navaho Mountain* (Salt Lake City: Albert R. Lyman Trust, 1986), pp. 55–56.
78. Platte D. Lyman, "Diary of Platte D. Lyman," Special Collections, Brigham Young University Library, Provo, Utah, p. 76.
79. "A Serious Conflict," p. 3.
80. Sam Todd to Glen Hanks, "A Pioneer Experience," Utah State Historical Society, Salt Lake City, Utah (March 2, 1925), pp. 1–5. Sam Todd is an interesting character. Born in Missouri in 1854, he soon moved to Texas, where he worked as a cowboy. By age eighteen, he contracted tuberculosis and ended a two-year bout with the disease by having a lung removed. Thereafter, he always wore a pad under his coat to compensate for the left side of his caved-in chest. In 1880 at the age of twenty-five, he moved to the "disappointment country" of southwestern Colorado, where he continued to ranch. He lived in this area until 1925, when he and his wife moved to Burbank, California, for the last four years of his life, returning to Cortez, Colorado, in 1929 long enough to breathe his last and be buried in the country that he knew and loved (from "Sam Todd Never Bragged–Could Have," *Montezuma Valley Journal* (April 22, 1987), p. 10A.
81. Ibid.
82. Walker, "Cowboys, Indians, and Cavalry," p. 257.
83. "Two More Victims," *Dolores News* (July 26, 1884), p. 3.
84. Walker, p. 257; and Report of Colonel L. P. Bradley to secretary of war, *Report of the Secretary of the Interior*, 48th Cong., 2nd sess., Vol. 1 (1884), p. 121.
85. "Two More Victims," p. 3.
86. Christian Soffke to Warren Patten, Consol. Ute Agency (July 12, 1884).
87. No name to Patten, letter, Consol. Ute Agency (n.d., but around 1884).
88. Patten to Hiram Price, Commissioner of Indian Affairs, Consol. Ute Agency (July [blurred] 1884).
89. "Capture of Six Indians," *Dolores News* (July 19, 1884), p. 3.
90. Walker, "Cowboys, Indians, and Cavalry," p. 58.
91. It is unclear whether this is a literary device invented by Lyman, a metaphor similar to the "war path" of Hollywood movies, or an actual physical trail imbued by the Utes with legend and lore from previous defensive and offensive campaigns, as Lyman asserts. In any case, the Utes were undoubtedly following familiar trails, components in a vast and complex network of ancient trails that spanned the region.
92. Identifying parts of this old Ute trail is difficult. In an attempt to tie Todd's account to the land, two days were spent looking for a likely trail off Elk Ridge. The most likely route followed by the Utes and their pursuers in 1884 is now marked by a major and developed stock trail that heads in a corral on the rim of the Pushout and descends via a knife-like ridge, with several level spots, to the valley floor. This trail has been significantly improved and maintained over the years and remains in active use as a drive trail. Most other sections of the Pushout and adjoining lands that offer the view described by Todd are impassable or would be difficult to negotiate by pack stock, with ledges, talus, dense vegetation, and rock walls making movement very inconvenient or impossible. Todd's statement that two Utes, half a mile away from the rim, lit signal fires to warn the main body fits very nicely with a level plateau on the ridge approximately half a mile from the top. The place is clearly visible from the likely Ute encampment on the Cheesebox/White Canyon bench to the southwest and offers an easy trail down to the valley floor after the fires were lit.

93. Todd, "A Pioneer Experience," p. 2.
94. Ibid.
95. Walker, "Cowboys, Indians, and Cavalry," p. 258; and Todd, "A Pioneer Experience," p. 2.
96. Lyman, *The Outlaw of Navaho Mountain*, p. 59.
97. Todd, "A Pioneer Experience," p. 2.
98. Ibid. People who travel to the battle site will find the terrain formidable. The trail to Piute Pass is dimly etched in the land and is not associated with the recently re-bladed, mid-twentieth century uranium road that traverses another part of the slope at a gentler angle. After leaving the bench along which Highway 95 runs, the Utes' trail winds over a ridge, with three step-like hills that ascend to the base of a steep talus slope approximately 300 meters long. Ascending at a 30°+ angle, the slope is covered with boulders, sagebrush, piñon, and juniper trees. At the top of the talus slope is the low saddle in the seventy-foot-high rimrock through which Piute Pass slices. There is no level place at the top of the talus slope for the maneuver of units, and the trail traversing the talus is too steep. The aforementioned bladed road has cut through the pass and widened the gap, apparently obliterating the actual narrow defile where the old trail passed and significantly disturbing the Utes' position.

There are two interesting points for conjecture. First, two unfired .50–70-caliber bullets have been found along the trail: one between the White Canyon bench and the upper talus slope, and the other in a protected location in the Ute position at the top of the trail. These were made to be fired by either an obsolete (in 1884) US Army Springfield rifle or a Sharps rifle. The placement of the bullets suggests the possibility that they may have been put in position as defensive "medicine" to invoke supernatural power in defense against the pursuers. A second issue is how the Utes brought all their livestock up such a steep slope and through the narrow defile. Most likely, they separated and tied into strings the large horse herd before leading them up the trail in groups. The ruggedness of the terrain precludes herding so many animals en masse.
99. Walker, "Cowboys, Indians, and Cavalry," p. 258; and Todd, "A Pioneer Experience," p. 2.
100. While the battlefield has been picked over by visitors to the site, the evidence that has been salvaged gives an indication of how both sides were armed. The soldiers carried .45–70-caliber trapdoor Springfield carbines with a maximum effective range of 500 yards. The cowboys had .44–40 Winchester center-fire rifles with a maximum effective range of 200 yards. The standing operating procedure for soldiers at the time was for each man to carry sixty rounds on his person and sixty rounds in his saddlebag. The Utes had a greater variety of rifles, including .45–60-caliber Winchester, .44-40 Winchester, a Henry rifle, and a Sharps. This analysis is based on the ten pounds of lead and the shell casings found at the site. Obviously, there were other types and numbers of firearms involved in the fracas.
101. Todd, "A Pioneer Experience," p. 3.
102. Ibid.
103. "Incidents of the Indian Fight," *Dolores News* (August 2, 1884), p. 3.
104. Ibid.
105. Todd, "A Pioneer Experience," p. 4.
106. Lyman suggests that the Ute trail led across Mossback Mesa before "skirting the Colorado River" via Red Canyon. This is probably an error on his part, based on the mistaken impression that the scarp at Piute Pass is part of Mossback Mesa, which is actually miles to the south and beyond Fry Canyon. A much more likely route leads directly southwest—from Piute Pass, across Red Canyon, and to the Moki Canyon sand slide via Mancos Mesa. The Ute trail across the Moki Canyon sand slide was inferred by Lyman's informants from the later discovery by Bluff stockmen of a pocket watch, believed to have been taken from one of the Piute Pass victims and dropped on the trail by the Utes (Albert R. Lyman, *Indians and Outlaws* (Salt Lake City: Bookcraft, 1962, p. 68). There is no independent evidence to support that inference.
107. Lake Pagahrit, or Hermit Lake, was an ancient natural reservoir formed behind a massive falling dune in the drainage now known as Lake Canyon. This was a favorite camp area for both

native people and Anglo stockmen prior to the failure of the dam and emptying of the lake in 1915, following several decades of severe impacts from cattle grazing. See David A. Miller, *Hole in the Rock* (Salt Lake City: University of Utah Press, 1959), p. 133 and photographs following, p. 112.

108. Lyman, *The Outlaw of Navaho Mountain*, p. 62.

109. Todd, "A Pioneer Experience," p. 4.

110. Ibid., p. 5.

111. Major R. H. Hall, 22nd Infantry, Fort Lewis Post Returns, *Returns from U. S. Military Posts from 1800 to 1916*, microfilm #624, National Archives, Washington, DC (October 1878 to August 1891).

112. Swaine to adjutant general, Fort Leavenworth, Letters Received—FLC (June 19, 1885).

113. Swaine to adjutant general, District of New Mexico, Outgoing Correspondence, Fort Lewis, FLC (August 10, 1883).

114. Warren Pyle, "The Story of the Beaver Creek Incident," unpublished manuscript (Cortez Public Library, n.d.); and Ignacio's statement cited in Earle R. Forrest, *With a Camera in Old Navaholand* (Norman, OK: University of Oklahoma Press, 1970), pp. 12–13.

115. Swaine to adjutant general, District of New Mexico, Letters Received—FLC (June 22, 1885).

116. Cowboy accounts testify of six dead, while the Indians' account say seven. Perhaps the reason for the discrepancy is due to the "sentinel" who, when shot, was said to have tumbled off a cliff. His body, therefore, would not have been located with those killed in the camp and so was not included in the count.

117. Swaine to adjutant general, District of New Mexico (June 21, 1885); and Swaine to Major David Perry, Letters Received—FLC (June 22, 1885).

118. Christian F. Stollsteimer, "Southern Ute Agency Report," *Report of the Secretary of the Interior*, 49th Cong., 1st sess., H.R. Exec. Doc. 1 (August 18, 1885), p. 241.

119. John H. Bowman to Southern Ute Agency, Bureau of Indian Affairs, Ute Agency, "Intertribal Difficulties, 1879-1926" (July 24 and August 1, 1885); and R. E. Crofton to acting assistant general, Fort Wingate, Consol. Ute (July 28, 1885).

120. Swaine to adjutant general, District of New Mexico, Letters Received—FLC (June 25, 1885).

CHAPTER FIVE

Fighting on the Fringes
Navajo and White Expansion into the Dark Corner, 1879–1887

Between 1868 and 1892, the Navajo population officially doubled to 18,000. In reality, it was much larger.[1] Water, grass, and landscape pushed these Native Americans all over their 20,000-square-mile reservation in mobile family units that made keeping track of most impossible. The territory on the northern part of the reservation was particularly challenging due to the distance from the Navajo Agency at Fort Defiance, Arizona; the rugged canyon country that divided the land; and the lack of geographical knowledge surrounding it. Army doctor Bernard J. Byrne, stationed at Fort Lewis during the 1880s, said it well when he wrote that local folks called the Four Corners area the "Dark Corner" because "a man makes his own laws there. There ain't no pertection [sic] 'cept what a man makes himself. . . . Down in the Dark Corner, if a man kills another man he just steps over to Utah. If he steals a horse in Arizona he slides across to New Mexico."[2]

Ute, Paiute, and Navajo factions, as well as lawless elements from white settlements, all appreciated the isolated tortuous canyon country, where resources to survive were available only if one understood the land and its escape routes.[3] Two primary examples of this fight-and-flight scenario are the Pinhook Draw skirmish and the battle at Soldier Crossing, both previously discussed.

Starting in the late 1870s, a tide of white settlement began edging its way into southeastern Utah and southwestern Colorado to take advantage of the land and its resources. A good example of the troublesome flotsam and jetsam that washed ashore in 1878 is Henry L. Mitchell, a cantankerous settler from Missouri, who settled at Riverview (now Aneth) on the San Juan River near the mouth of McElmo Creek. For seven years, he created, embellished, and fueled more incidents concerning Indian issues in this area than any other individual.[4] His importance lies in his correspondence. Mitchell wrote letter after letter to Indian agents, military commanders, and political personalities, relating—and often exaggerating—conflicts between white settlers and their Indian neighbors. By doing so, he provided a well-documented source of events while explaining how he was either directly or indirectly involved with almost every incident with Navajos in this area up until his departure in 1885.

Mitchell was born in Montgomery, Ohio, around 1820. He served in the Civil War, was wounded, and dishonorably discharged, which may explain his penchant for aggression. As early as 1879, he wrote to Utah Governor Arthur Thomas to request that the territory supply fifty rifles and two hundred rounds of ammunition for each weapon for protection against hostile Utes, Paiutes, and Navajos. The purported reason was to assist the eighteen families living along the river in resisting Navajo demands that the whites leave. The Navajos responded by aggressively herding 20,000 sheep around the Mitchell household, an act which "cleared away all grass several miles back from the river."[5] Each year saw other claims by Mitchell against the Indians, with a hope that he would receive some type of remuneration.

One of Mitchell's sons, Ernest, appears to have been of a similar nature as his father, but more interested in prospecting than farming or operating a trading post. On December 29, 1879, Ernest and his partner James Merrick met an advance party of Mormons heading to Montezuma Creek with the intention of settling there the next year. The two men invited one of the Mormons, George Hobbs, to join them in a search for silver mines in the Monument Valley area, but he declined.[6] The miners moved on to meet their fate. Two months passed, and Henry had not heard from his son or Merrick. The first indication that there had been trouble came when a Navajo, Boy With Many Horses, visited a Paiute camp sixty miles above Lee's Ferry. There, he saw four mules taken by Paiutes after they had killed the owners. Since the Navajos were often blamed for deeds they did not commit, they were anxious to have the affair investigated.[7] At the same time, Mitchell wrote to Navajo Agent Galen Eastman, saying that both the Utes and Navajos were acting "sassy" and that if fighting occurred, most of the settlers would be in trouble because the men were out looking for Merrick and Mitchell. If nothing happened in the next couple of weeks, however, there would be 200 men present to hold out against Indian attacks until soldiers arrived.[8]

As February drew to a close, Mitchell's fiery rhetoric grew more urgent. The search party found the two men dead in Monument Valley, adding to the anger and frustration. In the *Dolores News*, readers learned that "Merrick's body was riddled with bullets; from all indications it appeared he had fought nobly. The men found his body about three miles from his camp," beneath an overhanging rock in a deep and sandy arroyo.[9] Mitchell's body was nearer to their camp, but it had been devoured by wolves and could only be identified by the clothing on or near the carcass. Because there were Navajo families living nearby, they received the initial blame, which seemed to be confirmed when they turned over the dead men's weapons. The Indians protested, claiming the "Pi-Utes and White River Utes, fugitives from justice," were the culprits. Although it was a Navajo guide who led the search party to the corpses, no single group claimed responsibility, with the Navajos blaming the Utes, the Utes blaming the Navajos, and the Paiutes serving as a third scapegoat.[10]

Following the burial, Henry Mitchell launched into another tirade, claiming that five other men had been killed (although no bodies had been found), that the Utes were in league with the Navajos, and that both were equally bad. Eastman sent out representatives to investigate the murders. They returned with word that the guilty party was comprised of renegades who were not attached to any agency. A second inquiry by a Navajo and a Mexican named Jesus Alviso confirmed that three or four Indians of Ute-Paiute ancestry, living north of the San Juan, had killed the two miners.[11]

In November of the same year, the *Dolores News* headline read "Trouble near Home, and War in the Blue Mountains," claiming that a series of incidents gave proof "that the Indians have resolved to wage war upon the isolated miners and ranchmen. It is evidently their intention to steer clear of towns and large settlements, but to kill single families who are separated by miles from their nearest neighbors."[12] The paper published the story that a group of prospectors had left Parrott City that week and had been massacred in the Carrizo Mountains on their way to northeastern Arizona. It went on to say that the country was "overrun with renegade Pi-Utes and Navajos" and that although the fight was just a rumor, the prospectors had lost all of their horses and so were doomed. "The chances are that they are all slaughtered long before this time." The paper next called for the extermination of the Utes. "History will tell us that explosive bullets have more influence with savages than folios of vigorous editorials. We cannot appeal to an Indian's sense of justice or cause him to feel the pangs of remorse. Let us substitute Winchester rifles for brains and note the results."

A year later, another mining party comprised of twenty-five men from Rico and Durango converged at Mitchell's, then set off to search the Navajo Mountain area for the lost silver mines that Merrick and Mitchell were supposed to have found. The party met "Pah Utes" and was treated well, but the terrain and lack of water was more than they could handle, and they returned. The paper noted the formula for success with Indians: "Hitherto the savage Pah Ute has kept all out save a few adventurous souls, but this party went in well-armed and equipped."[13] Miners operating in small groups continued to comb the countryside for wealth. Not until the early 1890s would there be a gold rush along the San Juan River that threatened Utes and Navajos with loss of land.

The activities in the spring, summer, and fall of 1881 were not an anomaly. The next year, military forces of various sizes spent time at Riverview, Soldier Spring (near future Monticello), the mouth of Recapture Wash, and McElmo Canyon. In each instance, the soldiers selected the site for a specific purpose. At Riverside, the military stationed a "detachment of infantry of not less than 25 men to the Lower San Juan River to remain for a month to six weeks to give temporary protection and endeavor to restore confidence to the settlers. An equally important reason was to send an intelligent officer to investigate the trouble arising in that locality and report same to the District Commander."[14]

Given Mitchell's penchant for requesting assistance, fostering controversy, and sniffing out an opportunity to sell goods from his trading post shelves to troops stationed nearby, it is not surprising that he had the military at his settlement for five years in a row, until he finally departed.

On April 15, 1884, shots of conflict rang out at Mitchell's store. Some transient white men visiting the post killed a Navajo and wounded two others over a misunderstanding. Ba'álílee, a local medicine man whose home was approximately four miles east of the post, went to the store to trade, accompanied by three other men and two women. One of the Navajos took an unloaded rifle and aimed it at a calf outside, then at a boy, then at one of the white customers inside. Another white man saw the move and drew his pistol, believing a threat existed. One of the Navajos seized the rifle from the one pointing it around, showing it was unloaded. The disarmed Navajo called to Ba'álílee outside, saying, "These Americans are going to kill me." Ba'álílee strode toward the store, gun in hand. The threatened white men drew their weapons and opened fire. The Navajo who had done the pointing died instantly. The sound of gunshots brought Mitchell's son and another man from the nearby fields. Upon seeing the problem, one of them fired, hitting Ba'álílee on the forehead (most likely with a ricochet), knocking him unconscious. The Navajo men rushed out of the store, and the whites followed after, firing in all directions and hitting one Indian in the elbow as he jumped a fence. Mrs. Mitchell assisted the two Navajo women trapped in the store to escape out a back door. Although fired upon while running, neither was hit. Ba'álílee revived, then escaped, as did the remaining Navajo man.[15]

This incident is important for two reasons. First, when reporting his investigation of the incident, the Navajo scout Herrero Segundo said that when Ba'álílee started toward the store, he uttered, "All right, that is what I want." No doubt this was in response to the strong-willed personality of Mitchell, who seemed to grate on everyone's nerves. According to Left Handed, a Navajo living in the area, "After this shooting, the good Indians tried to give good advice, but he wouldn't listen to them and was always making trouble."[16] The issue of who followed Ba'álílee and who opposed him (i.e., the "good Indians") became increasingly magnified over the years.

The second point to draw from this incident is how fast the Indians mobilized once news spread. In a land of isolated settlements and little rule, problems quickly escalated.

The Navajos took advantage of the incident to run off twenty-nine horses belonging to Mitchell, while he saw it as an opportunity to claim the loss of fifty mounts, recruit twenty-three Colorado cowboys to stay at his establishment, and have a military force stationed there too. A group of Utes who had pitched camp nearby also joined in, riding four miles upriver to another post to tell two hired hands that a fight had broken out. The men fled the store, providing a wonderful opportunity for the Indians to appropriate an estimated $2,400 worth of supplies.[17] Another fourteen miles upriver, Oen Edgar Noland's post had its doors and windows closed in preparation for a Ute attack, also having been ordered to leave.

Six days after the confrontation, Lieutenant J. F. Kreps arrived with a detachment. One week later, Captain Hiram Ketchum from Fort Lewis descended on Mitchell's ranch with one company and a month's rations, as did Captain Allan Smith from Fort Wingate, New Mexico, with three weeks of rations. Once upon the scene, all agreed there was no need for this size force and that much of what had happened had been caused by Mitchell and greatly exaggerated. In the meantime, Kreps learned that the Indians wanted to "kill the white gentile [non-Mormon] settlers" and that the Utes desired plunder, while the Navajos wanted plunder *and* revenge for the previous shootings.[18]

By mid-May, Sergeant Christian Soffke, along with a corporal and ten privates from B Company, 22nd Infantry, received instructions to remain at Mitchell's, create a defensive position from which to "make a stubborn fight" if necessary, and prevent Indians from having access to his position.[19]

Other reports of discontent filtered in. Two cattlemen told of how Navajos and Utes had killed no less than 100 cows that spring, "actuated by pure deviltry, as the carcasses are usually untouched, save to cut out the tongue."[20] The newspaper rendering this report by "Messrs. Adams and Ptolemy" continued:

> They saw two or three Indians of Narraguinip's band who were shot by the Rico boys in the fight at La Sal. One of them, an old buck, is minus two or three inches of one of his legs, which shortened as it healed [possibly an Indian called The Sore Leg]. They have very little use for Rico. Oscar Carter, of the West Dolores, told them he came from Rico, and every one of his Indian visitors left the camp instantly. The Narraguinip band is composed of renegades from the Uncompahgre, Paiutes, Navajos, and other tribes and are not recognized at any agency.[21]

Still, Agent Warren Patten had the responsibility of keeping track of this group and took the jabs of discontent when things went wrong. He must have just shrugged his shoulders when E. L. Stevens, acting Commissioner of Indian Affairs, directed him to "take the necessary steps to have your Indians return to their reservation at once and remain there."[22] Within three weeks of the writing of that directive, the Indians were embroiled in the events of the Soldier Crossing incident.

As mentioned previously, some of them fled to the vicinity of Navajo Mountain, taking advantage of one of the darkest corners in the region to hide in. While a number of Navajo lived in the area, there had been very few white men to explore that country. Agent Dennis M. Riordan, sitting at the Navajo Agency in Fort Defiance, understood the problems created by this type of isolation. He had assumed control of the expanding Navajo nation in January 1883, leaving his home in California for the red-rock desert of Arizona and New Mexico. He was as impoverished as his charges, with a $1,500 annual salary, which encouraged him to submit his resignation six months later. It took a little less than a year to have John Bowman from Colorado replace him.[23] Even given his short time in office, however, it did not take long to learn of what a previous agent called "the land of death" to his northwest, that

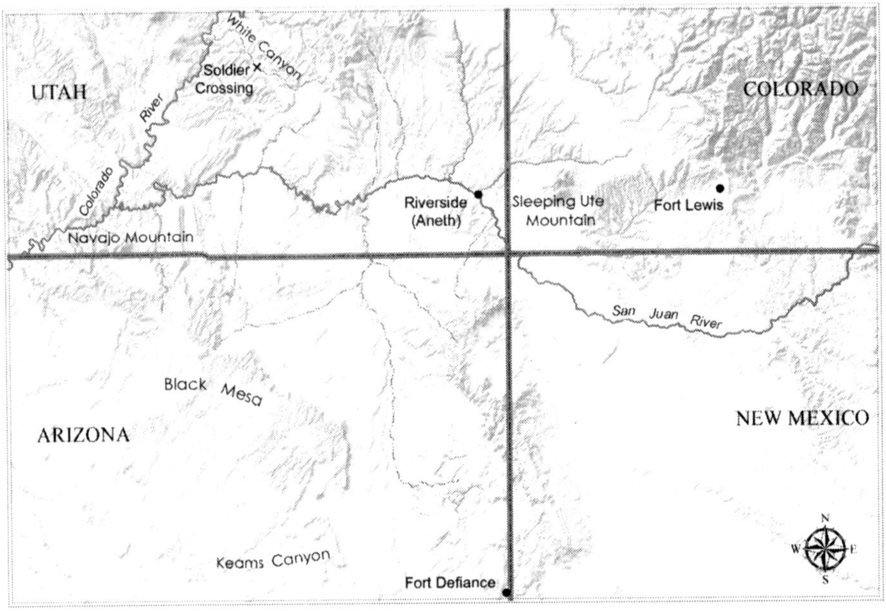

Fig. 21—The Four Corners region, with its vast canyon, mountain, and plateau systems, provided an ideal escape hatch for anyone wishing to evade the law. While each territory or state in 1884 had its hideouts, Utah and Arizona provided a particularly effective area for those wishing to avoid capture. This map gives a sense of the distance and broken topography to which one could flee. (Map by Mike Heagin, provided by Utah State Historical Society)

territory beyond reservation boundaries that primarily encompassed northern Arizona and southern Utah. In the 1882 annual report, he wrote about "a lawless remnant of the Pah Ute Indians and the Navajos affiliating with them," but still the agent had "hope that murders of prospectors and others in that heretofore land of death will be less frequent."[24]

Unfortunately, the outgoing agent had his hopes dashed on two counts. In early April 1884, word filtered south to Fort Defiance that Navajos had killed two prospectors—Samuel T. Walcott and James McNally—in the vicinity of Navajo Mountain, which sits astride the Utah-Arizona border. Riordan did what he could as he packed his bags, but left the main share of the chore to the incoming Bowman. The second issue was that now, what had not been part of the Navajo Reservation—and thus not of primary jurisdictional concern—was about to change. On May 17, 1884, President Chester A. Arthur signed two executive orders that made all the land in southeastern Utah between the San Juan River and the northern border of Arizona, as well as lands south of that border, part of the reservation. This did not encompass the "land of death," which included a triangle of territory with Moab at its northern tip, the Colorado River to the west, and the Colorado border to its east. It was, however, enough to add hundreds of miles of trackless terrain to the agent's responsibility.

Thus, it was not surprising that the short-termed Californian-turned-agent Riordan did not want to get involved in that tangle of canyons and ambush sites that would provide shelter for hostile elements. John H. Bowman was a different kind of man, however. Having previously been a sheriff in Gunnison, Colorado, he started the wheels of justice rolling toward Navajo Mountain as soon as he took office. This area was the preferred hiding spot for Navajos, Utes, and Paiutes fleeing retribution. Thus, when word first reached Riordan (and later, Bowman) that Navajos who killed two prospectors near the mountain were defiant, it was one more example in a long string of incidents that played off the isolation and lack of information concerning this territory.

This seemingly insignificant death of two prospectors provides a classic example of what the military faced when serving justice in an unknown and unforgiving land—a lesson repeated numerous times. The first news of the Walcott-McNally incident filtered into the agency via word of mouth. Riordan sent a Navajo scout named Pete to investigate. In the meantime, Mitchell sent a copy of a letter to the agent that he had previously mailed to a friend of Walcott. Mitchell reported two things.[25]First on the agenda was to make people aware that since February 8, when Walcott and McNally split from a group of prospectors and set out to find rumored rich deposits of copper, they had lost touch and were not following a planned schedule of contact. The two men, who had left a wagon and some other equipment at Mitchell's, were now almost a month late, suggesting something bad had happened; the other miners had arrived on the San Juan River but knew nothing about their companions. Mitchell, remembering the fate of his son, suspected the worst. Suggesting that "it is a common thing for the Navajos to kill white men that are travelling through the country," Mitchell felt it was time to teach them a lesson they would not forget.[26] The second incident he reported was the brush with Ba'álílee at his post the day before. In Mitchell's mind, it was time for the military to end this type of Navajo intimidation and deviltry.

Concern grew for the lost miners. Riordan wrote to the commissioner of Indian affairs that he had already had a run-in with the rumored Navajo perpetrators, who had once cornered him and another white man. The Indians had debated the two men's fates for several hours before letting them go. As far as the agent was concerned, "this band of cut throats in that region" needed to be punished, "and if the party sent out is not strong enough to bring them in, I propose to send the entire force at my command and if that will not do, I shall ask for troops. If my resignation was not pending, I would go myself and get those men or they'd get me."[27]

Several eyewitness accounts of the murders emerged and are provided below. As these various versions flowed into Fort Defiance, the presiding agent sifted through both fact and fiction, which could only be verified by action on the ground. The first account turned fears into fact on April 19, when the Navajo scout, Pete, returned with a detailed report provided by eyewitnesses. Near the southeast corner of Navajo Mountain lived the powerful headman, Hashkéneinii, and his son, Hashkéneinii Biye'. These men had held residence there for more than two decades, ever since the Long Walk period had begun. They were well-known and respected for both the physical and supernatural power they commanded. As Walcott and McNally camped in the Navajos' territory, it was only natural that members of this band visit them to find out what had brought the strangers there.[28] Man With White Horses (Hastiin Bilį́į́ Łigai) appeared first, learning that the white men wanted to trade for corn and meat, which he promised to bring the next morning. Slim Man (Diné Ts'ósí), along with White Horses's son, a "half-grown boy," reached the prospectors' camp and joined Hashkéneinii Biye', who was already seated at the fire. All three watched as the Americans ate breakfast, after which the younger McNally left to secure the prospectors' five horses. The Indians were ready to trade, but Walcott wanted to wait for his companion to return, and so the Navajos sat there, biding their time. Slim Man wondered if the white men would be interested in trading the rifle he saw lying on the ground for one of his horses. Hashkéneinii Biye' asked, but Walcott refused. This angered Hashkéneinii Biye', rekindling the resentment that had smoldered in his heart as he recalled that some of his relatives had been killed by white men in Utah ten years before.

As Hashkéneinii Biye' contemplated the loss, he remembered that there had been no satisfaction and no revenge on the perpetrators. He was still angry about it, and his wife knew that. That was why, the night before, she had hidden his moccasins: so that he could not go out and kill the two peacefully camped miners. But now, the time seemed right. Hashkéneinii Biye' said, "Let's kill these Americans. They are always mean and have no accommodation about them." The boy readily agreed, but Slim Man cautioned both that their relatives would not like them to do it. The other two, however, did not seem to care. Hashkéneinii Biye' told the boy to pick up the rifle while he, Hashkéneinii Biye', grabbed for an ax. Walcott went to the adult first, trying to wrest the tool out of his hands until the Indian told him he was just checking the blade for sharpness. He then went to the boy to get his rifle as the youth began to remove it from its scabbard. Walcott bent over to secure it, allowing Hashkéneinii Biye' to strike him in the back of the head with the ax, killing him instantly. Slim Man arose from his seat as two older Navajos joined the group, asking, "What have you boys been doing fighting?" Slim Man explained what had happened, which raised the question of what course to follow with McNally. The answer from one of the old men, Little Mustache (Dághaa' Yázhí), who had just joined the group was, "As long as one is killed, it is better to kill the other one too, for if they are murdered, no one will ever know anything about it."

The Navajos withdrew a short distance from the camp, but as McNally approached, Hashkéneinii Biye' began shooting at him with the newly acquired Winchester rifle. The prospector immediately tied all three horses he had together to form a standing breastwork—until all the animals fell, mortally wounded. McNally lay behind his dead mounts and returned fire. Soon, Hashkéneinii Biye' had used all eight cartridges in the rifle, so he decided that he and his companions needed to crawl as close as they could toward their victim, then engage him with their pistols. Little Mustache got the closest—twenty-five feet to the barricade—before they all began firing. When he raised himself up to see above a tuft of grass, the miner spotted Little Mustache, shot, and hit him in the head, with the bullet entering near his right eye and exiting behind his ear. The wounded Indian jumped up and stumbled away, occasionally falling. The others broke contact, secured their wounded friend, and brought him to a nearby hogan, where he could be warmed and cared for. They also sent word to Hashkéneinii's camp to make the headman aware of the incident.

Shortly after dark, the leader arrived with a group of followers. He sent an observer to see if McNally had moved and if so, where. The scout eventually returned, saying that the white man had left; the scout did not know when or in which direction, but the man was definitely gone. Father and son, along with a number of others in the group, took up the trail, lighting matches to follow the tracks. The next day, it was over; they killed McNally.

Pete reported that Slim Man buried Walcott; collected and burned the men's blankets, saddles, and equipment, all of it covered with blood; and captured their two remaining horses, as well as two others coming from the recent fracas at Mitchell's on the San Juan River. He accompanied the scout as far as Pete's home in Chinle Valley and planned to come to the agency with animals and equipment once the horses were able to travel again. Slim Man would also make a statement of the events he witnessed. Riordan appreciated the testimony, which corroborated that these murders added to "scores of white men during the past ten years [who] have paid the penalty of daring to examine the country outside of this reservation with their lives."[29]

Additional information trickled in. According to another Navajo scout with a less-convincing report, Walcott was much more the aggressor. He spoke sharply to the Navajos, was the first to draw his gun, and shot one of the Navajos who was sitting peacefully around the campfire. The scout also asserted that McNally was badly wounded before leaving his horse barricade and that other uninvolved Navajos, while looking for horses, found him dead. As for the badly wounded Little Mustache, he was still alive.[30]

Sharply at odds with this report is the eyewitness testimony of Slim Man, who came in to the agency on May 5. According to his account, when Man With White Horses had first approached the camp the night before, he and the two miners had shaken hands with the Indians and "hugged each other all around," followed by a gift exchange of tobacco. The next morning after breakfast, the white men had given all three of the new visitors tobacco, but Hashkéneinii Biye' "was moving around all the time while the other two sat by the fire." After the Navajo had killed Walcott, he removed a pistol and holster that he had tried to trade for earlier but had been refused. At that point, Man With White Horses returned to the camp, suggesting that they put a white rag on a stick, approach McNally, then point him in the direction he should go to get home safely. Another Navajo man disagreed, and so the group eventually decided to kill the remaining white man. Slim Man explained the next day's fight, adding that under the cover of darkness, McNally had left his barricade before departing and had gone into the camp, wrapped Walcott in some blankets, and piled his things around him. That night, although badly wounded, McNally travelled twenty-five miles before Hashkéneinii Biye', his father, and "an old Navajo" caught up and killed him. As for Slim Man, he felt sorry about the whole affair and did not hesitate to go against Hashkéneinii, who threatened to kill anyone who talked about it.[31]

Yet another actor in the drama came forth to testify—Hashkéneinii Biye'—who arrived at the agency with his father and "a large number of his warriors" on May 7.[32] The interim agent, S. E. Marshall, took his sworn statement, which both the young man and his father signed, then turned the pair loose. Hashkéneinii Biye's version of events started with his being sick and his friends "singing over me all night to make me well." Tired from the ceremony, he and his wife were returning that morning when they encountered the two Americans. Husband and wife received tobacco, offered to sell some mutton to the men, then went home. The next morning, Hashkéneinii Biye' traveled to the prospectors' camp, watched them eat breakfast before giving the leftovers to their dog (not feeding their guests was a very inhospitable thing), and waited for McNally to retrieve his horses. Hashkéneinii Biye' told Slim Man to tell the white man where the animals were, but twice Slim Man refused. Walcott took out a pair of binoculars and let Hashkéneinii Biye' look through them, but denied Slim Man the opportunity. White Horses's son went to look at the rifle on the ground, which made the white man angry, and he chased after the boy with an ax but never caught him. Next, the white man went after Slim Man, who was sitting by the fire. Fortunately, according to the account of Hashkéneinii Biye', Hashkéneinii Biye' wrestled the ax out of the white man's hand before he drew his pistol. The Indian "hit him on the back of his head—not very hard, but just enough to knock him down. When the American fell I was very much frightened and threw the ax away." Slim Man searched the prospector for things he might like, but as the victim gained consciousness, the Navajo took the ax and with three or four swings, killed him.

At that point, Little Mustache arrived on the scene, and in answer to the question of what had happened, Slim Man pointed to Hashkéneinii Biye', saying, "My brother. I would be dead now if it was not for this man—he saved my life. The American was just about to hit me with the ax when he stopped it." Later, Slim Man twice begged Hashkéneinii Biye' not to tell what he had done: "Dear brother [do] not give [me] away and tell that [I] killed the old American as he was not hurt badly when [I] took the ax and killed him." He also purportedly attacked McNally, trying to fire his pistol three times without success and later assisted the others in the multi-pronged attack against the barricaded miner. Slim Man did not finally kill McNally, according to Hashkéneinii Biye', but he was certainly in the party that went to search for McNally. Whether this reversed story had any impact on subsequent events is unclear, but Hashkéneinii Biye' was not arrested during his trip to Fort Defiance.

Once Bowman took charge of the Navajo Agency on June 30, he assumed responsibility for appropriate action on the ground. He sent word to the miscreants that they had ten days to travel the 175 miles to the agency and give themselves up, or he would assign Navajo scouts—or if necessary, the military—to apprehend them.[33] Things started to happen. Colonel L. P. Bradley ordered one of the officers of the 6th Cavalry, which operated along the San Juan River, to

Fig. 22—Hashkéneinii Biye' played a central role in the Walcott-McNally incident, as became apparent when details of the murders unfolded. He is pictured here over fifty years after the event, still a powerful medicine man and leader in the Monument Valley community. (Courtesy Utah State Historical Society)

find the graves of the two men in preparation for moving them to Fort Lewis once the weather was cold enough. Transporting them in the summer was too difficult. He also directed that a detachment of soldiers be available to Bowman on request, should it be necessary to ferret out the murderers.[34]

At first, this did not seem necessary. On July 10, within the ten-day ultimatum, Hashkéneinii Biye's father turned himself in, then traveled to Fort Wingate under guard; a day later, Little Mustache, described as a very old man still suffering from his head wound, came in with some Navajo scouts.[35] Before leaving for his incarceration, he provided a statement, insisting that Hashkéneinii Biye' and Slim Man were the two trying to kill McNally and that he, himself, had been wounded by chance as he had innocently walked near the battlefield.[36] A week later, Navajo scouts brought in Slim Man who, along with Little Mustache, joined Hashkéneinii in jail at Fort Wingate.[37] The effectiveness of the scouts was apparent, since according to Bowman, the "troops move so slowly that it is much easier to accomplish arrests with the scouts when the opposition is not too strong."[38]

It became too strong when the Ute and Paiute faction, prominent in southeastern Utah conflict, entered the ring. Fresh from giving the cavalry from Fort Lewis a drubbing in July at the Soldier Crossing fight, these warriors, along with their families, fell into their normal pattern of fight-and-flight-and-then-disperse, with some making their way to Navajo Mountain. The Utes "took charge" of Hashkéneinii Biye', promising to protect him. Bowman headed north with ten scouts, where he rendezvoused with forty soldiers of Troop K, 6th Cavalry, under First Lieutenant H. P. Kingsbury from Fort Wingate. On August 14, the agent met with 500 Navajos at Thomas V. Keam's trading post in Keams Canyon, Arizona, then moved toward Navajo Mountain.[39] One of the questions he wanted answered was if the killings had occurred in Utah or Arizona. With Navajo Mountain sitting on the Utah-Arizona territorial border, the lack of knowledge of the terrain, and some conflicting information, a definitive answer would help with future military jurisdictional control.

Kingsbury provides a detailed report of what happened.[40] Having traveled 122 miles from Fort Wingate to Keams' Canyon in three days, the officer learned that Hashkéneinii Biye' was camped with a band of Utes that had twelve men, while two other groups nearby composed a total compliment of thirty-two warriors. One of these groups had recently killed two of Captain Perrine's men at Soldier Crossing. The next day, August 19, in company with Bowman and his scouts, the lieutenant traveled thirty-eight miles over a very rough and indistinct trail. Another day of travel covered thirty-five miles, with little water available; after a few hours' rest, the command mounted at midnight and rode until daybreak. Kingsbury struck the reported camp only to find that the Utes had fled a few hours before, scattering into the desolate canyon country.[41]

From here, everything else turned anticlimactic. Kingsbury backtracked twelve miles to meet with his pack train, then established camp for the next three days while Bowman secured Walcott's remains to be buried later at Fort Wingate. Bowman also tried unsuccessfully to acquire any stock belonging to the murderers, only to find the animals had been "run out of the country and up into the mountains." Efforts to find McNally's body proved fruitless, since only the guilty knew where it was. According to one Navajo account, McNally made it "close to Kayenta," where he was caught and killed.[42]

As Bowman continued with his duties, the lieutenant had time to ponder his failure. In his mind it was easily explained:

> The reason I did not surprise the Utes is plain: the Navajos were cowards and politicians; being afraid of the Utes they did not want them killed for protecting the murderer; they were afraid the Utes would retaliate on them; they therefore kept the Utes posted every night as to my whereabouts; they persistently lied about distance; they were spies the entire route.[43]

Left Handed (Tł'ah), living in the area at the time, gave a first-hand account from the Navajo perspective. Everyone in the area was well aware of the killings and of the fact that the agent had sent word that troops would be coming if Hashkéneinii Biye' did not surrender. By this time, Hashkéneinii Biye' had received a new name: Át'íní, which variously translates as The One Who Did It or Had/Has Done It. He responded to the agent's threat by saying, "I don't want to go. I'd rather be dead right here on my land. If they want me so badly they can come and cut my head off and take it."[44]

At the same time, a group of Utes passed through the area, claiming they had killed soldiers and saying, "We did wrong and we're pretty sure we will all be killed." When he heard that soldiers were on the way, The One Who Did It traded a rifle and ammunition with the Utes and eventually left the area. The Navajos who remained feared the Utes as much as they did the approaching cavalry, both of whom brought back memories of the Fearing Time and Fort Sumner period.

Left Handed's mother panicked, "running around, saying, 'I want to go right now. I want to save myself.' "[45] Her husband took a calmer approach so that even after she had fled to another place, he leisurely gathered his livestock and prepared his camp for evacuation before leaving with a large group of Navajos and disappearing into canyon country. In the meantime, the cavalry had surrounded the empty Ute camp, with the Utes and Paiutes having moved out to a "big round rock" where they spent the night building a wall with firing ports. The One Who Did It with a friend, Hairy Face (Nii'ditł'oii), built their own defensive position where they waited. After the soldiers departed, Left Handed's father, Old Man Hat, took charge, persuading a group of fifty men to accompany him to visit the white men and find out what was to happen.

As they traveled, the Navajos discussed how they would respond if asked about the Utes. They decided to say they knew nothing, because they had returned to their country. The Navajos "did not want any of the troops to get killed. If they'd gone after them [Utes] they'd have been killed for sure, because the Utes and Paiutes were up on the big rock and had everything ready."[46] As they rode, the Navajos asked Old Man Hat to sing a war song for protection and to ensure the talks would go well. He agreed and had them swing their horses in a line that stretched across an open area before he began singing. By the time he had finished, they topped a hill and saw a camp of many tents in a row, established beside a pool of water in a wash. Old Man Hat put his men in line again and approached the quiet camp, which showed little sign of activity. As the Navajo arrived at the edge of the wash, the soldiers came running from their tents, "making some kind of noise, whistling or something," then forming their own line with rifles ready.

In the meantime, the commander, along with his interpreter, Chee Dodge, emerged from a tent in the middle of the encampment and approached the group. They invited Old Man Hat to get off his horse, shook hands warmly as a strong sign of friendship, had all the Indians dismount and shake hands, then ordered the soldiers to stack arms and return to their tents. Old Man Hat introduced himself and his purpose, saying:

> We came here to shake hands with you, and we came to talk in the kindest way to each other. We came here for peace. And now we've shaken hands and are talking to each other in the kindest manner, we're all friends now. That's what we came here for. Even though I'm old—you look at me, and you know I'm old; you look in my mouth and you know I haven't any teeth, and I'm about blind and about deaf; you see my hair is white, and my skin is wrinkled, my whole face is full of wrinkles; you know I look ugly—but

even though I'm this way I'm thinking about myself that I'll live many years yet. I want to be safe always. I don't want to die right now. Even though death from old age is coming soon I'm thinking about myself that I'll live for a long time yet. That's why I was chasing around, chasing away from you. I thought you were going to kill me. But here I've found out you are a kind man.[47]

The discussion continued in this same polite manner. After the officer reassured them of why the soldiers had come and asked for the Navajos' help, Old Man Hat said that if they assisted, The One Who Did It would start killing them. They were afraid of him. Plus, he was hard to find, and the military, in seeking him, would not know where to go. "From here on it's pretty dangerous all over. When a person does not know this country he'll surely get lost or die of thirst. It's dangerous to travel here, crossing the desert and the many canyons. A person has got to know where to get water, and water is scarce. There's no water for miles and miles. So I think it is dangerous to go after him."[48] Next, he asked that Hashkéneinii be released and was in turn assured that he was being well taken care of, that the military was not there to harm those who were living a good life, and that everyone should come down off the mountain and go back home to care for their gardens and animals. The meeting ended with another round of handshaking and the distribution of tobacco before the Navajos departed.

The military spent three days in this encampment, five more returning to Fort Defiance, then two more en route to Fort Wingate, arriving on September 1. This completed a round-trip excursion of 359 miles.[49] In Kingsbury's concluding remarks of his report, he commented that he would need 100 mounted men and 30 days to "run the Utes, who are protecting the murderer, to ground . . . [and that the] Navajos should be given to understand that condign punishment would follow treachery and tale bearing, and it should be meted out to the first caught going ahead of the marching column." This was not to be. Hashkéneinii Biye' remained at large; the government released his father and the other prisoners after about a year; McNally's body remained where it fell; and the military moved on to other pressing problems.

Utah historian Charles Kelly interviewed Hashkéneinii Biye' for a full week in April 1939. From this invaluable discussion came some of the best personal information about his father, their activities while escaping their enemies and hiding during the Long Walk period, later dealings with prospector Cass Hite, and aspects of Navajo culture and history in the Navajo Mountain-Kayenta region.

Fig. 23—Navajo Mountain, known to Navajos as "Head of Earth Woman," has a long history that reaches back to the mythology of Monster Slayer. It is seen as a place of protection—both physical and spiritual. Part of a Protectionway song that refers to it intones, "Beyond it, danger has passed by me; behind it, I will survive. I have survived here." This was certainly true for those Navajos involved in the Walcott-McNally incident. (Photo by author)

He said nothing about the Walcott-McNally incident except for what he implied as he talked about miners coming into his area to look for a silver mine. "If they refused to go, he [Hashkéneinii] had to kill them. Many white men have been killed around here; I have killed some myself."[50] Kelly went on to publish a couple of articles—"Hoskaninni" and "Chief Hoskaninni"—based on his interviews, but he apparently did not know about the Walcott-McNally incident.[51]

The One Who Did It went on to become a very powerful medicine man who understood how to use many supernatural powers. Numerous stories of his ability to control the elements—especially lightning—and other forms of power exist, but they take us far beyond the scope of this chapter. Perhaps the testimony of his maternal granddaughter, Susie L. Yazzie, given at the age of sixty-seven in 1991, will suffice.[52] Speaking of her grandfather, she said, "He was an excellent medicine man and kept things sacred. He would not allow anyone to circle the hogan he was using for a sing [ceremony]. He would tell the people to keep away because the holy people [deity] were present. It was the holy people who were performing through him, so it was very sacred. And for the same reasons, he did not expect to be paid a high price. He performed the Yé'ii Bicheii ceremony, the Hail Stormway (lóee), the nine day ceremonies, the fire dance and Enemyway (Anaa'jí), plus the Blessingway and Evilway (Hóchxǫ'ijí) ceremonies. He was recognized by many people."

Hashkéneinii Biye' died in 1941, a powerful and respected member of his community. There is no indication he was ever punished for the killing of the two prospectors.

A final incident between the Navajos and white settlers took place with the Mormons, who had settled Bluff on the San Juan River in 1880. The general tenor of interaction had been peaceful, far more so than with the non-Mormons (including Mitchell) from Colorado and elsewhere, who were living upstream.[53] Still, there were troubles. Church leaders had warned the settlers that they should remain in a relatively tight-knit community and not get spread out too far along the banks of the San Juan River. In 1883, William Hyde, who was involved in a profitable trade with the Navajos, built a post near where Comb Wash and Chinle Wash meet at the river in an area that is fordable for much of the year. Since the structures were on a "corner" of Comb Ridge where the water had carved through, it was called Rincon. The settlement had a ferry for high water, a water wheel as part of an irrigation system, and a number of buildings to include a house and trading post. All seemed prosperous and peaceful until June 9, 1887.

Although an industrious, resourceful, and physically powerful man, Amasa Barton (William Hyde's son-in-law) also had a temper. He and his wife, Feenie, were put in charge of running the post but had difficulty meeting the demands of their Navajo and Ute customers. On June 9, 1887, a Navajo named Bad Eye (or Old Eye) visited the store with a friend. Bad Eye had received his name from having been struck by a gad that had put out one of his eyes. He was well-known to the Hydes, working for them on Amasa's farm on the flood plain east of the rock shelf where the post sat. So it was not surprising that on that morning, the two Navajos ate breakfast with the Bartons before stepping into the post to conduct business. Bad Eye wanted to retrieve some jewelry that his wife had previously pawned. He offered an old pistol in exchange and demanded a reduced price of $2. An argument ensued, with Barton ordering the two men out of the store. As he stooped under the counter to enter the "bullpen," Bad Eye slipped a rope around his neck, jerked him to the floor, and began a tussle. The other man joined in the wrestling, strangling Barton with the rope and attempting to pin his arms. Encountering a tough opponent, the unnamed Indian drew his pistol and fired at Barton, but the shot went wild, hitting Bad Eye close to the heart. He ran outside, taking his last breaths behind the store. The next shot entered Barton's head as he lay on the threshold of the door. After the assailant learned that he had killed Bad Eye, he returned and placed another round in Barton's head, the brains oozing from the holes.[54] The trader clung to life.

Feenie, along with her mother-in-law (Angeline Harris Hyde) and two children, watched the horror unfold. Amasa, still alive, warned his family to stay away until the Indian left; he knew there was little they could do for him. The Navajo carried Bad Eye to the skiff, rowed across the river, left the body under a blanket, secured the boat, and went to tell others. Feenie prepared for the worst. She implored three Utes—Cheerpoots, Posey, and another man, all of whom were innocent bystanders—to move her husband to a shed where he could rest more comfortably, then offered one of them $15 to go to Bluff nine miles away for help. Cheerpoots, Posey's father, accepted the task, returning with Kumen Jones and Platte Lyman in a little over an hour. This represented a third of the men present in town at the time.

Word of the incident reached Joseph Barton at Recapture Canyon, where he was returning with freight. Other men were at the Milk Ranch or in the Valleys herding livestock. All made an effort to return to Bluff.[55]

Before any assistance arrived at Rincon, seven armed Indians crossed the river. Barton played dead, convincing them that there was no need to shoot him again or to molest the women. Instead, they demanded from Feenie the keys to the post and helped themselves to what they wanted. Warning shouts from nearby cliffs told of riders in the distance. The Indians gathered their plunder and rowed the boat to the far shore, then disappeared. Jones and Lyman assessed the situation. Rather than move Amasa to Bluff at that time, a group of five or six men cared for him but remained vigilant of the Navajo camps now established out of sight on the opposite side of the river. There was no hope for Barton's recovery. On June 16 he died, was brought to Bluff, and buried in the cemetery.

Shortly after, a band of sixty Navajos, their faces painted black, came to town ready for a fight.[56] The Mormons, now with only three men in town but still a lot of women and children to protect, barricaded themselves in some of the homes and waited for the worst. Bishop Jens Nielson, an old and crippled man at that point in his life, along with his son-in-law, Kumen Jones (who spoke Navajo), went to meet the group. Nielson pointed out that the Mormons had come in peace and had maintained friendly relations thus far and did not want war. Many of the younger Navajos were not interested in these sentiments, but some of the older ones agreed. Nielson shifted his approach, saying that although there were not a lot of men in town to fight right now, he could send for the soldiers, and they would do the fighting for them. This got all of the Navajos' attention, as they remembered the bitter pill they had swallowed during the Long Walk period. Suddenly, peaceful negotiations seemed more appealing. Nielson sat down and talked of the history of Bluff and what had brought the settlers there. He then had supplies brought from a community store, slaughtered and cooked a fat steer, and generally mollified the crowd. By the time the Navajos left, they had "a general handshaking, and the war was over."[57] The Mormon settlement of Bluff returned to its serene lifestyle.

Fig. 24—Navajos constantly came to Bluff to trade and visit. During the Amasa Barton affair, relations became fragile, as both sides blamed the other for the two deaths. Open communication and the threat of military intervention eventually cooled the situation. (Courtesy San Juan County Historical Commission)

The following examples from Mitchell and McNally to the Mormons provide interesting aspects of conflict in the "dark corner." Here are four points for consideration when examining Navajo and Anglo conflict during this time period. A number of these are applicable to not only the Four Corners region but also the general American West and Southwest experience. Space does not permit a comparative study, and this is not to suggest that the small scale of what is discussed here is comparable to a larger, more complex one, but only that the principles discussed fit in both instances.

Take for example the use of Navajo scouts. While no one would compare what occurred here to the US Army's use of Apache scouts against Geronimo—in terms of scale, difficulty of mission, or effectiveness—there is no doubt that Navajo scouts played a vital role. Whether reporting incidents, finding "enemy" camps, guiding the cavalry over unknown terrain, translating language, understanding cultural practices, or locating resources—water, in particular—these men played an invaluable role. Indeed, the previous chapter about the Utes shows what it was like during the same time period to *not* have Indian scouts working with the military. The scouts were also helpful in unraveling conflicting accounts to determine who the culprits were in both the Mitchell and McNally cases.

A second point is the power of tribal memory. The Navajos had recently been sorely chastened during the Long Walk period and were not ready to forget the lessons learned. In both the McNally and Mormon incidents, the mere mention of the Navajos fighting against the US military was enough to turn warlike intentions into peaceful negotiations. The fear that the Navajos felt is illustrated by Bighorse, a man living in the Navajo Mountain community when the McNally incident occurred. He and two other men actually saw part of the fighting take place but were reticent to get involved by reporting the incident. The three deliberated about going to Fort Wingate, yet feared that Hashkéneinii Biye' would find out and kill them. Bighorse said, "But if we don't tell the troops, they will be after everybody again. Like they did before. There will be a war again. Everything was going in their mind like that. Everybody was living in fear of another war."[58] The men eventually reported what they knew of the incident and returned to their homes.

Later, when Left Handed met the cavalry and "shook hands all around," Bighorse was present. His thoughts reveal that he was motivated out of fear for the welfare of his people, rather than for any love of the military or sense of justice. After Kingsbury told the Navajos they had nothing to worry about and to go home and live in peace, Bighorse commented, "All the time that this is going on, I don't feel like friends to the troops. What happened before with our people, I am thinking about it. And it really makes me mad. I see all these troops out here just because two white men die. And now they say it's against the law to kill. Where was that law when they were killing all of the Navajo people. . . . We have hearts to feel sorry for all our people that got killed, cry for them, miss them all our lives, as long as we live. But I just hold my temper. I just shake their hand, but I know I won't be their friend."[59] Hashkéneinii Biye' had also expressed an unforgiving sentiment toward white men because of his relatives that had been killed in Utah ten years before the McNally incident.

Navajo political organization at this time centered around headmen (*naataanii*), who were strong leaders over a community or a number of communities. These were often older men practiced in either making war or maintaining peace who knew the accompanying ceremonies to make them successful on both a spiritual and physical level. The people looked to them for guidance, and although they technically did not command a particular action, the headmen's stature was often enough to ensure their wishes were carried out.[60] Hashkéneinii and Ba'álílee were two such men. This type of dispersed leadership and simple government organization fit the Navajo lifestyle well. Moving about in search of resources, the role of an individual—as opposed to large group interaction—and the dependence on spiritual assistance as much as physical warfare, ensured these men had to take a considered approach to solving issues. On the other hand, personality played an important part in the turn of events, especially when considering Henry Mitchell, Ba'álílee, and Hashkéneinii (whose name translates as Giving Out Anger), all of whom were irascible. Unlike much of the friction with the Utes, Navajo problems were more individually oriented. It was fortunate that there were men like Kingsbury, Left Handed, and Nielson, who took a softer, more measured approach toward what could have been inflammatory.

Finally, these incidents underscore the differing cultural perceptions of the same events. Left Handed's first-person account is particularly helpful—one of the few detailed renderings of a conflict from the Navajo perspective that is equally well-documented from that of the white man. His concerns for family and community, evaluation of the military situation, the internal discussion and reasoning as to options with approaching troops, and his introductory speech to Kingsbury all give invaluable insight into Navajo thought. The Navajo scouts who reported different versions of the killing of Walcott and McNally also offer understanding. For instance, Hashkéneinii Biye' found it rude to give leftovers from a meal to dogs and yet not feed guests; he could not understand why the white men did not want to trade a particular item, since in Navajo custom, the person is more important than the thing. He also felt that all white men "are always mean and have no accommodation." The revenge of "an eye for an eye" for an event that happened ten years previous with people who were unrelated to

Walcott and McNally also made sense, allowing Hashkéneinii Biye' to kill two innocent men while maintaining a clear conscience. All of these points show the cultural differences between competing forces at the time. In some respects, the biggest chasm or "darkest corner" was not on the landscape but between the two cultures.

Chapter Endnotes

1. Garrick Bailey and Roberta Glenn Bailey, *A History of the Navajos: The Reservation Years* (Santa Fe: School of American Research Press, 1986), p. 28.
2. Bernard James Byrne, *A Frontier Surgeon: Life in Colorado in the Eighties* (New York: Exposition Press, 1935, 1962), pp. 153–154.
3. For examples of lawlessness in this area, see Robert S. McPherson, *As If the Land Owned Us: An Ethnohistory of the White Mesa Utes* (Salt Lake City: University of Utah Press, 2011); McPherson, *The Northern Navajo Frontier, 1860–1900: Expansion through Adversity* (Logan: Utah State University Press, 2001); J. Lee Correll, "Navajo Frontiers in Utah and Troublous Times in Monument Valley," *Utah Historical Quarterly*, Issue 39 no. 2 (Spring 1971), pp. 145–161; and Albert R. Lyman, *Indians and Outlaws: Settling of the San Juan Frontier* (Salt Lake City: Bookcraft, Inc., 1962, 1980).
4. See McPherson, "Navajos, Mormons, and Henry L. Mitchell," *Utah Historical Quarterly*, Issue 55 no.1 (Winter 1987), pp. 50–65.
5. H. L. Mitchell to Governor Thomas of Utah, Record Group 75, Letters Received by Office of Indian Affairs—Navajo Agency, New Mexico Superintendency, 1879, National Archives, Washington, DC (December 27, 1879) [hereafter cited as Letters Received—New Mexico].
6. David E. Miller, *Hole-in-the-Rock: An Epic in the Colonization of the Great American West* (Salt Lake City: University of Utah Press, 1975), pp. 92–94.
7. Galen Eastman to commissioner of Indian affairs, Letters Received—New Mexico (February 6, 1880).
8. H. L. Mitchell to Eastman, Letters Received—New Mexico (February 15, 1880).
9. "Murder by the Indians at the Field of New Discovery," *Dolores News* (March 13, 1880), p. 1.
10. J. Carpenter to Carl Schurz, Letters Received—New Mexico (February 28, 1880).
11. Mitchell to Eastman (February 27, 1880); Eastman to commissioner of Indian affairs (March 8, 1880); and F. T. Bennett to acting assistant adjutant general, Letters Received—New Mexico (March 22, 1880).
12. "Trouble Near Home, and War in the Blue Mountains," *Dolores News* (November 13, 1880), p. 1.
13. "The Navajo Mountain Explorers," *Dolores News* (January 28, 1882), p. 1.
14. Assistant adjutant general, District of New Mexico, to commanding officer, Fort Lewis, Calendar of Letters Received, Special Collections, Fort Lewis College, Durango, Colorado (June 12, 1882).
15. Report of Herrero Segundo, submitted to Agent D. M. Riordan, Letters Received—New Mexico (April 29, 1884).
16. US Congress, Senate, "Testimony Regarding Trouble on Navajo Reservation," 60th Cong., 2nd sess., Klah Testimony (March 3, 1909), p. 43.
17. Major R. H. Hall to assistant adjutant general at Fort Leavenworth, Record Group 75, Letters Received, 1881–1907, Bureau of Indian Affairs, National Archives, Washington, DC (April 18, 1884) [hereafter cited as Letters Received–BIA].
18. Second Lieutenant J. F. Kreps to post adjutant at Fort Lewis, Letters Received–BIA (May 1, 1884).
19. LT Theodore Mosher to Christian Soffke, Letters Received–BIA (May 18, 1884).
20. "The Ute Mountain Country," *Dolores News* (June 28, 1884), p. 2.
21. Ibid.
22. E. L. Stevens to Warren Patten, Esq., Records of Consolidated Ute Agency, Federal Records Center, Denver, Colorado (June 13, 1884).
23. William Haas Moore, *Chiefs, Agents and Soldiers: Conflict on the Navajo Frontier, 1868-1882* (Albuquerque: University of New Mexico Press, 1994), pp. 256–257.
24. Galen Eastman, "Reports of Agents in New Mexico," *Report of the Commissioner of Indian Affairs* (Washington, DC: Government Printing Office, 1883 (September 1, 1882)), p. 129.

25. See McPherson, "Navajos, Mormons, and Henry L. Mitchell."

26. Henry L. Mitchell to Fred Fickey, Jr., Letters Received—Adjutant General's Office, 1881–1889, Record Group 94, National Archives, Washington, DC (April 16, 1884) [hereafter cited as Letters Received—AGO].

27. Dennis M. Riordan to commissioner of Indian affairs, Letters Received—New Mexico (April 19, 1884).

28. The following account is based on information found in "Report of Pete," Letters Received—New Mexico (May 4, 1884).

29. Riordan to commissioner of Indian affairs, Letters Received—New Mexico (April 22, 1884).

30. "Report of Sam-Boo-ko-di," Letters Received—New Mexico (April 19, 1884).

31. Ten nai tsosi (Diné Ts'osi), "Story," as given to Riordan, Letters Received—New Mexico (May 5, 1884).

32. Hashkeneinii Biye, "Statement," Charles Kelly Papers, Library, Utah State Historical Society, Salt Lake City, Utah (May 7, 1884).

33. John H. Bowman to commissioner of Indian affairs, Letters Received—New Mexico (July 3, 1884).

34. L. P. Bradley to adjutant general, Dept. of the Missouri, Letters Received—AGO (June 27 1884).

35. Bowman to CIA, Letters Received—New Mexico (July 11, 1884).

36. Bowman to CIA, Letters Received—New Mexico (July 12, 1884).

37. Bowman to CIA, Letters Received—New Mexico (July 19, 1884).

38. Bowman to CIA, Letters Received—New Mexico (July 12, 1884).

39. S. E. Marshall to CIA, Letters Received—New Mexico (August 22, 1884).

40. H. P. Kingsbury to post adjutant, Letters Received—AGO (September 1, 1884).

41. Frank McNitt has a brief account of this episode in *The Indian Traders* ((Norman: University of Oklahoma Press, 1962, 1989), pp. 181–185). In it, he suggests that the site of the enemy camp (and hence, the place that Walcott and McNally were killed) was near Kayenta, Arizona, at a rock formation called El Capitan. Kingsbury's report, however, does not support this conclusion, even though he says, "I had traveled very nearly due north from Keams' Canyon, and as a crow would fly, I think about 80 miles, the highest northern point reached was about 20 miles a little south of east from Navajo Mountain." Military mileage estimates during this time were surprisingly accurate, and although there is a marked difference between how "the crow flies" and navigation over Indian trails, the lieutenant obviously knew where he was. A few facts support his statement: 1.) All the Navajo scouts who reported to the agents during the previous five months speak of the incident as being in the vicinity of the southeast corner of Navajo Mountain; 2.) straight-line distance from Keams Canyon to the southeast corner of Navajo Mountain is eighty-six miles (roughly the same distance that others have been citing), and from Keams Canyon to Kayenta is sixty-two miles, while eighty miles puts the site at the far northern end of Monument Valley, about ten miles away from El Capitan (this last distance is much closer to the vicinity of where the Mitchell-Merrick incident of 1880 occurred); 3.) the military, depending on the scouts, traveled trails with known watering places along the way, and if they traveled exactly due north (360°) they would be on course for Kayenta, while an azimuth of 340° (nearly due north?) would take them to Navajo Mountain, and perhaps 350° would take them "a little southeast" from this prominent landmark; and 4.) as a haven for escape (which the Utes were seeking at the time), the Navajo Mountain region was well known to them, while the flatter, better-known, and more-accessible terrain of the Monument Valley region would not hide them as well from pursuing forces (also, in August the higher elevations are cooler, and the resources of grass, water, and wood are more plentiful).

42. Tiana Bighorse with Noel Bennett (editor), *Bighorse the Warrior* (Tucson: University of Arizona Press, 1990), p. 62.

43. Kingsbury to Post Adjutant, Letters Received—AGO (September 1, 1884).

44. Walter Dyk, *Son of Old Man Hat: A Navaho Autobiography* (Lincoln: University of Nebraska

Press, 1938, 1967), p. 181.
45. Ibid., p. 184.
46. Ibid., p. 188.
47. Ibid., p. 190.
48. Ibid., p. 191.
49. Kingsbury to Adjutant, Letters Received—AGO (September 1, 1884).
50. Charles Kelly, "Chief Hoskaninni," Charles Kelly Papers, Utah State Historical Society, Salt Lake City, Utah.
51. Charles Kelly, "Chief Hoskaninni," *Desert Magazine*, Issue 4 no. 9 (July 1941), pp. 6–9; and Kelly, "Chief Hoskaninni," *Utah Historical Quarterly*, Issue 21 no. 3 (July 1953), pp. 219–226.
52. Susie L. Yazzie, in an interview with Robert S. McPherson and Marilyn Holiday (August 6, 1991).
53. See McPherson, *The Northern Navajo Frontier*, for a history of the Mormon settlement of this area.
54. Francis A. Hammond to Colonel P. T. Swaine, Record Group 94, Records of the War Department, Department of New Mexico, National Archives, Washington, DC (June 23, 1887); and Albert R. Lyman, "San Juan History," pp. 51–52.
55. Ibid.
56. Ibid.; and Kumen Jones, "Writing of Kumen Jones," unpublished manuscript, Special Collections, Brigham Young University Library, Provo, Utah, pp. 206–207.
57. David S. Carpenter, "Jens Nielson, Bishop of Bluff," master's thesis, Department of History, Brigham Young University, Provo, Utah (2003), p. 151.
58. Bighorse, *Bighorse the Warrior*, p. 62.
59. Ibid., p. 71.
60. See David E. Wilkins, *The Navajo Political Experience* (Tsaile: Dine College Press, 1999), pp. 68–71.

CHAPTER SIX

Soldiering in the Corner: Military Operations in Southeastern Utah, 1878–1891

There was nothing simple about being a soldier in the 1880s in southeastern Utah. Every aspect of military life in this environment exacted its toll. Each experience the soldier faced, whether in a tepee or across a barbed wire fence, called for ingenuity, patience, and skill. In 1880, Colorado boasted of having been a state for four years. Utah, Arizona, and New Mexico were still territories, with each perceived to have its own problems: Mormons and polygamy; Hispanic populations imbued with a foreign lifestyle; Navajo and Ute tribes on and off their reservations; and isolation enough to stymie many forms of progress. Trains, roads, and a growing surge of farmers, miners, and cattlemen gnawed away at the geographic seclusion, but there was still much to be done, and the military was often called upon to assist.

The post-Civil War army in the United States was the product of an immediate reduction in force following the cessation of hostilities, with a subsequent decrease. The boundaries of the continental United States were established, the South could not rise again, and relations with foreign powers were generally amicable. Consequently, the government reduced the 37,000-man army of 1869 again in 1874 to 27,000. Even with these impossible numbers spread over a vast geographic area, the army's tasks remained fixed. The first two—coastal defense on the Atlantic and Pacific Oceans and maintaining peace in the Reconstruction South—pulled the military to centers of large population. The third—keeping the overland trails open, placating Indians, and protecting settlers—was broad-ranging in scope and complexity and more difficult to logistically support.

The army in the West filtered its tasks through two large entities: the Division of the Missouri, headquartered in Saint Louis, and the Division of the

Pacific, headquartered in San Francisco. Geographically, this put the Four Corners area at the extreme end of both jurisdictions. Departments subdivided the divisions. The Department of the Missouri ranged over Missouri, Kansas, Colorado, and New Mexico; the Department of the Platte held responsibility for Iowa, Nebraska, and Utah, as well as parts of Montana and the Dakotas; the Department of California, one of two in the Pacific Division, controlled California, Nevada, and Arizona.[1] Again, what this meant for operational integrity is that three departments held responsibility for some part of the Four Corners territory, and for all of them, this area was at their extreme limits. Southeastern Utah was about as far away from the geographic center of the three commands as one could get.

To perform its many tasks across the continental United States, the army formed ten regiments of cavalry but shrank the infantry from forty-five regiments to twenty-five. These numbers rose and fell depending on the funding cycles of the US Congress, but compared to Civil War manning, the military was a sideshow to the much larger schemes of the Gilded Age. Each cavalry regiment had twelve companies, or troops, and each infantry regiment had ten companies. Each was commanded by a colonel and assisted by a lieutenant colonel, while within the cavalry regiment there were three majors, each of whom commanded a battalion; the infantry regiment had one.[2] The reasoning behind this was to give the cavalry more maneuverability with added control. Captains commanded companies with the assistance of a first and second lieutenant. The two platoons within each company served as individual maneuver elements, while four-man squads fought as a team working in support of the platoon, but not as a standalone tactical element.[3] On the larger scale, companies were the primary deployable unit that could be detached and sent on independent missions, and it was the company, not the battalion or regiment, which demanded the loyalty of the soldier.

In 1881, the enlisted strength of 120 cavalry companies on paper averaged 58 men, with the infantry companies at 41.[4] It was difficult for commanders to muster three quarters of their soldiers because of desertion, health problems, and extra duties. Part of the issue stemmed from the recruiting process. Half of the soldiers serving in the West came from foreign countries, with Ireland leading at 20 percent, and Germany at 12 percent between 1865 and 1874.[5] According to the Colorado census of 1885, the soldiers at Fort Lewis fell well within this demographic spread, led by the Irish and followed by Germans—in contrast to the officers who were native-born Americans.[6] Many of the enlisted men came from impoverished circumstances and had little or no education. Some did not speak much English. Accordingly, the monthly pay for these soldiers was low, with a private earning $13 and a line sergeant $22. Little wonder that the general desertion rate per year for many units was high. Between 1870 and 1891, there was an army-wide low of 6.2 percent and a high of 33 percent of the enlisted men in the army that deserted.[7] Over this twenty-year period, it has been estimated that one third of all enlisted soldiers would have deserted. Fort Lewis reflected similar trends. "Troop F of the Sixth Cavalry reported thirteen deserters from March 25 through June 24, 1887. From April into mid-May 1882, thirty soldiers stationed at Fort Lewis deserted their companies—nearly one per day!"[8]

Officers, while receiving higher pay, had their problems too. Promotions were based on seniority and not necessarily performance. They were also slow in coming within such a small force. For example, in 1877 a new second lieutenant might take anywhere from twenty-four to twenty-six years to move through the ranks to become a major. That same lieutenant could take from thirty-three to thirty-seven years to get promoted to colonel.[9] This graying of the officer corps meant not only slow promotion but also little upward mobility, few changes, and older men serving in maneuver elements that required the energy and reserves of youth.

The weapons and tactics used in the Civil War gave way to evolving technology that changed the battlefield. By 1873, the 1873 Springfield rifle and carbine replaced earlier models. This single shot .45/55-caliber breech-loaded rifle fired a metallic rim-fire cartridge, remaining in service for the next twenty years. Its maximum effective range was accurate to 500–600 yards, and its rate of fire, depending on the skill of the soldier, could be twelve or more shots per minute. The weapon was durable, accurate, and simple to operate. Shorter barrel carbines were easier to control on horseback and so became standard issue to cavalry units.[10] Repeating rifles, available by this time, were not issued due to their shorter range and requirement of more ammunition.

Fire discipline and the conservation of ammunition became major concerns, even for men armed with breechloaders. The basic load for most units was fifty rounds per rifleman. If firing twelve rounds per minute, a soldier in heavy contact could be out of ammunition in four minutes. Soldiers also carried the .45-caliber Colt 1872 army revolver with a six-cylinder capacity. The range of the "Peacemaker" was effective for fighting in close quarters but was relatively slow to reload under fire.[11]

In the case of both rifles and pistols, there was initially little ammunition for marksmanship training. By the 1880s, however, the men "took great pride in their skill and in the marksman and sharpshooter badges and certificates awarded to soldiers qualifying for them."[12] By the mid-to-late 1880s, the post returns of Fort Lewis show a very active program to increase weapons proficiency, with various elements reporting range fire exercises even while deployed in field operations.

In addition to equipment, tactical doctrine also received a facelift. In 1874, Lieutenant Colonel Emory Upton published his influential *Cavalry Tactics, United States Army: Assimilated to the Tactics of Infantry and Artillery.* For the next twenty years, his view of the battlefield determined how engagements would be fought and how troops would be deployed both at home and abroad.[13] His overall belief that the cavalry was merely mounted infantry who dismounted to fire their weapons was a basic tenet of his doctrine. General William Tecumseh Sherman, as the Commanding General of the Army, favored the development of the cavalry and was highly supportive of this new approach. Improved firearms demanded a change from the shoulder-to-shoulder-by-ranks assault popular ten years before. The dispersal of forces became mandatory, with a five-foot separation between each soldier and a fifteen-yard space between squads. Rather than massing fires through sheer volume, leaders placed more emphasis on selecting a specific target, aiming, then firing.

The four-man squad or "set of fours" became the fundamental tactical unit for independent employment with the platoon. The squad's horses were a determining factor. Three of the four soldiers dismounted, with the remaining rider taking the horses back from the firing line, preferably to a covered and concealed position away from direct fire and the loud noise of massed weapons. There was even a strap and snap ring on each horse's bridle to keep the animals close together and controlled. Skirmishing could be done either mounted or on foot, the latter being preferred for accurate shooting. An individual could seek cover as long as this did not affect the squad's volume of fire. Odd-numbered skirmishers in each squad fired a round on command and then reloaded, as even-numbered skirmishers reloaded and fired on command. Then everyone fired at will until told to cease. The two types of fire emitting from the skirmish line was either directly to the front or oblique. One or more squads could be held in reserve to the rear for exploitation of a battlefield opportunity or to plug a gap in the line.

The two platoons that comprised a company could take individual assignments during a fight. On the conceptually ideal battlefield, company commanders

Fig. 25—Men like these 22nd Infantry soldiers served in southeastern Utah and southwestern Colorado between 1880 and 1890. Many of these soldiers were foreign-born and relatively uneducated, but they served faithfully under trying circumstances. (Courtesy Montana Historical Society Research Center)

stationed themselves 80 yards behind the skirmishers, with the reserve forces 150 yards behind the line and centered on the formation. Battalions consisted of no less than two and no more than seven companies, with three or four being the normal size. The two basic formations used by the maneuvering companies were the line and the column. Usually, one or two companies remained in reserve about 300 yards behind the skirmish line for situational exploitation.

Command and control on the battlefield was of primary concern. The most obvious form was by an officer in front. Maneuvering units focused on the direction and speed of the leader of that element, and the men followed. Close to that leader was the *guidon*, denoting the location of an element and the general vicinity of its command during the ebb and flow of battle. A trumpet controlled soldiers' activities from the beginning of the day to the end. Boots and saddles, assembly, charge, retreat, etc. all rang out over the battlefield, directing the lowest- and highest-ranked soldier as to what his leader wanted. For long-distance communication, the telegraph became an integral part of railroad operations, and so Fort Lewis ran a line from Durango to the post. For elements in the field, messengers carrying reports sufficed until 1887, when the heliograph facilitated communication. With an average distance of thirty to forty miles on good days and a rate of speed of ten words per minute, the military employed the heliograph from Colorado to Utah. A tall ridge behind Fort Lewis provided a station that sent messages to Point Lookout twenty-three miles away and thence to Blue Mountain, another fifty miles away.[14] Though short-lived, southeastern Utah had its heliographic place in the sun.

In order to keep the military's horses fit, wagon trains or pack mules were necessary to carry enough fodder for the animals and supplies for the men. Unlike Indian ponies that could maintain their strength by eating prairie grass, soldiers' mounts required grain; extended campaigns took a heavy toll on horse flesh. Troop I, 9th Cavalry—comprised of the famed African-American Buffalo Soldiers (temporarily stationed at Fort Lewis in 1881 and again in 1883)—reported that the unit traveled 2,776 miles during that first year of operations throughout the Four Corners area, including southeastern Utah.[15] One can imagine the stress this placed on the cavalry's remuda. A surprising point to consider, however, arises from combined arms operations between infantry and cavalry. Colonel William B. Hazen, Commander of the 6th Infantry, noted, "After the fourth day's march of a mixed command, the horse does not march faster than the foot soldier, and after the seventh day, the foot soldier begins to outmarch the horse, and from that time on, the foot soldier has to end his march earlier each day to enable the cavalry to reach the camp the same day at all."[16]

When this issue is combined with differing rates of speed of moving elements to an objective, the problem of timing must be considered. The accepted planning estimate for horses at a walk was three miles an hour and at a trot, six. The length of a day's march varied according to terrain, time of year, and availability of wood and water. An average for many marches of infantry and cavalry indicates a usual distance of about twenty miles. Cavalry could move faster and farther than foot troops for a few successive days, but over a period of weeks, hardened infantry could outdistance horsemen on grain-fed army mounts.

In the 1880s, most supplies on tactical operations eventually ended up in horse-or-mule-drawn wagons. Each infantry company required at least 1 six-mule wagon, while each cavalry troop needed three, because of the grain to feed the horses. A wagon pulled by mules could travel up to twenty miles per day. If artillery pieces or Gatling guns became part of the mix, an even greater number of wagons and animals were necessary. Depending on the length of the operation and number of people participating, these trains were often slow, large, and cumbersome. Mule pack trains were an option to speed the logistical tail, but the animals could be temperamental, and the amount carried on the animal's back was much less than what fit in a wagon. The military often contracted with civilians to handle specially trained mules accustomed to a pack frame. Like the horses, pack mules required grain because they could not subsist solely on grass; they could eat all they could carry in twenty days.

The railroad alleviated much of the logistical burden between major military installations. The Transcontinental Railroad, established by the Union Pacific and Central Pacific, opened the West to large-scale movement of men and material for both military necessity and economic development. Trunk lines and spurs arose, with the Denver and Rio Grande Railroad branching its way through Colorado and by 1881, into the railhead established in Durango for the San Juan mine fields. With the Meeker massacre fresh in the minds of Coloradoans, the movement of the Southern Utes onto the Los Pinos Reservation, and the general unrest in the area, the military decided to shift a previously established (October 1878) cantonment at Pagosa Springs nearer to the rail line and the reservation. What had been called Fort Lewis after LTC William N. Lewis (who was killed by Cheyennes in 1878) now became Cantonment Pagosa Spring, a sub post under the new Fort Lewis near Durango.[17]

On July 9, 1880, Lieutenant General Phil Sheridan directed through Special Order 78 that companies A, B, C, D, and E, 13th Infantry, under the leadership of Lieutenant Colonel Robert E. A. Crofton from Fort Stanton, District of New Mexico, establish the new post in southwestern Colorado.[18] By October, construction was well underway, and the command settled in for a relatively uneventful winter. But for the next ten years, Fort Lewis played a prominent role in maintaining peace in the Four Corners region.[19] Different cavalry and infantry elements rotated in and out of the post on various assignments, with the average number of soldiers stationed there probably around 300 and a high for special circumstances of 600 to 700.[20] Spring, however, caused a spike in manpower due to friction: As the grass grew, Indian ponies strengthened, and both cattlemen and Indians contested for the same resources, giving rise to confrontation.

The first in a series of annual incidents surfaced on the border between Colorado and Utah. On May 2, 1881, Colonel Crofton received concrete glimmerings of what evolved into a long-standing feud between Colorado cowboys and Utah Indians. D. D. Williams, a rancher living near the Dolores River, penned the opening complaint: Southern Utes had stolen three horses, torn down his fences, allowed livestock to destroy his crops "beyond redemption," killed or mutilated thirty-five of his cattle without taking any meat, threatened him to the point of abandoning his home, and treated his neighbors in the same fashion. John Thurman, who lived near the Utah state line, reportedly had his home burned while Indians stripped another neighbor named Reese of six horses, then sent him packing on foot. Williams feared war was imminent with the "one hundred and fifty bucks with their squaws and families" who were heavily armed. Agent Henry Page previously described the Southern Utes as having 2,500 horses that were "always with them" and "all adult males" as being armed "with firearms of the best quality usually of the Winchester pattern . . . [with] a liberal supply of fixed ammunition." They were a formidable force.[21]

A week later, Williams reported to Crofton the deaths of Richard May and John Thurman, signifying the start of events that led to the Pinhook Draw Fight. The military learned its own lessons from the incident. The first was that it took too long to mobilize forces coming from three different posts in southern New Mexico: Forts Bayard, Cummings, and Seldon. What that meant in terms of travel time between when they left their duty station, arrived in Colorado, then rode to the battlefield was that the 190-man force averaged 22 miles a day for over 500 miles.[22] By the time Captain Henry Carroll arrived with four troops of 9th Cavalry (African-American soldiers), the Indians were long gone in various directions. The cowboys, on the other hand, had recruited locally, sensed where to find the Utes, and had a vested interest in supporting the operation. Poorly equipped, untrained as individuals and as a group, unfamiliar with much of the terrain, and underestimating their opponents, the Coloradoans still engaged the enemy. The cavalry did not.

One of the few recorded incidents of racial animosity with African-American soldiers temporarily stationed at Fort Lewis occurred during this incident. The whipped cowboys met Captain Carroll's command in the vicinity of Blue Mountain. According to Jordan Bean, one of the cowboys, the officer told the civilians they were under arrest for attacking the Indians. William Dawson, the leader of the group, drew his rifle (as did every other man), and "told Carroll he just didn't have 'niggers' enough to arrest his men."[23] Sense prevailed, with Carroll insisting he did not want a fight, but only some men to lead him to where the skirmish had occurred. He welcomed two volunteers, and the civilians and military parted company the next day.

This incident illustrates a second lesson learned—that the cowboys could be just as aggressive as the Utes, with no love lost between any of the groups within the triangle. Indeed, as the course of events unfolded over subsequent years, the military assumed a role of protecting the Indians from the settlers as much as it did the settlers from the Indians. Newspapers and correspondence testify that some citizens felt they were being discriminated against to the benefit of the Utes. A final lesson was the difficulty of identifying exactly who the enemy was. Peaceful bands of Utes living on the reservation made forays onto public lands to hunt, which was totally in keeping with treaty rights; some Indians involved in the fight melted into these friendly groups. Family and band relations demanded a certain level of loyalty, while other Indians felt no such allegiance. The Ute/Paiute/Navajo renegades flowed amongst their own tribal elements easily. In the mind of at least one officer, the answer was simple: "When west of the Rio Mancos, all Southern Utes become Piutes [troublemakers]. The above statement can be corroborated by every citizen living on the Rio Mancos and Rio Dolores."[24]

An army adage counsels, "Inexperienced leaders talk of tactics, [while] experienced ones discuss logistics." Field operations in Utah prove the point. As the 9th Cavalry remained on maneuvers during the summer of 1881, Second Lieutenant Charles A. Howard, stationed at Fort Lewis a minimum of 110 miles away, fretted over what it would take to keep the troops supplied. He started with 133 mules, eight of which either died or were unfit for service, leaving him 125. In order for the cavalry to have sufficient grain and rations, the lieutenant estimated a minimum need of twelve—six mule teams. Given the distance and amount of supplies necessary, he would not have enough animals for a rotating shift, thus requiring most of the same animals to remain in constant motion.[25]

Captain Carroll's battalion was on the receiving end. His travels in search of an elusive foe took him from Fort Lewis to the north slope of Blue Mountain, to the La Sal Mountains, across the Dolores River, then west to the Colorado River.[26] He respectfully urged "the necessity of full forage for our stock to put them in condition for field service. Ten days' hard service, now would, I believe, leave half of our horses on the trail. Many men of the command are about barefooted and need clothing generally."[27] Part of the battalion's problem was that many of the soldiers' "accoutrements" were stored in Santa Fe and impossible to retrieve. Carroll also believed that the paymaster would never venture to Utah to pay his men, so he offered to come part way, to Dolores, to obtain the funds. At the same time, he anticipated twenty-five new recruits and fifteen other men who had been left at Fort Lewis to join him. As with most extended field operations, logistical needs only increased.

Fig. 26—Fort Lewis, established in 1880 in southwestern Colorado, became the logistical and military hub for the deployment of soldiers in the Colorado-Utah portion of the Four Corners region. Infantry and cavalry units maintained peaceful relations between various Native American and white factions. (Courtesy Montana Historical Society Research Center)

One interesting question that arose early on was what to do with military prisoners. For at least two Utah Indians, a bizarre odyssey ensued. On July 20, 1881, some of the Southern Ute chiefs and Agent William H. Berry brought two "Pah-Utes" into the cantonment on the Uncompahgre. Having come from the "Sierra La Sal" region, the captives were branded as part of the band of Indians who had been committing depredations for a long time, and those two had "been bad men for years."[28] The recent Pinhook fight had not helped. The guardhouse door slammed behind them. A month later, the Commissioner of Indian Affairs, Hiram Price, wrote to the secretary of the interior, wanting to know what to do. While there was no proof to support specific charges, he repeated that "these two Indians have been bad men for years and should be sent to prison in the East" until enough evidence could be found to bring them to trial.[29]

In mid-September, the military sent the captives to Fort Leavenworth; a month later, the two men had become even more "evil." Characterized as "great rascals" with "as bad a character as words could set forth," the prison did not want to be "saddled permanently" with the Indians. The Interior Department, it was thought, should take care of them.[30] The new year brought little change. The Commanding General of the Department of the Missouri, John Pope, wrote that for the past four months, the presence of the "Pah-Utes" had been "a source of great annoyance and trouble and involves also, of course, the expense of their subsistence and other necessaries."[31] Commissioner Price responded that since the Indians were "renegades" and belonged to no agency, there were no funds to pay for their subsistence, no place to incarcerate them, and not enough evidence to bring them to trial. After presenting a litany of historic crimes by the renegades of Utah (some going back to 1875), the commissioner determined that the two could not be released and should remain in army custody.[32]

Commissioner Price at one point suggested that the prisoners be returned to their native lands when the proper time arose during scheduled troop movements. He saw no point in maintaining their "close confinement" and felt the humane thing to do was to put the past behind them. Sometime in the spring of 1883, the military shipped the two prisoners to Fort Riley, Kansas. There, they joined three Mescalero Apaches who had participated in a raid in 1879 and were also in custody. Correspondence finally identifies one of the Paiutes as Pah Gur. His captors learned that neither he nor his companion would stand trial in Colorado for any past wrongs and could be freed in the future. Mysteriously, on July 11, 1883, the two Paiutes "escaped," and though "the most vigorous measures were taken to pursue and recapture the fugitives, [this was] without success."[33] Just as miraculous was the "escape" three weeks later of the three Apaches, who were also going to be returned to their agency. They, too, were never found.

The spring, summer, and fall of 1883 simmered with tension. The military and Indian agents received complaints from almost every white community or settlement within a 100-mile radius of the Four Corners. The people of Colorado demanded soldiers be stationed at Navajo Springs and on the Dolores River to protect the growing population. Settlers in McElmo Canyon and on the Lower San Juan River grumbled about Ute travelers begging at the door; tearing down fences; destroying crops; running off, mutilating, or killing livestock; and threatening those who did not comply. Navajos joined the fracas, though they were not quite as militant, pushing livestock across the San Juan River, appropriating vegetables and fruits, and generally adding to the chaos. In one instance, a group of Indians attacked Peter Tracy at his home near Mitchell's ranch, requiring a military detachment to investigate the ruckus over some vegetables that resulted in his death.[34]

The Utes hit the large cattle companies the hardest. Why there was so much friction can be found in a newspaper article published in 1887, giving a few facts and figures that provide a telling picture of what was happening to the land over the years. W. J. Forham, an entrepreneur in Salt Lake City, noted in San Juan County alone there were 11,000 sheep and 32,000 cattle belonging to white stockmen on the range all year long—and another 100,000 cattle that came in from Colorado for winter grazing.[35] As a people dependent on hunting and gathering, the Utes ground their teeth as they watched livestock destroy their livelihood; plants not eaten were trampled and game not shot were scared away. Something had to give, and in 1884, it did.

As usual, the action started in the spring. According to citizen reports from Mancos, Navajos and Utes threatened their livestock, herders, and the mail carrier who traveled from there to Bluff. He would no longer ride the route without armed escort. A telegram from the District of New Mexico's commanding officer in Santa Fe notified Fort Lewis that the people in Mancos were capable of protecting themselves. Southern Ute Agent Warren Patten assured the local commander that the Southern Utes were moving on to the reservation to avoid any type of conflict. Cattlemen at Navajo Springs made a similar request for assistance, but the military told them that they could not protect them, since the cattlemen were trespassing on Ute lands. Besides, from five to eight feet of snow still blocked many of the trails over the mountains.[36] A month later, the Soldier Crossing fight occurred, adding another notch in the Indians' rifles.

Following Perrine's defeat, the Utes fled to the vicinity of Navajo Mountain while he remained in the field to prevent further incidents, establishing his camp near Noland's trading post at the Four Corners. This placed him "on the direct road from the Mancos River, and about twenty-two miles from Navajo Springs," as well as roughly eighteen miles from Mitchell's ranch.[37] It was as much a logistical consideration as a tactical decision. Here, there was "an abundance of fine grazing," whereas other places had been heavily cropped by flocks of sheep. The road network facilitated resupply from Fort Lewis: a key point, since there was continual correspondence about "returning," or "releasing," scarce wagons for transport.

At the same time, Captain J. B. Irvine of the 22nd Infantry established a camp at Soldiers Spring, 110 miles distant from Fort Lewis. He also had logistical concerns but of a different nature. Among other problems, he noted "men crippled by wearing shoddy narrow-toed shoes"; someone had failed to put kegs in the resupply wagons, and so the soldiers had insufficient containers for water;

and "no medical officer is with command which is a mistake."[38] In spite of the issues, life went on. Irvine and Perrine requested clothing for the men and horseshoes and forage for their mounts. They handled military discipline for deserters, conducted rifle practice, and created rough maps of the area. On August 12, new orders directed Perrine to break camp and move to Paiute Springs, located one mile west of the Colorado-Utah line and about five miles north of today's Highway 666. Among other tasks he had while assigned there, he was to build "barracks" for Troop F, 6th Cavalry, and other units who would replace his. By October 16, with the weather turning cold, he requested permission to move his men into the new facility.[39]

Other elements received missions to remain on the Mancos and go to the Big Bend of the Dolores Rivers, reconnoiter in the area of Blue Mountain, provide escort duty to Navajo Springs, investigate general rumors, man an outpost at Mitchell's ranch, and maintain a general presence. All of this was not good enough. Coloradoans sent reports to state authorities saying that the regular troops were not providing sufficient protection and that the situation was becoming so bad that some settlers had abandoned their homes to live in the brush for safety. They insisted the state militia be mustered for duty, since the regular soldiers were more interested in protecting Indians than whites.[40]

From the field came word that "the situation was never more quiet."[41] Even Mancos Jim, who had been one of the "Paiute" leaders in the Soldier Crossing fight the year before and who lived around Blue Mountain, said he wanted to avoid conflict, would stay away from the cowboys, and just wished to hunt. Mancos Jim's desire was not delivered from a position of weakness. Rather, Swaine believed that, "If we went to war with [these Paiutes/Utes], it is believed from the nature of the country [that] they could successfully defy a much larger force of cavalry than we have here."[42] The previous year underscores his point. Troops remained in the vicinity of Blue Mountain at least through mid-September.

Nagging problems of transportation and resupply continued. There never seemed to be enough wagons for hauling wood and water, freight from the railroad in Durango, infantry soldiers when possible, rations and equipment for troops in the field, and all of the day-to-day chores. Colonel Swaine complained the situation was so desperate that "when the force in the field has been longer, we have been much embarrassed to keep them supplied and have been obliged to suspend post training in a great measure. The contract for transportation is limited to hauling between here and the railroad at Durango and does not extend to the other matters."[43] More pack-train mules partially solved the problem.

Fig. 27—Training was an important but expensive necessity to maintain fighting fitness in infantry and cavalry units. Here, "D Troop volley fires at 800 yards." The men are shooting the .45-caliber Model 1873 Springfield carbine, preferred by cavalrymen because of its short length. Logistically, these single-shot rifles conserved ammunition. (Courtesy LDS Church History Library)

Whiskey was another issue. When the government created Fort Lewis, there remained a 160-acre parcel of land that had already been homesteaded and now belonged to a civilian, Edward Rebstock. He opened a saloon, selling to all comers but specializing in soldiers. He even loaded a wagon full of liquor and followed the troops to the field as they protected settlers against Indians. When the officers complained, he upped the ante by providing his saloon with "dance girls." Swaine requested special permission to allow his own post trader—a man he trusted who had previously sold alcohol until the army denied the privilege in 1885—to market whiskey to "thwart the evil designs of outside parties."[44] Request denied.

By August 1885, the Indian problems were quieting, but the people of southwestern Colorado and southeastern Utah were not. Taking it upon themselves to advise the military on departmental changes, groups of citizens circulated petitions, sending them to influential stewards back East. Forty-three citizens from both Colorado and Utah urged that the lands of southeastern Utah be placed under the Department of the Platte so that soldiers at Fort Lewis could be supplemented in providing more protection.[45] A second petition just from San

Juan County, Utah, followed that October.[46] G. G. Symes, a member of the House of Representatives, was the first to write a letter to the secretary of the interior, requesting such a change be honored. Recognizing that little help came from the Salt Lake area and hoping that the secretary of the interior would "not suffer us to be ruined by the delay of too much official etiquette," the petitioners pushed for a speedy solution.[47] All desired a firm hand with the Indians, who should not be coaxed with more "annuities and gratuities"; troops needed to be stationed somewhere along the San Juan River.

Government planners toyed with the idea of possibly establishing a permanent military presence in southeastern Utah. If enacted, it would serve to not only complement the efforts of Fort Lewis but also a number of posts in New Mexico that had their hands full keeping track of various Native American groups, including the Navajo and Apache. By placing a fort or cantonment in this area, the soldiers could cover a wide geographic region—the "land of death," as Agent Galen Eastman had called it—and get it mapped and controlled. Somehow, the "Dark Corner" needed to have a more permanent light shined in. The military decided to act by sending two officers from Fort Douglas to determine the feasibility of establishing a post and mapping the area. Lieutenant Colonel N. W. Osborne and First Lieutenant R.R. Stevens of the 6th Infantry received the mission and set out for southeast Utah. The two spent twenty-eight days on horseback researching the possibility of some type of installation and providing information to assist in determining whose departmental jurisdiction it would fall under.

On September 25, Oborne and Stevens boarded the Denver and Rio Grande in Salt Lake City and traveled to Blake (now Green River), then Moab, Blue Mountain, Bluff, and Montezuma Creek, Utah. From there, they went to Mancos, Fort Lewis, Silverton, and Montrose, Colorado before returning to Fort Douglas. Their findings were objective but with a few surprises. Based on many interviews throughout the white settlements, Osborne felt that the "Mormons are disposed to speak well of the Utes," while the Navajos were more involved in petty theft; the Utes had "a more predatory inclination of a more damaging character" when it came to outfits ranging cattle; the Beaver Creek massacre had led to more violence and increased tension; people who farmed or ranched and did not share with the Indians received most of the trouble; non-Mormon cattlemen felt the Mormons were encouraging the Utes to work against them, but "such stories may be received with a grain of allowance"; many of the Colorado settlers wanted the "extinction of the Southern Ute Agency," removing the Indians to "anyplace whatever"; and the land the Indians held was desirable for expanding white cattle ranches.[48] There was no mention that more soldiers meant increased sales that would offset losses in cattle, estimated by some as 10 percent of their herd. In summarizing the need for a post, Osborne concluded:

> The wish for a new military post in the Blue Mountain region is generally entertained by non-Mormon interests. Difficulty of access in winter leaves the country unvisited by government forces during a large part of the year—control of trails west and southwest of the Blue Mountain, are little known except by Indians. The reported disaster in the vicinity of Blue Mountain [Soldier Crossing] and limited supply of water, easily within the control of Indians, are reasons for establishing a post.[49]

Osborne went on to comment that the Indians also needed to be protected from white neighbors infringing on their lands. A continuous military presence would reduce the tension "growing out of the conflicting passions, prejudices, and greed of two races." If the government decided to place an installation in this region to control the "comparatively unknown section of southeastern Utah and adjacent parts of Colorado," then Blue Mountain offered the best location. "From there it is practicable to reach the San Juan settlements south and the Indian strongholds and trails west and southwest." In terms of logistics, water ran the entire year in the North Fork of Montezuma Creek at the southeastern base of the mountain. During summer months, supplies and troops from Fort Lewis had easy access to the region, and with the railroad stop at Thompson, necessities and personnel could be transported by wagon, horseback, and ferry twelve months of the year. In conclusion, "southeastern Utah can be as effectively controlled in a military sense by the Department of the Platte as by the Department of the Missouri."

By March 1886, the military began to consider a permanent garrison in southern Utah. Planners hesitated to make a full-blown commitment, given the recent problem a few years previous with Fort Thornburg (also in Utah). Established in September 1881, moved to a new spot in less than a year, then permanently abandoned a little over a year later, the fort represented what the military wanted to avoid.[50] With a constantly shrinking budget, planners wished to ensure that their expenditures were meaningful and somewhat permanent. What had appeared as a necessity for Fort Thornburg quickly became unnecessary. A good summer test for a Blue Mountain post would be worth the effort, so on April 7,

1886, Lieutenant General Sheridan issued the order tasking both departments to provide soldiers for the venture.[51] Company D, 6th Infantry (Department of the Platte), from Fort Douglas, received orders to take the Denver and Rio Grande Railway to Thompson, Utah, then move to the North Fork of Montezuma Creek (today's Monticello), establish a base, and protect the lives and property of settlers in the region. Troop D, 5th Cavalry, from Fort Riley, Kansas (Department of the Missouri), received the mission of patrolling Dolores and La Plata Counties in southwestern Colorado. As part of the response to the petition sent the previous year, this element was to monitor Indian activity in Colorado and coordinate its efforts with the troops from Fort Douglas.[52]

Company D left Salt Lake City on June 1, arriving in Thompson the next day after having completed their 220-mile train ride on the Denver and Rio Grande Railroad. The men stood on the sands of southeastern Utah contemplating the execution of a two-fold mission: to maintain peace among contentious factions of Utes, Navajos, cowboys, and settlers and to map a little-known section of country. To do so, they came well-equipped—perhaps too much so, since their first official act after re-assembling wagons and loading them was to leave grain, tents, ammunition, and hospital supplies behind with the stationmaster and "boarding mistress" at Thompson Springs. They had brought with them "two hundred rounds of ammunition per man; thirty days' rations; two six-mule teams and wagons complete; three four-mule teams with escort wagons complete; four saddle mules with equipment complete; and the necessary camp equipage."[53] This was the first of a number of subsequent caches made before they reached their destination on the southeast side of Blue Mountain, 100 miles distant.[54]

The first day's march of nineteen miles, an average distance for soldiers, brought the men to Court House Rock, a large spring of water, plentiful grazing for the animals, and abundant clumps of sagebrush for fuel. After a good night's rest, the cavalcade was on the road again, this time covering only twelve miles before the real work began. Once they reached Moab's valley floor, a wheel on the escort wagon broke, a small creek usually not worth considering now ran five feet deep, and the rough, curving road beyond made it difficult to maneuver wide-based wagons. After wasting a day to see if the creek's waters would subside, the command decided to transport the supplies across a half-load at a time, float the empty wagons, then move beyond to the ferry that traversed the wider Colorado River.

At 6:00 a.m. on June 6, the soldiers began crossing the fast-moving river just north of Moab. By 8:15 a.m., a third trip began, with Captain Murdock, the company commander, and six other men working the ferry attached to a cable that spanned the swollen waters. Frightened mules aboard the vessel shuffled about, shifted their weight, and rocked the boat and its pulley system. At the bow, Murdock attempted to muscle the main rope in order to prevent the ferry from swamping when, without warning, the rope snapped, sending him into the river. He was still holding the end of the parted rope attached to the cable. The commander desperately tried to pull himself up to the wire, but the current proved too swift, forcing him to let go of the rope. Down the Colorado River he swam, trying to reach the now-sinking craft, but 150 yards of struggle proved too much, and the raging brown torrent claimed him and 2,000 pounds of goods as its own. He left behind a wife who received small comfort from the $5,000 provided to her as the beneficiary of a life insurance policy.[55]

Second Lieutenant C. G. Morton, now in command of fifty-eight men, needed guidance. He left immediately for the telegraph key at the Thompson Springs station, arriving at 9 p.m. The next day at 4 p.m., he received orders to proceed with the mission and so made an all-night ride back to his men as their newly appointed leader.[56] This was hardly an auspicious start for a company ordered to bring peace to a troubled corner of the Colorado Plateau. Morton arrived at the river on June 8, happy to find that his soldiers had taken the initiative to repair the ferry. Wasting no time, he began the transfer of supplies across the high water, limiting loads to no more than three mules at a time—a process that took most of the day. Even though Moab lay only a short two miles away, the soldiers pitched camp on the south bank of the river and spent the night. By then it was apparent that the expedition needed to shed more excess weight and so left part of its 10,000-round allocation of ammunition and a broken wagon in Moab before continuing south on the first ten miles of good road. Eventually, however, the thoroughfare changed to loose sand, rocks, and sharp sliding curves, dictating another cache of 250 pounds of grain. In flat, open terrain, the oversized army wagons—with their long wheel base and six-mule teams—worked well, but once steep hills and narrow canyons had to be traversed, manhandling and roping the wagons reduced the rate of travel to a crawl.

On June 12, the party began its day by caching another 250 pounds of supplies and fixing a sheared wagon wheel a few yards out of camp. Although this expedition was supposed to have received the best wagons that Fort Douglas had to offer, wheel-related problems plagued the group from the beginning. Close inspection showed that most of the wagon axels contained cracks that had previously been repaired. By the time the soldiers reached Peters Hill (eight miles north of current-day Monticello), they were carrying 350 pounds of grain per mule. Although the command had discarded food and equipment all along the route, the wagons still had to leave half their cargo at the base of Peters Hill so that the men could pull the half-filled wagons up with ropes. On June 13, the soldiers reached the North Fork of Montezuma Creek below the southeast face of Blue Mountain, prompting Morton to send retrieval parties back along the trail to secure cached supplies and bring them to camp. The main party established headquarters in the vicinity of what would later be named Soldier Spring, very near the present town of Monticello.

On June 20, 1886, the Blue Mountain force met with Captain Edward Thomas, Troop D, 5th Cavalry. He had traveled from Fort Riley, Kansas, by rail to Durango, Colorado, and later to the camp in Utah. D Troop's assignment was primarily to watch for trouble in southwestern Colorado but also to cooperate with Morton should conflict arise, joining forces as necessary.[57] Both officers agreed that the Utes and Navajos were peaceful, mentioning that Mancos Jim, in particular—who seemed to be everyone's concern, given his past reputation—had moved his 120-member band from Blue Mountain when Morton arrived and was now down on the San Juan River, peacefully trading as he made his way east. Captain Thomas reported, "The Indians know that troops are out and will not commit any overt acts unless attacked by cowboys. . . . They will carefully avoid injuring any person unless in retaliation for injuries inflicted upon some one of their number."[58] Cowboys from various ranching outfits were in the midst of the roundup season, too busy to bother the mobile Indian groups, given that approximately 50,000 head of cattle—30,000 of which belonged to the Carlisle outfit—were spread from Fort Lewis, west to Blue Mountain, south to the San Juan River, and throughout southwestern Colorado.[59] Thomas concluded his report by stating that he did not anticipate any trouble for the rest of the summer and that the army's current position at Blue Mountain was the optimal location to conduct military operations if necessary.[60]

With the potential of Indian problems fading, it was time to begin initial reconnaissance of the area west of the encampment in the *terra incognita*. Ever since the birth of the Corps of Topographical Engineers in 1813, the army had an internal organization to assist its efforts in exploration and mapmaking. Military cartographers had many considerations that might otherwise be disregarded on civilian maps. For military purposes, there needed to be a detailed visual representation of the lay of the land to prevent poor planning, mistakes in maneuver, and errors in logistical support on unfamiliar terrain. For those units who chased

Navajos and Utes through canyon country, there was no doubt about the necessity of this type of accuracy. Mapmakers at the time used an aneroid barometer to measure ascent or descent of a hill (the device giving a reasonable estimate of altitude), while distance was calculated through horse paces, which proved fairly accurate.[61] Hachure lines indicated slope and where steep, a fall line. Proficient mapmakers were often talented artists who made preliminary sketches from the saddle, later adding watercolor washes to represent different terrain features. While there are no descriptions of the process that Lieutenant Morton used, his exploratory travel began the collection of necessary information.

On July 3, Morton, accompanied by a sergeant and a private, set out on a journey of 200 miles.[62] The small party headed southwest, first hugging the base of Blue Mountain, then on to Recapture Creek, next to the head of Cottonwood Canyon, and eventually to Elk Mountain (now known as Elk Ridge). There, they crossed. The men spent the next two days exploring the terrain to the west and traveling on two different Indian trails, one of which took them in the same direction that Captain Perrine had followed to his demise at Soldier Crossing two years earlier. Neither trail, however, led the party to where they had hoped to reach—the Colorado River. Morton's group re-crossed Elk Ridge and took what was then called the Settlement Road into Bluff. There, with their mounts fed and rested, the party mingled among Indians and settlers, collecting information.

From this trip came some important points for future travelers. The most important was the crucial knowledge of the location of "tanks": hollow pockets in sandstone that trap valuable rainwater coming from infrequent summer storms. Unless a person was intimately familiar with the land, there was no predicting their location; only a sure knowledge would do.[63] The complexity of the canyons and box canyons that run in all directions mired these travelers in a morass of rock that seemed impenetrable. Morton emphasized that the terrain, with its sand, canyon mazes, dead ends with drop offs, and limited springs all severely hampered normal travel time.[64]

More reconnaissance followed—fourteen days in July, sixteen in August, twenty-one in September, and fifteen in October. By the end of the summer, a far more complete description was given in a final report.[65] Much of this exploration was by Morton and two other lieutenants: R. R. Stevens and William P. Burnham, who had been assigned to help with mapping. Along with six privates, these three officers investigated the area between the San Juan River and Colorado River confluence; between the White Canyon and the Recapture Creek drainages; and north and east of Blue Mountain.[66] Morton, synthesizing the information he and the others found, correctly summarized what numerous fights had proven: "The country between Elk Ridge and the Colorado is a natural Indian stronghold, and in my opinion, is the place to which the Indians would go in case of hostilities. . . . If the Indians were hard pressed in the country I have mentioned, they could go into Arizona, slip back to their reservation or cross the Colorado. The country on the west side of the river is said to be quite as rough as that on the east."[67] Unlike the 1885 report of Osborne and Stevens, however, Lieutenant Morton felt there was no necessity for a post, only a spring-to-fall encampment, since that was the only time there seemed to be substantial conflict. He believed it was the Mormons who wanted a post to sell their products—not the cowboys, who thought a post would ruin their ranges, attracting more settlers and exposing the illicit activities of the cowboys.

For a summer encampment, the best place was on the North Fork of Montezuma Creek "near the place where the road from Moab to Bluff City crosses it" (on the outskirts of where today's Monticello now sits). The reason: "Water and grass are plentiful and of good quality; the best of wood is in abundance nearby, either for fuel or building huts; it is as near the Indian strongholds as wagons can easily go; trails start from there to all points not reached by road; [and] it is at the junction of roads from the north, east, and south so that information can be obtained concerning all parts of the country from Indians and whites passing through." Morton felt that a company of soldiers stationed there would be a sufficient force and that it was a good place to locate a heliograph station, since at least some food could be obtained locally for man and horse.

Morton's primary logistical concerns centered around access to the camp and keeping it supplied.[68] The route from Thompson Station to Moab in the 1880s was less than favorable. Flash floods were a problem when rain fell quickly and could not be absorbed by the ground, turning Courthouse Wash from bone dry one minute to nine feet deep with water the next. Travelers crossing the wash continued to be stymied until 1915, when an eighty-five-ton steel superstructure—supported by eighteen-foot pilings—provided a safer means to negotiate the streambed.[69] Next, there was the crossing of the Colorado River. Morton thought the heavy freight wagons too big for the available craft, posing problems with safety and efficiency; even if there were a larger ferry, the wagons were not maneuverable enough for the terrain beyond. Smaller wagons with a shorter wheel base and four-mule teams were more suited to negotiate the steep slopes and sharp curves encountered south of Moab. The downside to these smaller wagons was their limited carrying capacity.

Another logistical issue was how to obtain enough food for men and feed for horses to support field operations for an infantry company. Hay was not cut locally until August, while wheat, oats, and barley were not available until September. The road from Moab was so rough that in order to transport hay, it would have to be bailed; the 1886 price was $20 per ton, delivered. The easier route of travel did not require bailing, saving additional cost and arriving in only four to five days from suppliers in Mancos, Colorado. The same was true of food such as potatoes and vegetables, which commanded high prices but were more readily available from towns to the east. On the other hand, winter snow buried the toll road from Durango, making it inoperable until May, while the road from Moab was accessible year round.

For Lieutenant Morton and his group that year, it would not be a problem. On October 17, they returned to Thompson Springs to take the train back from their garrison duty on the North Fork of Montezuma Creek with "much valuable information obtained regarding this little known region."[70] As for the soldiers from Fort Lewis, they returned to their post in November due to the build-up of ice on the roads, which threatened the packers' ability to deliver food and supplies.[71] The experiment with the two units had received an answer, the military deeming a permanent post in southeastern Utah unnecessary.

Companies from Fort Lewis continued to provide security for settlers and cattlemen to prevent a low-grade fever of discontent from erupting into something larger. McElmo Canyon, a major thoroughfare for Indian and white travelers moving from the San Juan River to Sleeping Ute Mountain and a prime agricultural spot, turned into one such area of conflict. Mariano and Red Jacket camped near its mouth and intimidated the settlers living in its confines by demanding food, tearing down fences, visiting ranches when the men were away, grazing livestock on white-controlled ranges, stealing tools and horses, and killing cattle. Captain J. B. Irvine, 22nd Infantry, spent Christmas week sorting out the matter. Either Southern Ute Agent Christian T. Stollsteimer needed to get them back on the reservation, or a party of soldiers would have to be stationed there to keep the peace. Apparently, the agent succeeded, and Irvine returned to his post later in January. Stollsteimer did suggest, however, that for the next spring and summer, troops again should be stationed at McElmo.[72]

At the same time, there was a reverse situation on the Ute reservation. Cattlemen were grazing their herds at Navajo Springs. Ignacio, the Ute leader, demanded they be removed. Colonel Swaine insisted that they "do so without the use of a military force to eject them."[73] While Swaine appears willing to have used

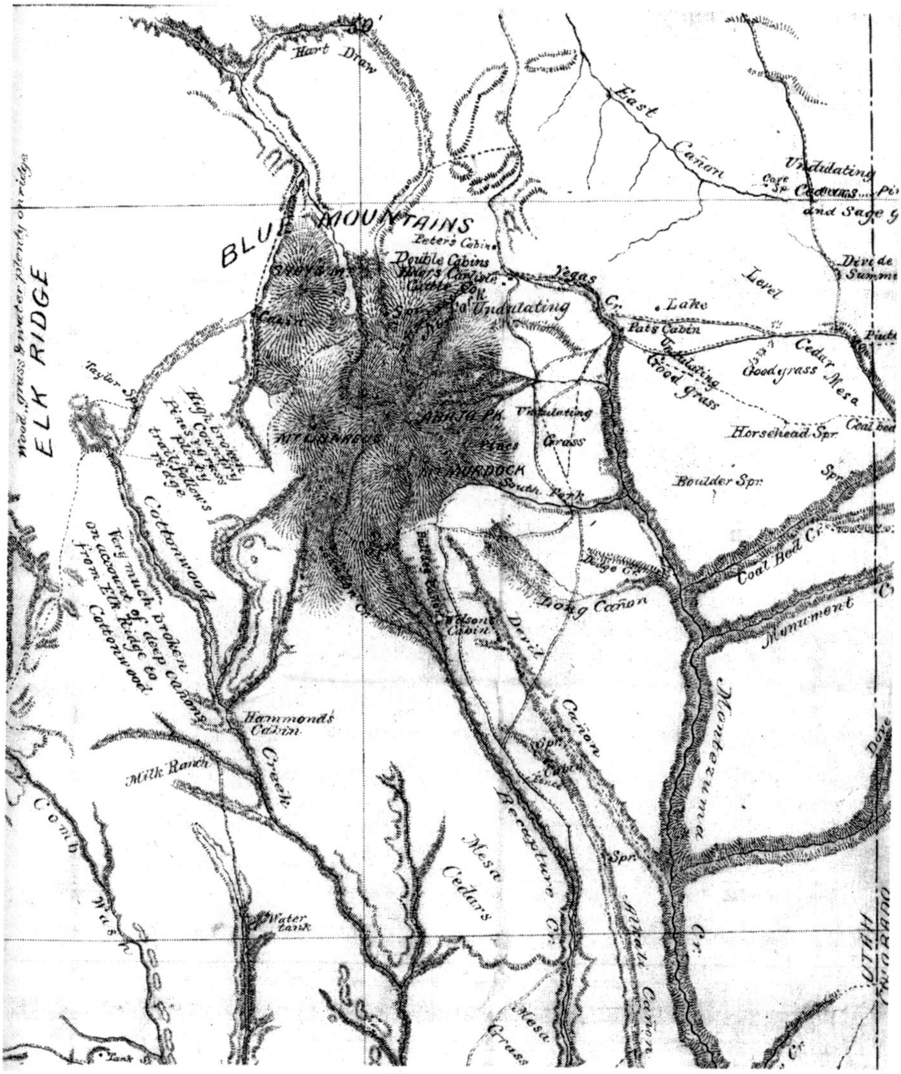

Fig. 28—A portion of the 1886 map created by three lieutenants—C. G. Morton, R. R. Stevens, and William P. Burnham—along with the assistance of six privates was the result of a summer's fieldwork. They explored and recorded land features, trail systems, and other features, creating this highly accurate feasibility study for creating a military post in southeastern Utah. (Reproduced from National Archives)

troops if the cattlemen did not comply with the agent's request, his commander was not as anxious. With Ignacio wanting to camp at Navajo Springs, along with the unrest in McElmo Canyon and the encroachment of livestock on Ute lands, Swaine's commander suggested the establishment of a subagency in that general vicinity. This allowed for monitoring problems, decreasing the use of troops, and providing a presence.[74] While the creation of this entity was ten years away, the seed had been planted, and the Navajo Springs Agency (later moved a short distance to today's Towaoc) eventually established government control in this troubled corner.

Another means of maintaining a presence when not responding to an actual threat was the "practice march." Captain Javan Irwin, 6th Infantry, participated in such an exercise in September 1888, providing lessons in training for his soldiers, a message to the Indians hunting around Sleeping Ute Mountain, and a good example of size, organization, tactics, and logistical concerns for units of this time and place. Captain Adam Kramer, battalion commander, led Troops E and F, 6th Cavalry, on this combined arms drill. He and three lieutenants, along with a surgeon, worked with sixty-nine enlisted men, three civilian packers and teamsters, one wagon pulled by six mules, seventy-six horses, fourteen pack mules, and two saddle mules—all of which were provisioned for a month. The maneuver element purchased fresh forage (at $1.50 per 100 pounds of hay) and fresh beef (at 10 cents per pound) locally.[75]

Companies A, B, C, D, E, and L of the 6th Infantry left on their march with the cavalry. "While the average length of daily marches complied with the orders, it was impracticable from want of camping ground, water, and thorough advanced knowledge, to comply exactly with the requirements of not less than ten miles per day."[76] The march simulated combat conditions, with advance and rear guards, as well as flankers. Upon reaching the campsite for that day, the command posted pickets (men emplaced to provide early warning) and vedettes (mounted sentinels in advance of an outpost). Other activities included a night "call to arms and to horses," as well as day convoy defense, "rapid concentration of the trains, deployment of cavalry and infantry as skirmishers, preparation of a field hospital," day-and-night signaling, and a march in the presence of a hostile force.[77] The only factor that marred the perfection of the exercise was that the men received their pay before leaving, there were many saloons on the route of march, and "the command was followed by whiskey peddlers," resulting in cases of drunkenness. "However, the precautions adopted to restrict sales were successful."[78]

The last few years of active soldiering from Fort Lewis centered upon keeping the Utes on their reservation and trying to allay the fears of settlers intimidated by the Indians who were constantly hunting off their lands. The continued demand for food at the cabin door, friction over access, request for troops, escort duty of dignitaries, practice marches, and days on the rifle range all filled the soldier's time. The era of larger troop deployments and possible pitched battles were over. In 1890, the Public Land Office declared the settling of the frontier closed, while the army re-assigned many of the troops stationed at Fort Lewis to a post in Montana.[79] With responsibilities elsewhere, the army moved to close its facility and shifted any further assignments to Fort Wingate, Arizona, 160 miles away. On May 28, 1891, the secretary of war signed the document closing Fort Lewis as an active army post, and on September 11, a civilian custodian, Mr. Lacombe, took charge of the grounds for $60 a month.[80] Less than a year later, the post became the Fort Lewis Indian School and assumed a different role in settling the West.

What can be said of this turbulent period of history, where southwestern Colorado and southeastern Utah became inextricably joined through cowboys, Indians, and cavalry? Most obvious is the fact that the military was at the right place and time to prevent an escalation of friction. It took an active and relatively impartial role in keeping things quiet. With cowboys, Utes, Navajos, Indian agents, farmers, and townspeople, there was plenty of need for diplomacy and understanding. Another point to consider is how well it did given the circumstances. With the exception of the fight at Soldier Crossing, the soldiers held their own against the Utes and gained their respect. In a number of instances, when the Indians learned that the cavalry would be called in, they insisted it was unnecessary and peacefully went on their way. The cowboys gave a similar message. Managing to travel long distances, remaining in the field for monthly stints, and solving the problems of resupply were all in a day's work. What came from these efforts, besides a quieted frontier, were maps and reports that describe southeastern Utah, improved road access to many parts of the land, an impartial view of events and personalities, and an attempt to understand issues underlying local conflict. The military's task was anything but simple or black and white. For the most part, they sided with right over wrong and did the best they could when soldiering in the corner, living on the fringe.

Chapter Endnotes

1. Robert M. Utley, *Frontier Regulars: The United States Army and the Indian, 1866–1891* (New York: Macmillan Publishing Company, Inc., 1973), pp. 14–15.
2. Ibid., pp. 16–18.
3. Douglas C. McChristian, *The U.S. Army in the West, 1870–1880: Uniforms, Weapons, and Equipment* (Norman: University of Oklahoma Press, 1995), pp. 33–34.
4. Utley, *Frontier Regulars*, p. 17.
5. Ibid., p. 24.
6. Duane A. Smith, *A Time for Peace, Fort Lewis, Colorado, 1878–1891* (Boulder: University of Colorado, 2006), pp. 71–72.
7. Utley, *Frontier Regulars*, p. 24.
8. Smith, *A Time for Peace*, p. 78.
9. Ibid., p. 20.
10. McChristian, *The U.S. Army in the West*, pp. 112–116.
11. Ibid., pp. 117–120.
12. Don Rickey, Jr., *Forty Miles a Day on Beans and Hay: The Enlisted Soldier Fighting in the Indian Wars* (Norman: University of Oklahoma Press, 1963), p. 104.
13. Richard Allan Fox, Jr., *Archaeology, History, and Custer's Last Battle: The Little Big Horn Reexamined* (Norman: University of Oklahoma Press, 1993), pp. 40–46
14. Smith, *A Time for Peace*, p. 55.
15. Ibid., p. 102.
16. Utley, *Frontier Regulars*, p. 50.
17. Robert W. Frazer, *Forts of the West: Military Forts and Presidios and Posts Commonly Called Forts West of the Mississippi River to 1898* (Norman: University of Oklahoma Press, 1972), p. 38.
18. Notes on file, "Fort Lewis—Calendar of Letters Received, 1880," Special Collections, Fort Lewis College, Durango, Colorado [unless otherwise specified, information cited with an "FLC" designation came from the Fort Lewis Library Collection].
19. Three major studies look at the role of Fort Lewis. In chronological order, there is Robert W. Delaney, *Blue Coats, Red Skins, and Black Gowns: 100 Years of Fort Lewis* (Durango, Colorado: Durango Herald, 1977); Duane A. Smith, *Sacred Trust: The Birth and Development of Fort Lewis College* (Niwot, Colorado: University Press of Colorado, 1991); and Smith, *A Time for Peace.*
20. These figures are estimates. Delaney gives an average of 200 soldiers, with a high of 600 for special occasions (p. 18). Smith, on the other hand, cites figures of 344 soldiers in 1887 and 439 in 1888 (p. 93). Given the operational tempo and the fact that entire units were shipped in for the spring and summer months due to Indian activity, an average (for winter and summer figures) of 300 soldiers seems reasonable.
21. Henry Page to Crofton, Calendar of Letters Received, 1880, FLC (October 24, 1880).
22. "Operational Returns," 9th Cavalry, microfiche #M774, National Archives, Washington, DC (1881–1887).
23. Jordan Bean, "Jordan Bean's Story and the Castle Valley Indian Fight," *Colorado Magazine*, Issue 20 (July 1943), p. 23.
24. H. G. Cavanaugh to commander, B Company 13th Infantry, Calendar of Letters Received, FLC (May 22, 1881).
25. Charles A. Howard to chief quartermaster, District of New Mexico, Calendar of Letters Received, FLC (July 2, 1881).
26. Assistant adjutant general, District of New Mexico, to adjutant general, Fort Lewis, Letters Received—AGO (July 8, 1881).
i Hiram Price to secretary of the interior, AGO (August 15, 1881).
27. Henry Carroll to headquarters, 9th Cavalry, Calendar of Letters Received, FLC (July 15, 1881).
28. Colonel R. S. Mackenzie to assistant adjutant general, Fort Leavenworth, Kansas, AGO (July

20, 1881).

29. Hiram Price to secretary of the interior, AGO (August 15, 1881).

30. Secretary of interior to secretary of war, AGO (September 29, 1881); and Major General Jonathan Pope to Colonel R. Williams, AGO (November 22, 1881).

31. Pope to adjutant general, Headquarters Division of Missouri, AGO (January 21, 1882).

32. Pope to adjutant general, Headquarters Division of the Missouri, AGO (January 21, 1882); and Price to secretary of war, AGO (February 16, 1882).

33. Price to secretary of the interior, AGO (August 9, 1883); and Assistant adjutant general, deparment commander to adjutant general, US Army, AGO (August 22, 1883).

34. For more information about this incident and others in southeastern Utah during this period, see Robert S. McPherson, *The Northern Navajo Frontier, 1860–1900: Expansion Through Adversity* (Logan: Utah State University Press, 1988, 2001), p. 46.

35. W. J. Forham, *Deseret News* (October 12, 1887), as cited in "San Juan Stake History," unpublished manuscript, Historical Archives, Church of Jesus Christ of Latter-day Saints, Salt Lake City, Utah.

36. Petition from Mancos to commanding officer, Fort Lewis, AGO (March 18, 1884); commanding officer, District of New Mexico, to commanding officer, Fort Lewis, AGO (March 18, 1884); and Warren Patten to commanding officer, Fort Lewis, Outgoing Correspondence, 1883–1885, Fort Lewis (March 24, 1884) [hereafter cited as OC].

37. Major Hall to adjutant general, District of New Mexico, OC (July 28, 1885).

38. J. B. Irvine, field report, AGO (July 24, 1884).

39. Perrine to commander, 6th Cavalry, AGO (October 16, 1884).

40. Ibid., FLC (July 2, 1885).

41. Ibid., FLC (July 5, 1885).

42. Ketchum to Swaine, FLC (August 7, 1885); and Swaine to assistant adjutant general, District of New Mexico, FLC (August 7, 1885).

43. Swaine to assistant adjutant general, Department of Missouri, FLC (August 19, 1885).

44. Swaine to adjutant general, District of New Mexico, FLC (August 11, 1885).

45. San Juan County, Utah, to assistant adjutant general, Department of the Platte, AGO (October 1885).

46. San Juan County, Utah, to assistant adjutant general, Department of the Platte, AGO (October 1885).

47. G. G. Symes to secretary of the interior, AGO (August 8, 1885); Petition to secretary of the interior, AGO (August 26, 1885).

48. N. W. Osborne to headquarters, "Official Report," Department of the Platte, AGO (October 26, 1885).

49. Ibid.

50. David L. Schirer, "Fort Thornburgh," in Allen Kent Powell, *Utah History Encyclopedia* (Salt Lake City: University of Utah Press, 1994), pp. 201–202.

51. Osborne, "Official Report."

52. Assistant adjutant general Samuel Breck to commanding officer, Fort Douglas (May 10, 1886); acting Assistant Adjutant General J. C. Kelson to commanding general, Division of the Missouri (April 9, 1886); Ibid. (May 8, 1886); and Special Orders No. 56, Headquarters Department of the Missouri, Fort Leavenworth, Kansas AGO (June 3, 1886).

53. Special Orders No. 49, Headquarters Department of the Platte, AGO (May 10, 1886).

54. C.G. Morton to adjutant general, Department of the Platte, AGO (June 25, 1886).

55. Ibid.

56. Ibid.

57. Special Orders No. 56, Headquarters Department of the Missouri, AGO (June 3, 1886).

58. E. D. Thomas to assistant adjutant general, Department of the Missouri, AGO (July 13, 1886).

59. Ibid.

60. J. H. Carter(?) [Illegible] to adjutant general, Department of the Missouri, AGO (July 7, 1886).
61. Earl B. McElfresh, *Maps and Mapmakers of the Civil War* (New York: Harry N. Abrams, Inc., 1999), pp. 32–33.
62. Morton to assistant adjutant general, Department of the Platte, AGO (July 15, 1886).
63. Ibid.
64. Ibid.
65. C. G. Morton to assistant adjutant general, AGO (May 2, 1887).
66. "Record of Events," Fort Douglas Post Returns, Fort Douglas, Salt Lake City, Utah (July 3–August 28, 1886).
67. Morton, "Report: Southeastern Utah," AGO (April 30, 1887).
68. Ibid.
69. "The Crossing at Courthouse Wash –A Year Ago and Now," *Grand Valley Times* (October 15, 1915), p. 4.
70. "Report of Brigadier General Crook," Headquarters Department of the Platte, *Report of the Secretary of War,* 50th Cong., 1st sess., Vol. 1 (Washington, DC: Government Printing Office, 1887 (August 27, 1887)), p. 133.
71. P. T. Swaine to acting adjutant general, Outgoing Correspondence #334, 1878–1891, Southwest Center, Fort Lewis College, Colorado (November 5, 1886).
72. J. B. Irvine to commanding officer, Fort Lewis, Record Group 75, Consolidated Ute Agency, Federal Record Center, Denver, Colorado (December 26, 1886).
73. Stollsteimer to adjutant general, Fort Lewis, FLC (January 11, 1887); and Swaine to Irvine, FLC (January 16, 1887).
74. Assistant adjutant general, Department of the Missouri to Swaine, FLC (January 22, 1887).
75. Post commander, Fort Lewis, to assistant adjutant general, Department of Missouri, FLC (September 18, 1888).
76. Ibid., FLC (September 17, 1888).
77. Ibid.
78. Ibid.
79. Helen M. Searcy, "The Military," in Sarah Platt Decker Chapter, *The Pioneers of San Juan Country*, Vol. I (Durango, Colorado: Daughters of Colorado Pioneers, 1942), p. 70.
80. Assistant adjutant to chief quartermaster, Department of the Platte, FLC (September 11, 1891).

CHAPTER SEVEN

Ba'álílee and the 1907 Aneth Brawl Power, Progress, and Principle[1]

Moonlight turned the yellow cottonwood leaves silver as they drifted in the gentle current of the San Juan River. Hogans, livestock corrals, and summer shades rested in the shadows under the now-naked tree branches. Sheep bleating in the cool autumn air, the smell of juniper smoke and manure, the stomp of tethered horses' hoofs, and an occasional coyote's bark were all that rose above the gurgle of the river to disturb the night's peace. Inside the hogan slept the Navajo Ba'álílee, The One With Supernatural Power.[2] Confident in his ability to remain safe, he lay next to the west wall: the place of honor. He had spent the evening working against the sickness of a patient bewitched by a man and his family for winning a horse race. Through divination, Ba'álílee had uncovered the evil, identified the culprits, and worked hard to ceremonially return the curse and heal the sick man.[3] Now, the weary medicine man slept, secure in the knowledge that he had done his best and that he, himself, was protected from harm. Or so he thought. He was actually resting on a stage about to erupt in conflict, having no idea that troops were on the way.

Born *of* the Water Edge (Tábąąhá) Clan and *for* the Salt (Ashįįhí) Clan around 1859 in Canyon de Chelly, his earliest recollections were of war and fear.[4] His mother died shortly after his birth, and little is known about his father, Happy Man (Báhózhóní). Caught in the clash of cultures, Ba'álílee watched the United States military—with its auxiliary forces of Utes, Hopis, and other tribes, as well as New Mexican citizenry—fight the Navajo during the Fearing Time (Náhonzhoodąą'). Kit Carson's foray into Canyon de Chelly with a large body of soldiers must have been part of his experience before joining 8,000 of his tribal members at Fort Sumner on the Pecos River in New Mexico. Still a child, he managed to survive the ordeal and return to the lands set aside by the government in what is today New Mexico and Arizona.

Fragmentary evidence that survives in the written record suggests Ba'álílee spent an errant early adulthood. Hastiin Klah (Left Handed, or Tł'ah), a policeman at the Northern Navajo Agency in Shiprock, New Mexico, testified that he had known Ba'álílee since he was a boy, "and he was always bad."[5] Klah recounted how Ba'álílee had employed witchcraft to kill a sick woman by shooting hair into her body. His witchery had led to four days' confinement, perhaps at Rock Point, Arizona.[6] Other Navajos spared his life after he confessed his guilt and promised to leave the reservation. Ba'álílee then spent a couple of years in "Mormon country," presumably southern Utah, before returning to his people. Perhaps this is where he gained some proficiency in English, starting the rumor that he had guided the Mormons to Bluff, Utah, in 1880.[7] Shortly after returning to the reservation, he attended a dance with three friends, all of whom had revolvers and "witch knives," which scared the participants away.[8]

Ba'álílee grew increasingly powerful as a medicine man. Most chanters might know two or three ceremonies, indicating a high degree of intelligence given the learning required just to know one. He knew six: Evilway (Hóchxǫǫ'jí), Blessingway (Hózhǫǫjí), Mountain Topway (Dziłk'ijí), Windway (Nílch'ijí), Shootingway (Na'at'oyee), and Night Chant (Tł'éé'jí).[9] Navajos accepted his ability to see into the past and future through stargazing (déest'įį'), during which he perceived events in his mind's eye. To control that much knowledge and power allowed him to use it against those he wished to intimidate. He also could use it to help those seeking aid. Among the Navajo, even the *knowledge* of witchcraft and that type of supernatural power is usually denied.[10] Not so with Ba'álílee, who spoke openly of his ability.

His interesting personality provides a glimpse into a specific type of conflict already touched on in previous chapters. In Navajo culture, the use of supernatural power is as real and destructive as the powers that are solely physical. Ba'álílee provides a clear example of how he used his religious knowledge to fight against those who opposed him—regardless of ethnicity. He amassed a group of followers who felt protected by his abilities and who were equally anxious to fight against the increasing control of the government and its influence over the Navajo lifestyle. Unlike the Utes in the next chapter, who squared off against their opponents in a primarily physical sense, the medicine man used the unseen to intimidate and control as much as he did armed force.

By 1884 and the shooting at Henry L. Mitchell's trading post, Ba'álílee was well on his way to having other run-ins with both Navajo and Anglo people. In

1900, he broke into a store owned by Howard Ray Antes, an independent Methodist missionary, and stole a silver belt from which he fashioned bracelets and other merchandise.[11] Antes, fearing repercussions, refused to press charges.[12] Shortly after this, James M. Holley—owner of the Aneth Trading Post from 1899 to 1905 and later a government farmer—went to a Yé'ii Bicheii dance at Ba'álílee's camp. Many spectators were drinking whiskey, waving bottles over their heads and yelling, " 'Where are the police? Where are the chiefs? Where is the agent? Where are the soldiers?' saying they [were] not afraid."[13] Eventually, the agent from Fort Defiance visited them to demand they send some of their children to school. Ba'álílee, as a local spokesman, refused, then told the people that if the reservation police or soldiers came after the children, his men would kill them as fast as they came. The agent balked and did nothing. It did not take long, however, for the federal government to answer the questions of "Where is the agent? Where are the police?"—much to Ba'álílee's chagrin.

In 1903, Superintendent William T. Shelton established the Northern Navajo Agency in Shiprock, a little over thirty miles from Ba'álílee's camp, and instituted an aggressive policy of change. Espousing the ideals of Progressive reform prevalent at the turn of the century, the agent enforced the mandate to improve the Navajo economy, provide education for the children, remove vices on the reservation, and create stability in a region prone to lawlessness. Shelton, a man of sobriety and strong religious conviction, surged forward on all fronts. While many people have characterized Tall Leader (Naat'áanii Nééz, as he was known among the Navajos) as puritanical and heavy handed in enforcing government programs, he faced an almost overwhelming task.

Speaking of the agency's early years, Shelton recalled taking a thirty-five-mile trip to Farmington, New Mexico. During this travel, he met "eighteen drunken Indians" coming from Durango. There were also those selling liquor to the Navajos, while everyone seemed involved in gambling. He noted that "fifteen to twenty, and sometimes more, would congregate at each of the trading posts during the day and waste their time and money gambling. At some of the posts the traders kept a 'tin horn' gambler at their store for the purpose of getting a crowd together and beating them out of their money."[14]

By the end of 1905, Shelton claimed to have put a lid on this activity by gaining the "cooperation of the older and more influential Indians, convincing them that gambling was bad business and detrimental to the best interests of the reservation." For battle trophies from the war against gambling, he collected more than three bushels of playing cards. As for the whiskey traffic, he slowed it by assigning first-time offenders ten days of work at the agency; second offenders twenty days; and an additional ten days for every other infraction. In the next ten years, agency police brought in only eleven drinkers for punishment, leading Shelton to boast, "I doubt if there is a community in the United States more free from whiskey, drinking, and gambling than this reservation."[15] This claim may be naïve, but his control was something that had not been possible before the government established the agency to quell the liquor traffic on the northern boundaries of the reservation.

Four years of Progressive change brought substantial alteration in many aspects of traditional Navajo life. Briefly, Shelton's jurisdiction extended over approximately 3,000 square miles of territory that spanned parts of New Mexico, Arizona, and Utah. He was responsible for the welfare of an estimated 8,000 Navajos, 2,500 of whom were school-age children ages 6–18 and 100 of whom attended the Shiprock School.[16] He supervised government farmers hired to improve crop production, expand irrigation systems, issue all types of farm equipment, construct and maintain roads, increase the quality and production of wool, eliminate diseases such as scabies through sheep dipping, and provide individualized agricultural counsel. The agent worked with traders to ensure fair practices and encourage blanket weaving, quality silversmithing, and an improved lifestyle.

Changing values, however, is not always easy or pleasant. Social issues—the practice of polygyny, abolition of Indian hairstyles, consumption of alcohol, and general law enforcement—proved more problematic than incorporating material goods. This effort struck at the heart of cultural practices or aberrant behavior that had not been challenged, in some cases, for centuries.[17] The three Navajo policemen initially assigned to the agency were far too few. Shelton bemoaned the fact that "crimes such as wife beating, whiskey selling, horse thieving, and even murder have gone unpunished. . . . But one of the worst things we have to contend with is that when a man dies his relatives come in and rob the widow and children of all their belongings and leave them homeless and destitute. One case has been brought to my attention where the woman resisted and was murdered."[18] Armed with this type of justification, he requested funding for two more Indian judges, a captain of police, and eight additional policemen, bringing his force to twelve. He received only five.

If there was an antithesis to Shelton and what he stood for, it was Ba'álílee. Much of what follows is reconstructed from personal testimony obtained by the government in sworn statements from Navajos and whites alike. They paint a highly negative picture of this medicine man. There is sufficient testimony from unofficial sources, both Navajo and white, not given under government direction, that indicates Ba'álílee was very much a power broker. While the sworn statements may not be exaggerated, they are at times uninformed as to traditional Navajo practices. Nevertheless, all accounts provide a telling story that shows Ba'álílee did all he could to resist government intervention and consolidate his power. More than just a clash of personalities between him and Shelton, his resistance forced a final answer as to who controlled the lives and future of hundreds of Navajos in the Aneth area.

A medicine man in traditional Navajo culture plays a prominent role in his community. Viewed as a person of wisdom, he is often the repository of religious learning and local history, as well as a spokesperson for those who adopt his point of view. Equally important is his control of supernatural powers, which is dependent upon the number and type of ceremonies he practices. The more he knows, the more he controls, and the more powerful the man. As a leader, his position may at times become politicized, and the more power he wields, both in a spiritual and political sense, the greater his following. Ba'álílee was exceptionally powerful and did all he could to employ that power in a political agenda.

Many Navajos in the Aneth area believed Ba'álílee controlled rain and lightning. He charged a fee to bring showers to the parched earth and threatened to withhold them if his terms were not met. According to Holley, Ba'álílee was "a medicine man of the worst type, [making] the Indians believe that he has power to cause rain to fall at his will and has made the greater part of his living requiring the Indians to pay him for singing."[19] When it did not rain, he blamed it on the Navajos who followed Shelton's advice and patterned themselves after the white man. He also threatened to kill those who opposed him with lightning, especially any soldiers who dared attack. As for their bullets, they could not touch him. Community members credited Ba'álílee with killing those who worked for Shelton. He threatened The One With Muscles (Dohii) and Left Handed (both Navajo judges), warning that he would kill them with "darts" shot into their bodies by witchcraft. Shortly after, Dohii died, while Left Handed spent $700 for a protective ceremony.[20]

Even after Ba'álílee's death, stories about his powers persisted. Mary Blueyes remembers, "My grandfather said he performed a prayer for a Mud Clan woman. Sometime while performing the prayer, he saw Ba'álílee in a brief flash. The supernatural spirit probably said this is the person that is doing this [witchcraft]. The prayer ended and he told of what he had seen. He said, 'I saw Ba'álílee.' "[21]

Fig. 29— Ba'álílee, a proud and powerful medicine man, confronted the forces of change in traditional Navajo practices at the turn of the twentieth century. His extensive ceremonial knowledge gave him the ability to use both physical and spiritual force against his adversaries. (Courtesy Utah State Historical Society)

There were plenty of other, more tangible things that directly opposed Shelton's plans. Not only was Ba'álílee involved in excessive drinking, gambling, and bootlegging on the reservation; he also stole livestock from the Utes at Towaoc, cowboys in Colorado, and Mormons from Bluff. Saloons and individual entrepreneurs in Cortez supplied his whiskey trade, which provided a handy profit when charging up to $8 a bottle. His polygamous marriage to two wives was a common Navajo practice, but bothered the puritanical Shelton, who espoused the Indian Bureau's belief of monogamy.[22] On many occasions, Ba'álílee told anyone within earshot that he would have as many wives as he pleased and that the agent had no say in the matter. There were also charges laid against him and his cohort of selling wives and young girls to older men. In fairness to Ba'álílee, this may have been confused by Shelton for certain legitimate marriage practices found in traditional Navajo culture. These include marrying at the young age of thirteen or fourteen, honoring the practice of bride price in recognition of losing a family member, marrying both a mother and her daughter to the same man, and dissolving relatively fragile marriage bonds common in matrilineal societies. For whatever reason, Shelton wanted it all stopped.

Ba'álílee gathered about him a growing circle of followers who basked in his power and gave legitimacy to his being leader and spokesman. Estimates vary, but most sources suggest that he had between thirty and forty men to call upon for support.[23] There is no mistaking that at least a dozen of them appropriated some of his power and reputation to create their own, becoming a law unto themselves. Short Hair (Bitsii' Agodí) was such a man.[24] In the spring of 1906, he came upon a young Navajo girl, Hattie, herding sheep. Seizing her horse's reins, he dismounted, tied her hands behind her back with a quirt, and assaulted her. Hattie eventually untied herself and went home, where she remained sick for several months before going to the agency for help. Soon after this incident, Short Hair raped her sister too.[25] Many of the law-abiding Navajos were shocked and intimidated by these criminal events.

The San Juan Agency School in Shiprock opened its doors on February 8, 1907, to 106 students.[26] Traders, government farmers, Navajo police, and community leaders helped in the recruiting efforts for this new experience. Some families willingly sent their children; others were coerced into filling an established quota. Ba'álílee refused to send his children and raved against what he saw as a loss of Navajo rights. He threatened to harm or kill anyone who gave their children over to the government. As a reason, he proffered that when children had been sent to the school at Fort Defiance, many had died from disease, but the government had kept requesting more. As a headman, he declared this would not be repeated in his region.[27] Parents needed children at home to herd livestock, help with sheep shearing, haul wood and water, and perform a myriad of other camp chores. Turning them into white men was undesirable at best. Navajo police and Holley, who was now the government's "Additional Farmer" in Aneth, received the brunt of Ba'álílee's antagonism. Fourteen children were waiting at the Government Station, ready to travel to Shiprock, when Ba'álílee and a heavily armed contingent arrived and "persuaded" all but four that they had better head home.[28]

Equally disturbing was his refusal to dip sheep in medicine that removed the debilitating livestock disease called scabies. Shelton placed fifty vats of medicine throughout the northern Navajo Reservation to eradicate the sickness. Many of the people in Aneth welcomed the program, but Ba'álílee refused and warned others not to participate. The vat arrived in the fall of 1906, and dipping commenced, but not without threats and refusal. Shelton also provided better breeding stock to improve herd quality. He admonished the recipients to not sell these animals, warned the traders not to buy them, and encouraged the Navajos to not slaughter them for food. Ba'álílee sold his for a song and told the agent that he would do whatever he wished because they were his.[29] Others in his group did likewise.

With a final burst of bravado, he and his followers armed themselves heavily against any kind of intervention. Ba'álílee had never seen soldiers in his part of the reservation and was quite sure that Shelton did not have the nerve or the ability to order them to his location. If Shelton did, however, there would be a fight.[30] Shelton, Holley, and the Navajo police received death threats at different times. Local traders were also put on notice. Four Navajo friends approached Hambleton B. Noel, trader at Teec Nos Pos, and warned him that if trouble arose and soldiers appeared, Ba'álílee would rob and burn the post, kill Noel, and take everything he could on his way to the hinterlands of Navajo Mountain.[31] With his armed force in Aneth, Ba'álílee controlled a formidable position not to be taken lightly.

Shelton measured his response to these challenges. Realizing that Ba'álílee had clan relations with another dissident group around Black Mountain also opposed to change, Shelton approached the Aneth situation carefully.[32] He sent local Navajo leaders and police on a number of occasions to invite Ba'álílee to the agency to discuss problems. Ba'álílee refused. Shelton dispatched other messengers and worked through Holley to convince Ba'álílee that he and his following would benefit from what the government was providing. Ba'álílee strenuously resisted. Finally, both Special Agent R. S. Connell and Shelton set off on March 30, 1907, to tour the area and see for themselves. Connell's report is an interesting example of agent hype, providing a graphic picture of their encounter with the medicine man. The two unescorted agents went to Ba'álílee's "stronghold," where they found him with thirty-six warriors. Shelton spoke tactfully and encouraged friendly relations.

> Fortunately, Mr. Shelton and the agency doctor had at one time cured the mother of one of By-lil-le's warriors, who had a boil on her neck, and who was under By-lil-le's treatment until she got maggots into her head and face and was a terrible sight even to the Indians. This Indian was the first to take

> our side, and Shelton, recognizing another Indian whom he had helped, got them over and called all the Indians' attention to the improvements on the roads, etc., that he had made. Working along this line, we got the band divided, and finally By-lil-le had only three left on his side and then I went after By-lil-le rough; told him he was sick in the head and proved it to the other Indians. The sweat just rolled off his face, and I thought possibly he would try a gun play, but he stood the truth as long as he could and then he went off with only two friends following him and the rest of the Indians giving him the laugh; then we had a horse race, and the Indians left with a different feeling toward the Government and the Government's officials.[33]

This eyewitness account flies in the face of every other indication of how Ba'álílee would react in such a situation, but it does indicate the feelings of superiority that at least one agent felt. Connell summarized his sentiments by saying Ba'álílee was on the "edge [including the Black Mountain group] of the worst district of bronco Indians in the Southwest" and that as long as the government is "slack with these Indians and it does not interfere with their raping, stealing, and depredations upon the friendly Indians, [then] there will be no open hostilities."[34]

While Shelton appreciated Connell's report, he was not fooled. The meeting did not produce the desired effect, with Ba'álílee being as troublesome as ever. The agent again sent some of the most influential Indians he could muster to visit Ba'álílee's camp to quiet unrest, only to have the medicine man emerge from the brush, demand a fight, and challenge everything the leaders said or offered. While the leaders parleyed, Ba'álílee's men remained close by, shooting pistols and rifles for an intimidating effect. Holley did not fair much better. He sent word that a Navajo judge and policeman were coming to talk to Ba'álílee, who announced his intent to kill them both. The medicine man arrived at the Aneth Trading Post with thirty-five heavily armed supporters. The judge and policeman never appeared, so Holley staged a horse race for a purse that he generously provided to the winner. Following the contest, the group disbanded. There were still other peacemakers who traveled to Ba'álílee's camp but with no success.[35]

Shelton removed his velvet gloves. Realizing that his Navajo police force was woefully out-numbered and unprepared for a confrontation, he fired off a letter to the commissioner of Indian affairs, requesting two troops of cavalry to either arrest Ba'álílee or remain in the vicinity of his camp to suppress his activities. Shelton even suggested the soldiers come from Fort Wingate in New Mexico, 150 miles away, because the roads were excellent and hay could be delivered to Aneth at $15 a ton, along with grain for $2.25 per 100 pounds. That was Shelton's recommendation in a letter dated September 18. By October 15, the commissioner of Indian affairs, the secretary of war, the regional commanding general, and the commander of Fort Wingate had signed off on the plan. At 8 a.m. on October 22, Captain Harry O. Williard, along with Troops I and K of the 5th Cavalry, began their ride to southern Utah.[36]

Williard's force—comprised of four officers, seventy-four enlisted men, a surgeon with two medics, and three Indian scouts—arrived at Shiprock four days later. The next morning, October 27, the soldiers moved again, fearing that word would spread amongst the Navajos that a military force was present. Shelton and Williard devised a plan that capitalized on speed of movement, secrecy, and a night march to decrease the probability of detection. Shelton let slip a rumor that the troops were in the area to control the unruly Utes and Paiutes in Bluff, masking the real intent.[37] All excess baggage remained at the agency. The quartermaster issued each man 100 rounds of rifle ammunition and 20 rounds for his revolver. Wagons loaded with six days of rations and additional equipment rumbled toward their first stop at the Four Corners Trading Post, estimated by Williard as thirty-two miles distant.[38] The cavalry accompanied them on the first leg of the journey.

At this point, a basic understanding of places and distances is helpful. Many of these historic locations are no longer identified on maps. Using estimates given by Shelton and Williard, one gets a sense of the route taken and sites encountered. The road from Shiprock was an improved dirt road, having been a product of Navajo labor. The first stop along the route was the Four Corners Trading Post, a rock structure on the north bank of the San Juan River. Charles Fritz operated the post. Approximately ten miles down the road—and mid-point between the Four Corners and Aneth posts—sat another store run by M. R. Butler.[39] From there, the road continued roughly three and a half miles downstream to the vicinity of Ba'álílee's camp, which was then four miles to the Aneth Trading Post run by J. A. Heffernan. The Government Station, recently built by Holley, lay on the flood plain below the post. The road continued to follow the general course of the river along the north side to Montezuma Creek, ten miles away, thence through the washes and over the rolling hills to Bluff.

Ba'álílee's camp sat in a sandy flood plain extending approximately two and a half miles on the south side of the river.[40] Two washes— the larger being Among The Rocks (Tsé Bitah-on today's map, Tsitah) and the smaller being Rough Canyon (Tségi Hóchxǫǫ'jí)—feed onto this flat, where groves of cottonwood trees grow interspersed along the banks.[41] Both canyons wend their way south, away from the river. Large surrounding hills create a cove-like space known as A Place Reserved or Set Aside (T'áásahdii Náhásdoon). To the north of this flat, the San Juan River flows against the base of a hill, channeling access. It is called Close Against The Rock (Tsé Nitah). Over a dozen hogans, corrals, agricultural fields, irrigation ditches, and heavy log fences around two of the larger camps sat against a backdrop of rough ridges and boulder-strewn hills. One of Ba'álílee's wives had a hogan on the north side of the river near a ford opposite the main settlement.[42]

Ba'álílee's camp was large, with relatives living in or near his home. He enjoyed a log and a stone house, as well as a number of hogans next to his fields that were serviced by an irrigation ditch. There was also a "medicine lodge" that was a hogan in which he performed ceremonies.[43] Around his camp—and sectioning off parts within—was a heavy log fence that kept his livestock out of the gardens, confining them to the corrals where they belonged.

So it was here on that October night, following the healing of a man sickened by witchcraft, that Ba'álílee rested peacefully. October, however, is a time of change and is known in Navajo as Ghąąjį': a term that means more than "parting of the seasons" or "back-to-back." When the holy people created the twelve months—six of summer and six of winter—Coyote the Trickster spoke up, reserving October, the first winter month, for himself. Ghąąjį' fills the space between the ending of one way (summer planting, harvest, and ceremonies) and the beginning of something new (winter activities and a different set of ceremonies).[44] It is a time of change, when it can be both summer and winter, and with it comes confusion. In that particular October, Ba'álílee's life soon experienced confusion and change on a scale he had not felt possible.

Shelton, all his police, and a contingent of Navajo leaders reached the Four Corners Trading Post an hour before the military force arrived. In the interim, Shelton secured any local Navajos who came to the store, preventing them from leaving before 11 a.m. the next day. Security and surprise were paramount. Among those detained was Sisco, one of Ba'álílee's followers and a persistent troublemaker.[45] He remained in custody and eventually joined the group sent to jail. Shelton ate lunch, then moved on to Aneth to determine the exact location of Ba'álílee. He would inform Williard as to the medicine man's presence, but if he did not, the soldiers were to proceed on their own. The captain arrived in the afternoon, shortly after Shelton departed. Williard and Fritz discussed the situation at Ba'álílee's camp, agreed that a night march offered the greatest chance of surprise, and felt that a direct assault (rather than a diversion through Aneth) would net the best results.

At 1:30 a.m. on October 28, the command awakened its soldiers. They ate a hurried breakfast, quietly saddled their horses, and started down the road an hour later under the light of a half-moon. Navajo police and headmen took the lead. The logistical trains remained behind with orders to break camp in the light of day and move to Aneth. The cavalry horses trotted rapidly over the fourteen miles to a spot near what the Navajos called Close Against The Rock, where the San Juan River was fordable.[46] Known as Soldier/Police Move Across (Siláo Ha'-naa Ninínáá), this place was still some distance from Ba'álílee's camp but inhabited by a number of Navajo families. Once across, the horses' paces quickened. The troopers pressed forward, and a half mile from the objective, the formation fanned out to surround Ba'álílee's hogan.

Dawn was breaking when Williard, Navajo interpreter Robert Martin, and some of the soldiers rushed inside the hogan. Ba'álílee, Polly (a staunch supporter also known as The Man From Spreading Water Who Is Tall, or Tó Háálíinii Nééz), and a third man all stumbled to their feet. A scuffle ensued, with increasing numbers of soldiers piling into the fray. Several women, a child, and a sick man avoided involvement, but in Williard's words, "The Indians strenuously resisted arrest and capture to such a degree that it was necessary to use considerable force before they were overcome, secured, and handcuffed."[47] Navajo accounts verify this statement but focus on different aspects. A man called Old Mexican reported that once the soldiers took Ba'álílee outside, he refused to stop growling like a bear. "They tried to make him stop, but he wouldn't, so one of the soldiers took his six-shooter and hit him over the head with it three times and knocked him cold. They then tied him up. He was covered with blood."[48] Polly knocked down three soldiers before they subdued him.[49] And Son Of Red House Clansman noticed how Ba'álílee's medicine pouch had been carelessly discarded. "Rattles and feathers and many other things were lying scattered out there."[50]

By now, people in the community were gathering. Surrounded by relatives' camps, Ba'álílee was sure to draw assistance. Some came with weapons, while others were armed only with curiosity. Williard took no chances; he arrested everyone and "all resisted." Finding eight hogans in Ba'álílee's camp alone, with other Navajo homes spread over a larger area than he had planned, the captain directed Martin, the Indian police, and Troop I to secure the more distant parts of the objective. Within minutes, gunfire erupted in their direction. Ba'álílee's son-in-law, Little Warrior (Naabaahii Yázhí), also known as Smarty, opened fire and received a shot through the torso. Although the soldiers dressed his wounds, by noon the next day he was dead. J. A. Heffernan, the trader, buried Smarty in a shallow grave where he had fallen.[51]

A detachment from Troop K spurred their horses toward the sound of firing, followed in a short while by Williard, who had remained behind to ensure all the prisoners were secured. The shooting lasted only a few more minutes, then there was silence. On his way to Troop I, the captain heard a cry for help and dispatched soldiers to investigate. They found the first sergeant afoot without his rifle, which had disappeared beneath his wounded horse shot out from under him. The Indian assailant, Little Wet One (Ditłéé'ii Yazhí), Ba'álílee's son-in-law, was out of range of the first sergeant's revolver. Another sergeant drew his rifle and shot the man in the head, killing him instantly.

Ba'álílee's camp continued to buzz with activity. In some of the hogans, women and children wailed that the soldiers were taking their men and moving them across the river. Others fled into the brush nearby, behind the rocks on the hills, or up the slopes, taking what they could with them.[52] Soldiers pursued Fuzzy Hat (Ch'ah Ditł'oii) also known as Ba'álílee's Nephew (Ba'álílee Bidá'í), a medicine man. He fired two shots from his Winchester, and the soldiers returned fire, wounding him in both legs before he escaped into the brush and fled through Among The Rocks Canyon. Friends provided a horse and helped him over the rough terrain.[53]

News spread to other camps. Florence Norton recalls, "My father was extremely upset over the incident. He planned to encounter and kill the troops who were on their way up there [Aneth]. He had a big shotgun ready. But a woman showed up on her horse and pleaded with him and some others to please leave the place before the troops arrived. . . . He said he had really wanted to shoot all the troops."[54]

Williard returned to the ten prisoners, moved his force a half mile to a ford on the river, and sounded assembly. Following roll call, the officers reported that they had met resistance from some of Ba'álílee's followers. They had opened fire on the police, not noticing the approach of the soldiers. The fifteen-to-twenty-minute battle resulted in the death of Little Warrior, Ba'álílee's son-in-law, and the cessation of all opposition. The command crossed the river with its walking prisoners and by 7:30 a.m. arrived in Aneth. The soldiers established camp near the post, secured the prisoners in a log house, purchased three sheep for lunch, and awaited the supply trains to arrive in the late afternoon. The captain took the opportunity to explain to local Navajos why he had come:

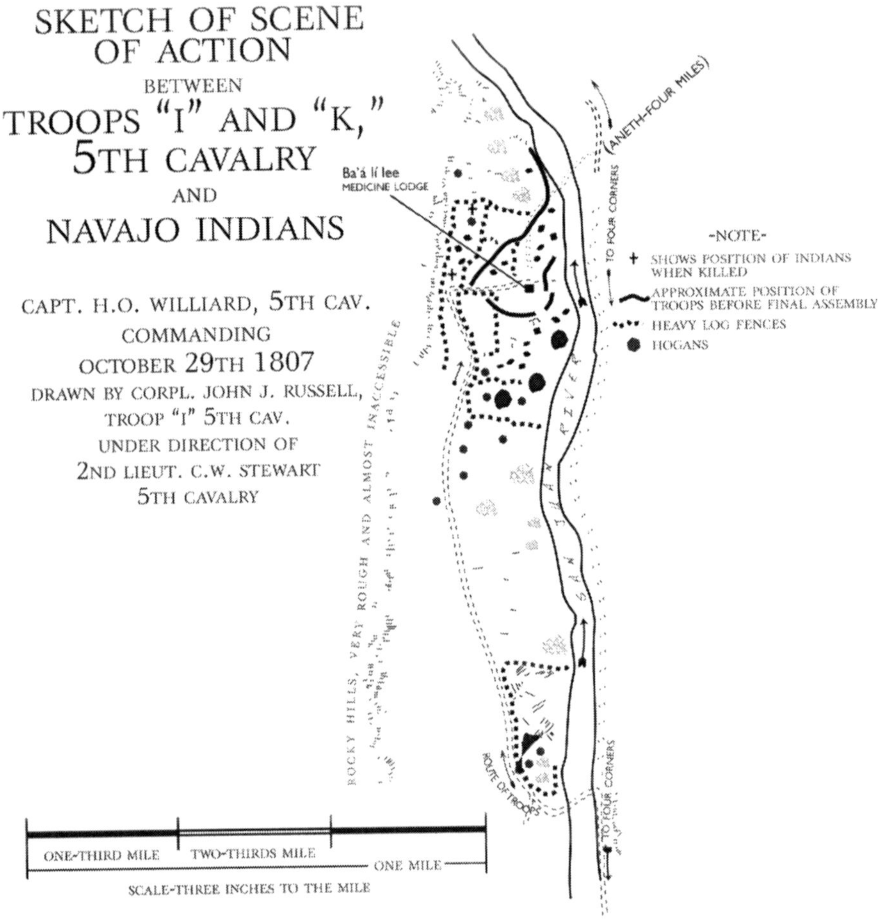

Fig. 30—This sketch of Ba'álílee's camp four miles southeast of Aneth, Utah, was drawn the day after the battle. Today, the floodplain is bare of any dwellings, but the place name—Soldier Crossing—remains to identify the location where the last cavalry charge against "hostile" Indians took place in the United States. (Refurbished sketch by author)

Supernatural Power spoke as though he could lick anybody. We heard that he said that whenever the soldiers came after him they were going to get struck by lightning and be killed all at once. That was the reason I came, to see if he was right. I have been looking forward to being struck by lightning. Now we are going back to see if anybody is going to take a shot at us again.[55]

Shelton and Williard then discussed the morning's events. They were pleased with the results in that no soldiers or policemen had been hurt and that resistance had been light, with few Navajo casualties. That afternoon, the two men and part of the force returned to Ba'álílee's camp and surrounding area to search for the wounded Fuzzy Hat and to allay fears. Williard reported that the Navajos he talked to were relieved of the threat that Ba'álílee had imposed.

Rumor of a night attack faded with the dawn of a new day. At 7:30 a.m., the command rode toward the Four Corners Trading Post with prisoners in tow. The next day, they arrived in Shiprock and began to refit. Word from the field filtered back to the agency. The disgruntled remainder of Ba'álílee's group insisted that the troops had fired first, there had been indiscriminate killing, and property had been wantonly destroyed. Those opposed to Ba'álílee, however, breathed a sigh of relief. Heffernan and Holley reported a calm along the San Juan that had not existed for years. Jim Joe, a Navajo living near Bluff, related that he was supportive of the action and encouraged others to be peaceful. John Wetherill, a trader in Kayenta, visited the Navajos in his area after collecting all the facts of the incident. He, along with Williard, Shelton, and others, were concerned that the Black Mountain Navajos might force a confrontation. It never materialized. Charles Goodman, a photographer living in Bluff, wanted Williard to bring the troops there and tackle some of the Ute, Paiute, and Navajo issues that community faced; Will Evans, a trader in Farmington, New Mexico, wrote a lengthy article dispelling rumors and false allegations.[56]

By November 12, Williard received orders to return to Fort Wingate with his prisoners who, in December, continued on to Fort Huachuca, Arizona, to serve their sentences. His recommendation was that Ba'álílee and Polly spend ten years at hard labor, while the rest of the group should serve two years. The ten slated for prison were Ba'álílee; Ba'álílee's Nephew (Ba'álílee Bidá'í); Silversmith (Atsidii); Many Goats Son (Tł'ízí Łání Biye'); Mister Coat (Hastiin Éé'tsoh, also known as He Who Smells Himself); No Teeth (Biwoo'ádinii); Polly (also known as Big Tangle People Clansman (Ta'neeszahnii Tsoh)); Son of Mexican (Naakaii Biye'); Sisco; and Mele-yon.[57] Shelton felt that Mister Coat was too old to withstand the rigors of prison life, so he was released from Fort Wingate to return home. The agent was apparently right. By the time Mister Coat arrived at One With An Open Mouth (Aneth), he was exhausted. Navajos changed their local name for this settlement from that of a trader to one that honored the returning elder: Barely Enough Pep To Make It. In January 1908, the government also released Mele-yon from Fort Huachuca because of his advanced stage of tuberculosis.[58]

Everyone seemed to be at peace with the settled issue except for Howard Ray Antes, minister of the Navajo Faith Mission in Aneth. He seized upon the opportunity to wage a crusade against Shelton. Why their relationship had deteriorated is not entirely clear. Perhaps it was because of the disagreement over building a riprap dam to protect the mission property; perhaps because Shelton had lost interest in purchasing this site; perhaps because of a growing misunderstanding over an adopted Navajo boy; or perhaps because Antes received inaccurate information from biased sources. Whatever the reason, the missionary sent vehement letters to H. M. Teller, a senator from Colorado, and the editor of the *Denver Post*. In his communications, he charged the soldiers with opening fire on "the poor, defenseless people," abusing the prisoners, shooting the Indians in the back, destroying crops, stealing corn, scaring the Navajos into the hills, and withdrawing the troops while leaving "the settlers to the mercy of bloodthirsty Indians coming from Cortez."[59]

Within six months after the incident, Colonel Hugh L. Scott, Superintendent of the United States Military Academy and investigator for the government, received word to proceed to Utah and determine the truthfulness of the charges. He arrived in Aneth on April 19, 1908, found Antes was staying on his farm in McElmo Canyon, Colorado, and sent for him. On the 21st, the investigation started. Captain Williard, Agent Shelton, Navajo interpreter Robert Martin, Colonel Scott, and Reverend Antes were present in the mission school house. The burden of proof rested with the minister, who first called forth Navajo witnesses. Many of them had trouble understanding what it meant to be sworn in. Antes clarified the procedure through Martin, saying, "Does he [the witness] know God heard what he said and is strong enough to punish him if he told a lie?" Antes received the reply, "He does not think so."[60] Eventually, some of the witnesses understood enough to be acceptable to all concerned; with others, the panel just agreed to let them speak.

Old Mexican told of his experience before the court. He had been in the midst of lambing season when a man had approached him and his older brother to attend the hearing. Although reticent, he relented and met with "an old man with white hair, dressed up in a uniform with an eagle on his shoulder." Two Indians—one an Apache, the other a Kiowa—"dressed up all in feathers," plus five Navajo policemen and Shelton comprised the group. Old Mexican then commented on how the agent and the missionary had argued long and hard and how he was reluctant to say much of anything about Ba'álílee because he did not know him that well. As far as he was concerned, the matter was already settled. He blurted out a stronger reason when Shelton asked him if he was still afraid of Ba'álílee, to which Old Mexican replied, "I'm afraid of him all right. . . . That's all I'm going to tell you. No more."[61]

Antes eventually requested the session adjourn to Mancos, Colorado, where a white witness named Oliver lived, but Scott denied it, saying that this man had been summoned, had not shown up, and so was "unwilling." The investigation dragged on until almost midnight. The colonel closed with a question to Antes, asking if the missionary had the right to talk to Indians, even if a government agent forbid it. Antes said he had the right to talk to anyone he pleased when his home was off the reservation, and even though a recent boundary change had encompassed his property, it did not change that right. Scott disagreed and believed that the whole problem resulted from this type of attitude.

The following day Williard and Shelton built their defense. For nine hours the two men systematically destroyed the allegations brought against them and proved that previous Indian testimony was inconsistent and inaccurate. Williard summarized his position in a detailed statement showing the absurdity of the claims that the Navajos carried high powered rifles but supposedly had no ammunition; that one of Antes's witnesses was too sleepy to recall certain details, but could conveniently recount specific information when necessary; that Indians had been shot in the back; that the soldiers had not taken steps to bury the dead; that his men stole things; and that the crops, purportedly destroyed during the fight, had not already been harvested. Summarizing his feelings, Williard spat out, "that those statements made by him [Antes] were willfully and deliberately false and malicious, groundless, based on hearsay of the flimsiest character, without an iota of truth. . . . [and that Williard] had been made the butt and scapegoat of a personal feeling of animosity between Mr. Shelton and Mr. Holley on the one hand and the Reverend Mr. Antes on the other. . . ." [62]

The captain next offered testimony that shed surprising light on attitudes concerning the minister. He asserted that he had made an inquiry as to Antes's character "all the way from Gallup, New Mexico, to Aneth, Utah, and failed to develop one person who spoke well of him." Dr. W. F. Fish, whose statement Antes cited as part of his defense, said that he had been misrepresented. Even after the doctor made clear the misunderstanding of events, the minister retorted, "'. . . but I will make them a whole lot of trouble anyhow; I will write every paper and magazine in the country.' He said something about doing all he could to get Shelton and Holley fired."[63] Fish also caught Antes lying about a supposed police force coming to arrest the minister.

The reverend was defeated. Lack of evidence disproved his charges, his witnesses had either not testified or were shown unreliable, and his motives were questionable. Rather than struggle further, he tried to back out gracefully, scraping together as much dignity as possible under the circumstances. Using the guise of protecting his witnesses from the ravages of an irate Shelton, Antes chose "to suffer the humiliation of falling down on this prosecution personally rather than let any injury come to them [i.e., the witnesses]."[64]

While still in prison, Ba'álílee garnered more attention. The Indian Rights Association (IRA) sprang to his defense once Antes's efforts died, arguing that use of troops was illegal and that the prisoners had not been properly charged yet still arrested for questionable crimes.[65] The Commissioner of Indian Affairs, Francis E. Leupp, sustained direct attack for both his handling of the situation and accepting the recommendation of Captain Williard in determining the jail sentences. Part of his defense is found in an article he penned entitled "Law or No Law in Indian Administration." In it, he argued that the incident was well handled and that there were not a lot of options in dealing with the recalcitrant medicine man.[66] The IRA fought back and managed to have the case tried before the Arizona Supreme Court. They argued that an Indian person has a right to a fair trial, the government had overstepped its legal bounds, the prisoners were unfairly incarcerated, and they should be freed. On February 4, 1909, the government released six of the eight prisoners; on March 20, 1909, the Arizona Supreme Court unanimously voted to also return Ba'álílee and Polly to the reservation. The federal government abandoned the appeal process and in June, ordered a noncommissioned officer to escort the two Navajos to Shiprock, where they were released to go home.[67]

Fig. 31—Opposing forces after the "brawl." Standing fifth from left, Robert Martin (Navajo interpreter); sixth from left, Agent William T. Shelton (with badge); and seventh from left, Captain Harry O. Williard. Seated fourth from left, Ba'álílee, with Polly immediately to his right. (Courtesy National Archives, Washington, DC)

Ba'álílee returned a changed man. He continued with his medicine practice, but there was no more head-butting with Shelton. Two years later, the medicine man was dead, drowned when crossing the San Juan River on his way to conduct a ceremony. Even in death, Ba'álílee attracted controversy. He had become embroiled in a fracas with a man named Cream Colored Horses (Biłį́į́' Yishtłizhii). Ba'álílee had resorted to his previous tactics, saying, "You are going to be struck by lightning. I have mastered witchcraft and am filled with it up to here (gesturing to his throat), and according to this witchcraft you are going to be struck by lightning."[68] Cream Colored Horses replied, "You aren't in command of lightning. You, Ba'álílee, are going to be swallowed by a big snake, and I place the San Juan River as the Big Snake."

Accounts vary as to exactly what happened next. In May 1911, when the river ran exceptionally high even for flood stage, Ba'álílee crossed with another man, He Hunted It Near Those Rocks (Tsét'ah Neiskah). The boat capsized, and the other man swam to shore, but Ba'álílee, wearing his cartridge belts and pistol, never surfaced. Some say he was chanting a witchcraft song as he crossed, but family members believe he was not involved in it. Some say his body was never found; others testify it washed ashore downstream at Rock Nose (Tsé Achį́įh). "There was a little bit of him showing and two buzzards were there. They [Navajo searchers] got him out and washed him and took him back."[69]

Jane Byalily Silas, Ba'álílee's granddaughter, who was born the night before the attack, believes her grandfather has been falsely accused of practicing witchcraft. Her family tells of stories shared by those captured by the government. For instance, the troops challenged Ba'álílee to use his powerful songs. At one point, "he prayed for rain and it rained until the camp was nearly washed out; he had to pray again to stop it. Moving on to another camp, Ba'álílee was asked to pray for a bear to come to it. He prayed, and sure enough, a bear showed up. Ba'álílee asked one of the white men to wrestle the animal, but he [the white man] was afraid. The soldiers paid Ba'álílee to call it off."[70] After performing other miracles, the troops let him go because they realized "the natives truly had a powerful God." Another person told of Ba'álílee's resistance against government programs and Shelton. When the cavalry pursued the medicine man and his people, he used his powers to part the rain-swollen river so that his followers could safely cross.[71] These stories and others say as much about the people sharing them as they do of the man.

What can be learned from these events of 100 years ago? Besides the fact that this fight is purported to be the last cavalry charge against "hostile" Indians in the United States, are there lessons to consider? There is no missing the rapidity of cultural change that challenged traditional Navajo beliefs and practices. When physical powers overwhelm, spiritual solutions become an obtainable means to address challenges. Ba'álílee was adept at playing upon the deeply religious nature of the Navajo people to resist both physically and spiritually. How much of it was self-serving or justified remains for the reader to determine. But Holley, who spoke Navajo, reported that "Ba'álílee repeatedly had told his people, 'We are Navajos; we are Navajos; we want nothing to do with the agent, the Government, or the whites but want to stay away from them;' but to continue all their old Indian customs."[72] It was an uphill climb that the tribe is still addressing today: How does one maintain the values of traditional culture in a sea of contemporary change?

Shelton, on the other hand was a spokesman for the Progressive Era, with Shiprock as his flagship. When he bemoaned Ba'álílee's presence and negative impact upon the Indians trying to follow the agency's lead, Shelton viewed the struggle in terms of diametrically opposing forces. There was no gray. The conflict was "between the two classes, the progressive and the unprogressive," and for the latter, "something more than kind talk and persuasion would have to be used."[73] It was, and after the troops returned to Fort Wingate, the government increasingly intensified imposed change. Regulation of trading posts, further dependence on a federally sponsored Navajo government, more programs to assist in agriculture and livestock production, additional boarding schools with greater enrollments, oil and mineral exploration, the nascence of the wage economy, heightened desire for consumer goods—the list goes on. Shelton took the first step of introducing change in an isolated and heretofore ignored area of the vast Navajo reservation. Conflict soon arose.

There is another way to look at this struggle. Historically, Aneth has seemed to attract people with strong personalities. Henry Mitchell, Ba'álílee, his followers, William Shelton, Captain Williard, James Holley, Howard Ray Antes, and others were distinct in their approach and did not hesitate to speak their mind. In an area where people did not have many restrictions placed on them, it had not been necessary for them to feel a bit in their mouths and the pull of restrictive reins. Once enforcement of change began, personalities took over, playing a prominent role in issue resolution. Shelton wanted peace and quiet; Ba'álílee thrived on confrontation. His power came from magnifying conflict and enlisting, either willingly or otherwise, his army to oppose the government. Shelton refused to accept intimidation and drew the line. Mexican Man (Naakaii Diné), a resident of Aneth, summarized the situation succinctly when he testified that, "There was too much noise in that bunch [Ba'álílee] across the river."[74] Shelton quieted it.

Chapter Endnotes

1. Portions of this chapter were previously published in Chapter Four of *Dineji Na'nitin: Navajo Traditional Teachings and History* (Boulder: University Press of Colorado, 2012).
2. Spelled in various primary sources as Bai-a-lil-le, Bah-leel, Be'élilee, Bia-a-lil-le, By-a-lil-le, Bylillie, and Ba'ililii. The name has been translated as The One With Supernatural Power, He Who Knows Many Ceremonies, and The One With Magic Power. Using contemporary standardized rules, the name is spelled Ba'álílee. The basis for this name comes from the Navajo term *álílee k'ehgo,* meaning literally "according to his supernatural/magical power" and referring to his ability to use unseen power for either good or evil. It is the force by which things are done supernaturally. For instance, Jesus walking on the water or a Navajo skinwalker (witch) running at superhuman speeds are examples of a divine ability to control this force. The power is not discussed or flaunted, and its existence is recognized with reverence (Marilyn Holiday, in a conversation with the author (September 23, 2007); and Jim Dandy, in a conversation with the author (September 24, 2007)).
3. Walter Dyk, *A Navaho Autobiography* (New York: Viking Fund Publication in Anthropology, 1947), p. 138. Another explanation of what happened the night of October 28, 1907, is offered by Jane Byalily Silas, Ba'álílee's paternal granddaughter. She claims that he was assisting another medicine man named The One Who Sucks Out The Evil (Ats'ǫǫsí). The two sang songs and prayed to remove an object shot by witchcraft into a woman's body by her jealous husband. At one point, a scuffle broke out between the medicine man and the patient's husband. They exchanged blows before the distraught husband left, allowing the ceremony to continue late into the night (Jane Byalily Silas, in an interview with the author (February 27, 1991)). Ba'álílee is Jane's paternal grandfather; she was born the night before this incident. Her story is corroborated by Son of Red House Clansman, who said that the two medicine men were "singing over a woman who was sick" (Red House Clansman, "The One with Magic Power," in Robert W. Young and William Morgan, *Navajo Historical Selections,* Navajo Historical Series #3 (Lawrence, KS: Bureau of Indian Affairs, 1954), p. 35.
4. Silas interview; Florence Begay, in an interview with the author (April 29, 1988). Navajo society is matrilineal, emphasizing the mother's clan for descent (born *of*) with the father's clan (born *for*) as a secondary source of kinship ties.
5. US Congress and Senate, *Testimony Regarding Trouble on Navajo Reservation,* 60th Cong., 2nd sess., Klah Testimony (March 3, 1909), p. 43 [hereafter cited as *TRTNR*].
6. Florence Begay interview.
7. J. Lee Correll, *Bai-a-lil-le: Medicine Man or Witch?* (Widow Rock: Navajo Historical Publications, Biographical Series #3, 1970), p. 4.
8. The reference to "witch knives" most likely refers to a ceremonially treated piece of sharpened flint, perhaps one that has been touched by lightning or a bear. This is "shot" through witchcraft into an individual. Cures for this include prayers that reverse the evil, sweating or sucking the object out, or with some kinds of witchcraft, induced vomiting (see Gladys A. Reichard, *Navaho Religion: A Study of Symbolism* (Princeton, New Jersey: Princeton University Press, 1950, 1974), pp. 610–11 and 727).
9. Ibid.; Silas interview; and Correll, *Bai-a-lil-le,* p. 49.
10. See Clyde Kluckhohn, *Navaho Witchcraft* (Boston: Beacon Press, 1944, 1970).
11. See Robert S. McPherson, "Howard R. Antes and the Navajo Faith Mission: Evangelist of Southeastern Utah," *Utah Historical Quarterly* (Winter 1997), pp. 4–24.
12. Statement by James M. Holley, government farmer—Aneth, J. Lee Correll Collection, Navajo Nation, Window Rock, Arizona (n.d.) [hereafter cited as JLC Collection].
13. Ibid.
14. William T. Shelton to commissioner of Indian affairs, Record Group 75, Letters Received, New Mexico Superintendency, National Archives, Washington, DC (December 5, 1913) [hereafter cited as Letters Received—N.M.]; and Major James McLaughlin papers, Assumption Abbey Archives, microfilm #5, on file in the Denver Public Library, Denver, Colorado.

15. Ibid.
16. William T. Shelton, "Report of Superintendent of San Juan School" (July 23, 1907); and Shelton to commissioner of Indian affairs, JLC Collection (July 23, 1907).
17. Ibid.; and George W. Hayzlett to commissioner of Indian affairs, JLC Collection (July 25, 1902).
18. William T. Shelton to commissioner of Indian affairs, JLC Collection (October 20, 1903). What Shelton did not understand is that a man or woman's family can claim ownership of the property that belonged to their deceased relative as long as individual ownership had been recognized when that person was alive.
19. Holley Statement, JLC Collection.
20. William T. Shelton to commissioner of Indian affairs (March 29, 1907), as cited in *Report on Employment of United States Soldiers in Arresting By-a-lil-le and Other Navajo Indians*, 60th Cong., 1st sess. (May 25, 1908), p. 7 [hereafter cited as *ABONI*]; Harry O. Williard to adjutant general, *ABONI* (October 30, 1907), p. 17; Shelton to James M. Holley, JLC Collection (September 3, 1907); Williard to adjutant general, JLC Collection (November 3, 1907); *TRTNR*, Frank Mitchell Testimony, p. 49; Dyk, *A Navaho Autobiography*, p. 134; and Klah Testimony, *TRTNR* (April 25, 1908), p. 44. The One With Muscles was also known as Black Horse (Łį́į́ Łizhiní).
21. Mary Blueyes, in an interview with the author (March 20, 1992).
22. Sworn Testimonies from Sis-co, By-a-lil-le Bida, Mele-yon, Frank Mitchell, Pit-ce-cote, and Att-city, JLC Collection (March 19, 1909).
23. R.S. Connell to commissioner of Indian affairs, *ABONI* (April 6, 1907), p. 9.
24. Short Hair was also known as Ba'álílee's Son In Law (Ba'álílee Bidá'í).
25. Hattie Testimony, *TRTNR*, p. 51.
26. Shelton, "Report of Superintendent" (July 23, 1907).
27. James R. Garfield to commissioner of Indian affairs, *ABONI* (November 22, 1907), p. 26; and Dyk, *A Navaho Autobiography*, pp. 111–12 and 124.
28. Shelton to commissioner, *ABONI* (March 29, 1907), p. 7.
29. Dyk, *A Navaho Autobiography*, pp. 122–26.
30. Nah-ki-Den-Na testimony, *TRTNR*, p. 50; and Statement of Jimmie Noland, JLC Collection (March 19, 1909).
31. Frank McNitt, *The Indian Traders* (Norman: University of Oklahoma Press, 1962), p. 344.
32. In 1905, Agent Reuben Perry, reacting to a rape incident, traveled from Fort Defiance to Winslow, Arizona, where two Navajos met and forced him to sign a pardon for the accused man, Black Water (Tółízhiní). Perry returned to the agency, requested soldiers from Fort Wingate, then marched with Captain Harry O. Williard and K Troop to Chinle to make the arrests. Eventually, seven Navajos went to Alcatraz, then Fort Huachuca, Arizona, to serve their sentences. Williard was the officer who arrested Ba'álílee, who was also sent to Huachuca. The seven men arrested from the Black Mountain area left others behind who resisted encroachment by the government. This region, like southeastern Utah, was isolated from the main population of Navajos. Many of those living in these locations had never known the chastening lesson of Fort Sumner. For a synopsis of the incident, see Bill Acrey, *Navajo History: The Land and the People* (Shiprock, NM: Department of Curriculum Materials Development Central Consolidated School District No. 22, 1988), pp. 171–75.
33. Connell to commissioner, *ABONI* (April 6, 1907), p. 9.
34. Ibid.
35. William T. Shelton to commissioner of Indian affairs, *ABONI* (September 18, 1907), p. 11; and Statement by Holley, JLC Collection (n.d.).
36. Shelton to commissioner, *ABONI* (September 18, 1907), p. 12; and Adjutant general to commanding general, Department of Colorado, *ABONI* (October 15, 1907), pp. 13–14.
37. Correll, *Bai-a-lil-le*, p. 20.
38. Unless otherwise noted, the information concerning the movement and attack on Ba'álílee's camp is taken from Captain Harry O. Williard's report to the adjutant general, Headquarters Department Colorado, *ABONI* (October 30, 1907), pp. 14–20.

39. The post was most likely located on the flood plain at the mouth of Marble Wash and along the San Juan River. On a 1903 map located in the Wetherill–Grand Gulch Archives (Edge of the Cedars Museum, Blanding, Utah), the old road from the Four Corners Post to Aneth is shown following the river on its north side. Midpoint is a trading post called Berlin. This is most likely the post operated by a man named Spencer, as well as where M. R. Butler traded at the time of the Ba'álílee conflict. The site is now called Burned House (*Kin Díílidí*) by the Navajo. Mary Jay (see below) said, "A trader named Silver (Béésh Łigai) used to live there until he got mad at some people who threw him out. This store was located by the river below the gray hill." Florence Begay noted that the Utes used to trade there too.

40. Today, the flood plain is covered with tamarisk and has been scoured by the San Juan River during past floods so that nothing remains of its historic buildings. Once one moves off the flood plain, there is a twelve-foot-high bank that buttresses the historic flats not cut by the river. Above that is a second plateau and then a number of large hill masses, creating the "cove" effect. The entire flood plain bench is now known as Soldier Crossing, coming from the Ba'álílee incident.

41. *Tségi Hóchxǫǫ'jí* is a difficult term to translate. The first word means a narrow canyon that is a defile through high rock walls. The second term means "evil," but in this case is such rough terrain that it is very difficult to pass over it. In English, one might say, "It is a devil of a canyon to pass through" (from James Benally's conversation with the author (November 19, 2007).

42. As one travels downstream, there is a collection of ruins atop a mesa and along the bank, which is called Scattered Anaasazi Remains (*Bits'iil*). Opposite Aneth is the prominent Tall Mountain (*Dził Ninéézi*), sitting on the south side of the river. Leading to its plateau-like top and with a truncated appearance is Reclining Rock (*Tsé Biyaají*), a long ridge that inclines from the flood plain (from Baxter Benally's conversation with the author (September 24, 2007); Florence Norton, in an interview with author (March 6, 1991); Mary Jay, in an interview with the author (February 27, 1991); and Isabel Lee, in an interview with the author (February 13, 1991). North of this mountain lies Aneth, which was then called The One With An Open Mouth , having been named after a trader. Howard Ray Antes was the first to apply the name Aneth, a Hebrew word meaning "the answer," in 1895. There were other Navajo names given to Aneth and Montezuma Creek, many of which are tied to traders who were operating there at the time. It is not clear if The One With An Open Mouth refers to Holley, Heffernan, or another person.

43. The difference between a male (*hooghan ałch'įadeez'ą*) and female (*hooghan nímazí*) hogan is determined by the shape of the structure, not who uses it. The male hogan has a passageway that leads into the area where people live. The main space is constructed by using three forked poles that interlock at the top where the smoke hole is located. There is not as much space in the male hogan, due to the conical shape of this tepee-like structure. The female hogan is more prevalent today. It is round, more spacious in height and width, constructed with a cribbed roof, and has a greater seating and storage capacity. Both hogans have doorways that face east. The male hogan, because it was the first to be created by the holy people, is said to have more efficacy for ceremonial purposes, although either male or female hogans are acceptable for ceremonies. Ba'álílee's "medicine lodge" could possibly have been a large male hogan.

44. Jim Dandy, in a conversation with the author (October 29, 2007).

45. This phonetically spelled name is untranslatable and does not sound like a Navajo word.

46. Lee interview.

47. Williard to the adjutant general, *ABONI* (October 30, 1907), p. 16.

48. Dyk, *A Navaho Autobiography*, p. 131.

49. Ibid., p. 132.

50. Son of Red House Clansman, p. 35.

51. Ba'álílee's Wife testimony, *TRTNR* (April 22, 1908), p. 19–20; and J.A. Heffernan testimony, *TRTNR* (April 22, 1908), p. 32.

52. Lee interview; and Son of Red House Clansman, p. 36.

53. Florence Norton interview; Dyk, *A Navaho Autobiography*, p. 132; and Mikinly Chinee Nez testimony, *TRTNR*, p. 45.

54. Ibid; and John Norton, in an interview with the author (January 16, 1991).
55. Dyk, *A Navaho Autobiography*, p. 131.
56. James A. Holley to William T. Shelton (November 5, 1907); Shelton to Jim Joe (November 7, 1907); Joe to Shelton, JLC Collection (November 20, 1907); Frances Gillmor and Louisa Wade Wetherill, *Traders to the Navajos* (Albuquerque: University of New Mexico Press, 1934), pp. 136–138; Charles Goodman to Holley, JLC Collection (November 1, 1907); and William Evans, "The Actual Situation," *Farmington Enterprise* (November 29, 1907), p. 1.
57. As noted previously, some Navajo names were written phonetically and are either untranslatable or may have more than one meaning, depending upon inflection and how attuned the ear of the writer was to the language. Navajos often had more than one name, which explains how the list of the ten men who went to jail differs between eyewitness native speakers. Most of the names presented here are confirmed, but there are still two or three that are a best guess or left as they were found in the historic record.
58. Son of Red House Clansman, p. 37; and Commander Thomas, in a telegram to adjutant general of the army, JLC Collection (January 29, 1908).
59. Court Proceedings, *TRTNR*, p. 29.
60. Ibid., p. 11.
61. Dyk, *A Navaho Autobiography*, pp. 133–34.
62. Court Proceedings, *TRTNR*, p. 31.
63. Ibid., pp. 40–41.
64. Ibid., pp. 24–25.
65. For an excellent review of the political fracas surrounding the Ba'álílee incident, the Indian Office, and the Indian Rights Association, see Donald L. Parman, "The 'Big Stick' in Indian Affairs: The Bai-a-lil-le Incident in 1909," *Arizona and the West* (Fall 1978), pp. 343–60.
66. Francis E. Leupp, " 'Law or No Law' In Indian Administration," *The Outlook* (January 30, 1909), pp. 261–63.
67. Interior Department to secretary of war, JLC Collection (June 25, 1909).
68. Cited in Correll, p. 47. The San Juan River has many teachings and specific sites that are connected to Big Snake: a powerful Navajo deity who participated with other holy people during the creation of this world. He is not a benevolent god but rather one connected with protection and conflict.
69. Silas interview; Mary Blueyes, in an interview with the author (March 20, 1992); Florence Begay interview; Martha Nez, in an interview with the author (August 10, 1988); and John Joe Begay, in an interview with the author (September 18, 1990).
70. Silas interview.
71. Jerrold E. Levy, *In the Beginning: The Navajo Genesis* (Los Angeles: University of California Press, 1998), pp. 229–30.
72. Holley testimony, *TRTNR*, p. 7.
73. Shelton to commissioner, *ABONI*, p. 8.
74. Nah-ki-Den-na (Naakaii Diné) testimony, *TRTNR*, p. 50.

CHAPTER EIGHT

Settling the Ute Issue
The Last Indian Fights in the Twentieth Century[1]

The frontier was closed; the last cavalry charge against hostile Indians over; most Native Americans were on reservations living in the nadir of their tribal existence; Progressive Era politics were in full swing; and the twentieth century seemed to most Americans to dawn with a new, technologically sophisticated march into the future. Or so it appeared to those not living in southeastern Utah. There, it seemed the opposite. Homesteading was still *de rigueur*; the San Juan Utes and Paiutes were not on the reservation; meaningful politics were mostly at the hometown level; and technology—electricity, phones, treated water, and automobiles—was slow in arriving on any meaningful scale. The old days were giving way to the new, but not before some interesting combinations of the two made the first quarter of the twentieth century distinct from what was transpiring in the rest of the country. Few other places can claim chasing belligerent Indians in a Ford Model T, requesting aircraft armed with bombs to suppress Native Americans, building a barbed-wire stockade for prisoners in the middle of town, or fostering a string of events that eventually reached the White House and President Woodrow Wilson at a time when the country was embroiled with incidents along the Mexican border and Europe was fighting World War I.

This chapter examines two conflicts concerning the Utes and their white neighbors living primarily in Bluff and Blanding. It was a difficult time for these Indian people. They had lost most of what they had once depended on and had been pushed into poverty while trying to survive without going onto the Ute Mountain Ute Reservation in Colorado. Unlike the Navajo, whose reservation had done nothing but expand, the Utes' land holdings had done nothing but shrink. They had no choice but to be beggars in their own home. And unlike the

Navajos, who approached conflict on a more supernatural level, the Utes settled their difficulties through a totally physical confrontation. As in the past, they depended upon their knowledge of the land as to where they could go to hide, but this advantage, which had been so helpful previously, was now greatly diminished. White settlement and industry had changed much of that. Times had changed.

Moving from the nineteenth into the twentieth century, there continued to be low-grade conflicts. The Utes pastured their horses in farmers' fields; they begged at white men's doors and used verbal intimidation and threats against men, women, and children; they did things that irritated their neighbors as revenge for all they had lost; and they had to adjust to an ever-shrinking land base. On both sides of the cultural fence, people lived in grinding poverty, but the Utes had it far worse, trying to survive as impoverished second-class citizens on the outskirts of the white settlements. Both groups were tired and exasperated with the state of affairs that had persisted for thirty to forty years. Underneath the relatively peaceful exterior were seething emotions of anger and frustration waiting to erupt. Tse-ne-gat, a young twenty-six-year-old Ute, unwittingly ignited the fuse that burned slowly, then exploded in an armed conflict that caused death on both sides.

The affair started simply enough in mid-May 1914, when two Utes approached Superintendent Claude C. Covey stationed at Navajo Springs.[2] They reported a body buried in a wash southwest of Cowboy Springs six miles north and six miles east of the New Mexico and Utah state lines.[3] The agent, along with a coroner and an attorney, went with a group of Indians to determine identity and manner of death for the man killed in March. Articles on the body quickly confirmed that he was Juan Chacon, an Hispanic herder returning home to New Mexico with a large paycheck earned in Utah. He had fallen in with some Utes, spent the night at Mariano Springs in successful gambling, and then was ambushed by a member of the group, Tse-ne-gat, who had lost at cards with him.

Ute testimony from five individuals painted a detailed picture of how events unfolded.[4] One man, Ca-vis-itz's Son, told of returning from the agency when Tse-ne-gat reined in next to him and inquired if he had seen Chacon and how far ahead he (Chacon) was. The Mexican had passed that way just a short while before. Tse-ne-gat said he was going to kill him and when asked why, replied it was for the large amount of money Chacon carried. Three other witnesses testified that while they were looking for cattle near Sleeping Ute Mountain, they heard three shots from a .30-30 rifle in rapid succession. They hastened to see what was happening and ascended the crest of a hill in time to see Tse-ne-gat pulling and pushing something into a ravine. Once he knew they had spotted him, he mounted his horse, took in tow a second animal, and quickly rode toward the agency. Upon investigation, the three Utes found the body of Chacon lying faceup in the wash with three bullet holes in him. They did not report their find because the agent was on a trip and "we were afraid of this Indian and his father as they are known as bad men, the father, Polk, having killed a number of Indians, including two of Rooster's sons and that we now fear that he will try to kill us for having told this. . . . [W]e believe that Polk knows that the Mexican was murdered; that Polk and his son have said that they would kill Indians or white men who tried to arrest them."[5] Other witnesses confirmed all that had been told, with one man saying that when he ran into Tse-ne-gat, who was heading toward the agency, Tse-ne-gat had made the comment, "I did not think anybody saw me."[6]

Superintendent Covey sent word for Tse-ne-gat to come in to discuss the matter; he and his father almost did but turned around before reaching Navajo Springs and returned to Allen Canyon, Utah. Polk (or Billy Hatch, as he was known on tribal roles) struck fear into the hearts of the Utes at Towaoc and was believed to hold supernatural power that made him bullet-proof.[7] "Billy Hatch is said to have killed five or six other Indians. The Indians living here received word that the Hatches, with a number of friends, were coming to the agency in force and if an attempt was made to arrest young Hatch and take him away they will kill anyone making the attempt."[8] The agent realized his Indian police were totally ineffective in a situation like this and could not officially operate off the reservation, so he suggested that a US Marshal serve the warrant to arrest Tse-ne-gat.

In September, Deputy Marshal David Thomas appeared in Bluff and confronted Tse-ne-gat in Frank Hyde's store but failed to arrest him, fearing there would be an uprising and bloodshed. To the locals, this just emboldened an already impudent father and son, especially considering that there were "thirty men ready to help the marshal if necessary and that they could have taken him without serious resistance."[9] From the marshal's perspective, the townspeople were "unwilling to cooperate . . . for fear that if assistance was rendered, revenge might be taken on some of the people later," and so he returned empty-handed.[10] Tse-ne-gat was allowed to go to his camp with the understanding that he would surrender the next day, but when the time came, he refused and said he would resist any attempt to take him. The marshal,

Fig. 32—Tse-ne-gat (Činigatt, or Silver Earrings) was born in 1888 and died in 1922. During his short life, he created a stir that brought attention to southeastern Utah from as far away as the White House. Both whites and Indians feared his father, Polk, which Tse-ne-gat capitalized on for his own benefit. (Courtesy San Juan County Historical Commission)

feeling unsupported by the white community and outgunned by the Indians, chose discretion and departed.[11]

Mormon Stake President and cattleman L. H. Redd met in Salt Lake with Lorenzo D. Creel (Special Agent for the Scattered Bands of Indians in Utah) and Governor William Spry to determine what could be done. Creel had met Tse-ne-gat on a number of occasions and concurred that something needed to happen before serious conflict resulted. Louisa Wetherill, John Wetherill's wife and a trader in Kayenta, knew Tse-ne-gat well enough to go to Bluff with a group of Paiutes from her area and ask him to surrender. He absolutely refused. Local papers questioned how the murderer of Juan Chacon could hold the authorities at bay for eight months with no decisive action. Around the same time, James E. Jenkins replaced Covey as superintendent at Navajo Springs, inheriting a pot of trouble about to boil over.[12]

By now, the commissioner of Indian affairs, Indian agents in both Colorado and Utah, the US Marshal's office, Governor Spry, and local citizens were all well aware of the Indian resistance, more symbolic than real, mounting in San Juan County. The irritating pimple of Polk, Tse-ne-gat, and perhaps thirty followers needed to be pinched before the infection spread, and it needed to be done quickly and with stealth. But stealth was elusive. Colorado and Utah papers soon became aware of actions underway and reported in great detail any plans they heard (some of which was fiction but made interesting reading). Portrayed as an old-fashion Indian war, the yellow press leaped into action. Any type of operational security flew out the window. In the early part of February, Marshal Aquila Nebeker went to Cortez to raise a force he could deputize and move into Utah without alerting the Indians. Its mission: Capture the twenty-seven-year-old Tse-ne-gat and avoid fighting the estimated twenty-five warriors who sided with Polk. The marshal expected a hard battle. As newspapers amplified their stories, the number of Indians who might resist quickly inflated to fifty, then seventy-five, and eventually one hundred fifty.[13]

The marshal next traveled to Grayson to recruit local men, many of whom were ranchers, and to be closer to his objective. He also sent five men to Bluff to spy on the Indians and track their movements. In the meantime, twenty-six Colorado volunteers under Deputy Sheriff A. N. Gingles camped in McElmo Canyon during a major snowstorm. Many of these men had been involved in brushes with the Utes and were ready to polish their tarnished record of previous defeats. Rumors were rampant, declaring that the Indians had been forewarned, were digging entrenchments, and had vowed to fight to the last man—all of this in spite of Nebeker "having taken elaborate and effective measures to conceal the fact of his destination from everyone but those sworn to secrecy when he left Salt Lake."[14] He apparently forgot to swear in the newspapers that revealed his every move. Fortunately, the Utes did not read.

The storms, said to bring the heaviest snowfall in twenty years, continued blowing in during the next week, leaving an accumulation of four feet in northern San Juan. Jenkins had traveled from Colorado in this weather to be the first Indian agent arriving in Bluff on February 22, the day after, as he put it, "the eggs had been scrambled," while Lorenzo Creel traveled by train to join him. Jenkins felt he could get Polk and Tse-ne-gat, in spite of the warrants, to come in to the agency peacefully, but if Nebeker was going to do something, he should at least wait for the weather to mellow. The agent assumed responsibility for the two Utes and their band, although he recognized that they were not on the Navajo Springs rolls. One of his primary goals was to separate visiting Colorado Utes from those Utes and Paiutes who had never enrolled on his reservation. Estimating there were about fourteen adult males in Polk's group, Jenkins complained that "it was a serious mistake to permit other departments to undertake the handling of Indians. They don't understand the Indians and the Indians resent the interference of officials other than their own agents."[15]

Wayne H. Redd from San Juan agreed. He knew the Polk and Posey groups, who had worked for many of the people in Bluff. He felt that "[t]he Indians are known to be friendly and there are only a few perhaps who would fight. The Indians are in no condition to aid Tse-ne-gat to resist arrest. Their ponies are poor at this time of the year and the snow on the ground leaves them with no surplus food sufficient to last them in a siege."[16] Contrary to reports of entrenched Indians preparing for battle and Polk selecting defensive terrain, the Utes were actually strung out over a three-mile distance, from Sand Island to Bluff. Many of their camps occupied the south-facing sand dunes below the bluffs because the snow did not accumulate for any length of time. If Polk was expecting trouble, he did not show it, since his camp was just to the west of Bluff with some of his people living near the Navajo Twin rock formation on the other side of town.[17]

In spite of those suggesting a more cautious approach, Nebeker moved forward with his plan. He placed strict censorship on the use of phones by civilians and posse members in Grayson and Bluff, greeted the deputized Colorado volunteers on February 20, traveled that night to Bluff, and began a partial encirclement of Polk's camp on the west side of Cottonwood Wash at first light on February 21.[18] Chester Cantsee recalls his parents returning from Bluff to their camp near Posey's home at Sand Island the day before the attack. They commented there were "different kinds of horses" in town but did not attach any particular significance to them until the events of the next day.[19] According to Gingles, when the marshal's force reached the wash, it split. Half headed north, and half headed west in order to encircle the small encampment where Polk and Tse-ne-gat had been playing cards most of the night. The converging elements awoke the camp dogs, whose barking gave the first indication that something was amiss. Gingles tells of "Poke [sic]and his boy in front of the wickiup dancing, whooping, and yelling" before they opened fire on the posse, then dashed with another Indian north, up the wash, to take position behind a sandbank.[20] From there, they delivered a steady fire as members of the posse maneuvered.

Joseph C. Akin crawled to a high part of an embankment and raised his head to get a fix on a target. In a split second before lifting his rifle, a bullet entered his skull over his left eye and lodged behind his right ear. Less than two minutes later, he was dead. Years later, Polk claimed the kill, telling trader Ira Hatch how he still had the old Model .35 Winchester he had used. The man was far away and so Polk "used all of his sights and the bullet landed on line but about twenty-five yards short. The next time he shot he used the end of his barrel for a sight and shot the man right between the eyes."[21]

The rest of the posse west of this fighting encountered Posey and others coming from their camp at Sand Island. Once Posey was in range, he shot José Cordova through the torso and began skirmishing against the rest, eventually breaking contact to return to the women and children. Frank Pyle recalled that "the rest of that morning there was no organization, white men and Indians were just shooting everywhere. . . . Posey's men cut five of the white men off from their horses and took them. The five men escaped and walked back to Blanding."[22] Uriah Butt, a young boy at the time, remembers how the "cowpunchers" did not want to remain out there much longer and so came to his house for breakfast. When Polk realized he was not under pressure, he and others gained a defensive advantage by climbing into the rocks nearby. "Those three Indians stood up there on the hill and motioned to the Bluff people to come up and fight. A whole bunch of us fellows were out in the street; I was just a kid, but I was out there among them, and the Indians could have shot all of us. They could have killed some of us if they had kept shooting, but they didn't keep shooting."[23]

There were also Indian fatalities. Many of the Utes just wanted to stay out of the fracas. Chicken Jack, unarmed, was making his way to town and crossing Cottonwood Wash when he ran into members of the posse, who gunned him down. To Alma Jones, "He was a favorite Ute in this area. He was friendly to everybody. He was no trouble; he never did get into any trouble at all."[24] During the initial outburst, Jack Ute dashed into the open to rescue his six-year-old daughter, who was caught between the two skirmishing sides; both father and daughter sustained wounds. Fortunately, other Indians were allowed to surrender and come under protective custody. Eventually, six men—Jack Ute, Havane, Joe Hammond, Jack Rabbit Soldier, Noland May, and a Mexican named Bruno Seguro— were incarcerated in the dance hall on the second floor of the San Juan Co-op.

Two days after the fight began, Havane (who, like Posey, was Polk's son-in-law) felt threatened by all the talk and behavior he was seeing. Convinced he was about to be murdered, he slipped off his handcuffs and ran to the window, hoping to leap to the ground twenty feet below. A guard named Honaker shot and mortally wounded Havane with a .45-caliber revolver, the concussion from which was powerful enough to blow out all the kerosene lamps on that floor and leave a large gaping wound in Havane's kidney and spleen. Twenty-three-year-old Charles Burke from Cortez, acting as a reporter for the *Rocky Mountain News,* went to Doctor E. E. Johnson, who had arrived from Cortez, Colorado, and obtained a hypodermic needle filled with a sedative. He recorded the scene:

> I went down there [to the co-op] and he was lying on the floor. I said, "Havane, how are you?"
>
> "Oh heap sick, heap sick, heap sick."
>
> And I said, "Well I'm going to give you something to make you sleep. Pretty soon sleep." I rolled up his sleeve and gave him a shot. . . .
>
> "You my friend," [he said,] and I said yes. I told him as best I could that I wasn't there to do any fighting. I was not a friend of the white man, [but] a friend of the Utes, see.
>
> He said, "Well you kill 'em. Me heap sick, you kill 'em [for] me, please kill 'em [for] me."
>
> It was a pitiful scene.[25]

Havane died three days later. Alma Jones said, "There were two peaceful, unarmed harmless men who lost their lives."[26]

There were also members of the posse actively searching and questioning local Utes who might be assisting or at least knew what the hostiles were doing. Edward Dutchie remembers as a toddler the fear that four men brought to his home as he, his brother, sister, and mother stirred at daylight: "Early in the morning my mother awoke me. She got me on her lap and held me down. She told me to keep quiet and don't cry. I saw riders outside . . . four people on horses with guns lying across their saddles. Before I could say anything, holler or anything like that, my mother put her hand over my mouth. . . . She was afraid the white men were going to kill her. She thought they might take us away or maybe kill us right there. So that is when we moved out."[27] By the next day after the attack, all of the Utes had fled down the San Juan River to Comb and Butler Washes, where they remained for some time without further engagements.[28]

A second group of "106 friendly Utes" were camped nearby in Butler Wash, then moved to town to avoid association with those fighting. Navajo scouts from the Northern Navajo Agency in Shiprock escorted them. As the Indians conversed, the "friendlies" learned they were actually slated to only pass through Bluff on their way to the Ute Reservation. "They halted in their march and refused to come in. Leaders of the band declared [that] rather than leave their ancestral hunting grounds they would resist the white authorities and join Old Polk and his bunch of renegades."[29] Further suggestion of their removal was quickly swept under the rug.

Fig. 33—All the Utes pictured in this 1921 photograph were involved in the 1915 and 1923 fights. Inspector El Fago Baca (standing third from left) visited Bluff to determine why there was constant low-grade conflict between white settlers and these people. Utes photographed here include (*back row, left to right*) Mancos Jim, Posey, Baca, unknown, Jim Mike, Washington Dutchie, Anson Cantsee, Posey's Little Boy, Jesse Posey, and Joe Hammond; (*front row*) Johnnie Peterson, Johnny Cockeye's wife and baby, Charlie (interpreter), Jack Fly, Joe Bishop's Little Boy, Havane's Son, and Johnny Cockeye. (Courtesy San Juan County Historical Commission)

Nebeker began depending on local help. He recruited the services of Mancos Jim, who he sent to the fighters, asking that they surrender peacefully. But they let it be known they would fight to the death. One eyewitness said of Mancos Jim, "He was one of the Mormon's main men to trust. He'd come into town and then he'd go back and tell what they wanted him to tell some of these Indians. He always worked in the dark [because] he didn't want anybody to follow him."[30] Nebeker also sought help from Grayson and Monticello, the former providing seventeen men ready to fight and the latter, twenty-nine, raising the total posse size to over seventy. Newspapers carried the word that

Bluff was surrounded, in imminent danger, and needed help, encouraging people from southwestern Colorado to further mobilize. Nebeker requested from Superintendent William T. Shelton at Shiprock twenty Navajo policemen to assist with tracking. They arrived in Bluff on the 25th, just as Nebeker suspended field activities to give Jenkins and Creel an opportunity to work with the Utes.[31] Besides, now that the initial hysteria was over, the cut telephone lines between Bluff and Grayson were restored, and the flight of the Indians to the west was an accomplished fact, the white participants felt comfortable remaining close to Bluff for the next two weeks in spite of what the press churned out for a good story. Newspapers also falsely reported that Posey had killed his brother, Scotty, who wanted to go to Bluff to surrender.[32]

On the night of the initial attack, Lorenzo Creel arrived in Moab. Spurred on by the news, the agent "traveled alternately from stage to stage by wagon, sled, sled to wagon, through mud often hub deep, and again in snow from three to four feet deep, with but little sleep until we reached Bluff on the night of the 24th."[33] The next day, he, Jenkins, interpreter Jim Allen (Ute), and "Catombet" (a Ute policeman) all went in search of non-combatant Indians. Creel found evidence strewn along the pathway of hasty flight, which convinced him that they had fled in sheer terror, since "the posse and citizens did not seem able to draw the line between combatant and peaceful Indians."[34] Fifteen miles outside of Bluff, the party encountered an old Indian acting as a lookout. Once he determined this group meant him no harm, others joined them, shaking hands all around, then listening to Jenkins' message that the Navajo Springs Agency was a refuge with food and assistance readily available. Eventually, all but Mancos Jim agreed to go, but the next day, he, too, fell in with the departing group of sixty Indians under Jenkins' and Ute police supervision. Creel bid farewell and returned to Bluff to collect the property and livestock as well as the sick Utes left behind by those fleeing. He also urged that regular troops be brought in to handle the situation, feeling that the posse members were "a bunch of greenhorns out for glory."[35] Before this was enacted, a better solution appeared.

On March 1, Nebeker summarized the situation. He believed he now faced fifty Indians under Polk and Posey, fifteen to twenty of whom were warriors, while the rest were women and children. Mancos Jim's band numbered 115, while another group of about fifty in the McElmo area was peaceful. All of these groups "commingled."[36] Those at large, however, had checkmated the posse. The same day that Nebeker made his assessment, Brigadier General Hugh L. Scott, Army Chief of Staff, was implementing his own plan of action.

He received plenary powers to draw upon the government resources of the War Department and Indian Office and also legal rights granted by the Justice Department in order to convince the Indians to surrender of their own volition. He also requested that the Navajo Bizhóshí, whom he had arrested the previous year, meet him at Bluff to assist in negotiations; a living testimonial of Scott's character and veracity could go a long way. With President Woodrow Wilson directing his subordinates to support these efforts, Scott started to the field on March 3 with approvals in hand, arriving in Bluff with his aide, Lieutenant Colonel Robert E. Michie, and orderly Private Paul Randolph on March 10.[37] Nebeker received word of Scott's role; the newspapers, noting the shift, congratulated their "boys who have done their full duty and done it well"; and the five manacled prisoners boarded the Denver Rio Grande Railroad for Salt Lake City to stand trial.[38]

Now it was Scott's turn to assess the situation. Louisa Wetherill, who had been in communication with Polk's group, sent a telegram asking for assurance that the father and son would not be hung if they surrendered. Could Scott guarantee them a fair trial? Creel and Jenkins reported that the Indians had crossed the San Juan River and were now around Douglas Mesa. The people in Bluff were afraid for the general and quoted what a Navajo had heard Polk promise to Nebeker: "Only bullets talk now."[39] Undaunted and unarmed, Scott set off the next day with John Wetherill, Bizhóshí, and four other Navajos, as well as the two agents and his aides.

Hardy Redd, son of L. H. Redd of Bluff, predicted failure, saying that the Indians would withdraw and that when the weather cleared, they would go to Navajo Mountain, where they would never be found. But Redd had a grudge to bear, noting that the previous summer, Posey had drawn a gun on him when the cattlemen let down the bars of the Indian's fence in order to drive livestock through. His take: "We would like to see the Indians driven out of this country."[40] Redd was right about one thing: It would be some time before Scott encountered the Utes. The general established a headquarters at Mexican Hat and waited for a parley. In the meantime, Nebeker bid farewell to his posse, who returned home on March 19. The next day, Scott sent a telegram to the secretary of war: "Successful. Have four Paiutes desired by Marshal Nebeker, and at their desire am personally conducting them to Salt Lake to turn over to Marshal Nebeker."[41]

People were elated. Scott explained what happened and how Bizhóshí had played an important part. At first, the Navajo and his two sons had hesitated to go, reciting a story about how since the beginning of time, Paiutes were mean. Scott had cajoled him into agreeing after promising "that when we were both killed we would be buried together."[42] Once the party had reached the trading post at Mexican Hat, they found only Arthur H. Spencer and family. Eventually, Wetherill and Scott recruited a Paiute from Kayenta to find Polk and Posey and invite them to come in for a talk. Several days elapsed before the messenger returned with news that the next day, the "outlaw Indians," about thirty in number, would be in. They were, but not before carefully glassing the situation from afar and posting armed lookouts on the surrounding mesas.[43] After listening to their complaints, Scott asked them what they were going to do and welcomed their reply, "We are going to do just what you tell us to do."[44] With this music in his ears, Scott agreed to accompany the four recalcitrants to Salt Lake City to ensure they had a fair trial and that Tse-ne-gat successfully arrived in Denver for his hearing. In the general's mind, he was going to "prevent those four Indians from being legally murdered."[45] Just as clear in Scott's view was the belief that when the posse had attacked these Indians, they had made no attempt to identify themselves, show a warrant, or give any explanation. The Colorado cowboys had attacked the Indians, and the Indians had just defended themselves. John D. Rogers, a local cattleman, later told of how Polk had explained this fact to him long after the incident was over.[46]

Praise poured in for Scott, who enjoyed the dramatic situation. The secretary of war sent congratulations, as did the adjutant general of the army, commissioner of Indian affairs, and President of the United States. The Indian Rights Association was also quick to applaud, believing the Indians had an advocate looking out for their welfare. But the Utes captured even more of the spotlight. From the time they arrived in Moab and then in Thompson to board the train for Salt Lake, press coverage ran continuously. The train ride was a new experience, the reporter playing on the "curious savage theme." Scott, "The White Father," assumed a paternal role with the Indians, who admired him and depended on his friendship, remaining close to their advocate. The large crowd at the station jockeyed for position to catch a glimpse of the prisoners, who were sporting dark glasses when they got off the train.

Their reunion with the other Utes awaiting them in the cell was a "genuine joy," countermanded only by the sadness they felt at Scott's eventual departure for the east. There were car rides in a Studebaker Six, church services in LDS and First Church of Christ chapels, and a deputy marshal caught by reporters learning the Ute "war dance." The daily walks about the city were enjoyable, except in the case of Polk, who suffered from rheumatism. And a few weeks later, when Tse-ne-gat went to a hospital in Denver for treatment of tuberculosis, the newspapers

Fig. 34—Participants in the surrender at Arthur Spencer's Trading Post in Mexican Hat, 1915: (*left to right*) Robert Martin, Agent Lorenzo Creel, General Hugh L. Scott, Polk, unidentified, Lieutenant Colonel Robert Michie, Posey, Ute Agent James E. Jenkins, and (*kneeling*) Jim Allen (Ute). (Special Collections, University of Nevada-Reno Library)

were sure to report his reaction to a white female nurse: "Me no sabe white woman. She funny, she heap pretty—no got man."[47]

On a more serious side, the government released the seven Indians in Salt Lake to return with Superintendent Jenkins, having promised to remain at Navajo Springs, forsake their connection with southeastern Utah, encourage others in their band to join them, send their children to school, and no longer carry weapons.[48] All signed or placed their thumb print on the paper in agreement. "Old Polk put his hand on his heart and declared he now saw clearly that he had been blind before, that his heart was bad, but that he now knew his duty and would do it."[49] The group went to what had become Towaoc.[50] Tse-ne-gat, still facing trial and badly sickened with tuberculosis, departed for Denver, entered Saint Anthony's Hospital, and received a five-year prognosis for his life.[51]

While Tse-ne-gat's trial is an interesting study in the complexity of external sources affecting the legal system, there are a number of other salient points to also consider. Both sides made every effort to exert pressure through expert testimony that played well in the press as well as in the court. Before the trial started, US District Attorney General Harry B. Tedrow traveled to Towaoc and Bluff to gather evidence and evaluate the strength of his arguments. He correctly divined that if it were just a matter of presenting evidence, he had a very strong case. He was also a realist. Recognizing that the victim was a Mexican, Scott was a hero who sided on behalf of Tse-ne-gat, the Ute people were afraid of Polk, the interpreters struggled to make their points, and the defendant was gravely ill, it all added up to an emotionally biased case in favor of the defense. "The old time prejudice against Indians has been replaced in the locality of the trial by a general feeling distinctly in the defendant's favor. Denver representatives of Eastern Indian Societies [Indian Rights Association] are much interested in Hatch and his case."[52] All the evidence indicated Hatch was guilty, but convincing the jury would be another story.

During the collection of eyewitness statements in Bluff, Polk, Posey, and twenty other men all appeared at the hearings and intimidated those providing information against Tse-ne-gat. Jenkins was supportive of the two leaders, even suggesting they might become part of the agency police force, while at the same time publicly declaring his opinion that the defendant was innocent. The agent could also take no actions against witchcraft or other "methods peculiar to themselves [Indians] to intimidate witnesses," giving an open hand to Polk's faction.[53] Indeed, there were even white men afraid to testify against Tse-ne-gat, knowing full well that both Polk and his wife might appear on behalf of the defense. The attorney general in Washington, DC, intervened to ensure Jenkins would keep the two testifying sides separate at all times and would not allow them to influence each other.[54]

The trial started on July 6 and ended on July 15. Judge Robert E. Lewis presided, and Henry McAllister, Jr. and Charles L. Avery served for the defense. The latter's strategy was to discredit the witnesses, who testified of Tse-ne-gat's actions on the day of the murder. From Tedrow's perspective, the defense received a great deal of help from Jenkins, who took one of the Indians, Harry Tom, to Avery's office and coached him. Antonio Buck, interpreter for the defense, offered him money; Jenkins had made his pro-defense position clear, which threatened the Indians under his charge; and Tom became confused by some of the questions, responding only to the parts he understood. The prosecutor also claimed that Jenkins had not followed instructions and had brought only a portion of the information requested from the agency files. The superintendent had gone to the scene of the crime, fired a rifle three times, and then reported in court that the person accompanying him, who was stationed at the place where the body had been found, had not been able to hear the shots, which subsequently discredited the Indian witnesses. Finally, Jenkins claimed that the three Utes testifying for the prosecution belonged to Mariano's faction, were untrustworthy troublemakers, and were at odds with Polk's band. Subsequent testimony by Covey, the previous agent, and local whites countered this assertion, saying the men were of good character and entirely credible. Tedrow concluded that Jenkins had done this because of his promise to Polk that the trial would turn out favorably for his son; if it did not, then the Indian would exact revenge, a theme mentioned a number of times during the trial.[55]

The defense enjoyed a strong ally in the press. Billed as "the most thrilling criminal trial ever held in Denver," activities inside and outside the courtroom grabbed the public's attention. Titles and subtitles captured the imagination and fueled the fires of public spectacle: "Mother of Tse-ne-gat Braves Terrors of Railroad Engines to Be at Son's Side" [Polk was subpoenaed to appear but refused]; "Mournful Eyes Turn on Mother"; "Indian Simplicity Baffles the Court"; and "Existence of Feud Admitted by Agent." Written like a dime novel, the text reeked with description:[56]

> 'Ma Polk' mother of the defendant [was] brown, worn, aged; this Indian mother watched the opening proceedings ignorant of what was being said, [and] what was being done, her twinkling black eyes fixed steadily on the melancholy face of the young man at the head of the table in the middle of the room. Now and again Tse-ne-gat turned his mournful eyes toward his mother. For long moments they gazed at each other [and] then the glance was broken, not by a smile of sympathy, but by a woman lifting the loose end of her red calico sleeve and wiping her lip. 'Ma Polk' is dressed to kill in turkey-red calico edged with orange yellow. She wears white leather moccasins and her bronze colored hands are covered with silver rings set with stunning turquoise.[57]

Nine days after the start, the twelve-man all-white jury reached its verdict of not guilty, following seven hours of deliberation. Tse-ne-gat and his mother remained unmoved after the pronouncement, but they were the only ones. Antonio Buck, interpreter for the defense, grasped the hand of his friend; Mary Baker, graduate of Haskell and court interpreter, smiled broadly; each juror shook Tse-ne-gat's hand in congratulations; Scott, when he received the news that night, expressed approval, declaring he knew Tse-ne-gat was innocent; crowds of people in the corridors surged around the Indian, giving an ovation; and no doubt the "women in Denver [who had] sent red neckties and pink stockings, love notes and sweetmeats," were elated.[58] As for Tedrow, he fumed and demanded an investigation into Jenkins's behavior; Juan Chacon's widow "sprang up like a tigress and went for Tse-ne-gat," only to be stopped by a deputy; and those who had testified for the prosecution shuddered at what this tacit approval would mean back in southeastern Utah.[59]

All that remained was a dramatic farewell from Denver. Tse-ne-gat boarded the train the next day with a "string of cheap medals pinned on one side of his breast," no doubt as he had seen Scott attired, with an American flag draped over his other shoulder. "Ma Polk" sported a new dress that had safety pins attached all over the front. In one hand she carried an American flag and in the other, a bag in which well-wishers, many of whom were women, had placed presents and food. Her son took his position on the rear of the last car and bid farewell to the people of Denver, while, according to the newspaper, "Polk, his father, wait[ed] in the front of his tepee, his aged eyes shaded from the sun, watching for his son."[60]

Polk may have been facing east and awaiting his son, but where he had pitched his tepee was becoming an issue. The Utes who had gone to Salt Lake City returned and went to the reservation but soon traveled with Jenkins to San Juan to get their wives and possessions. Polk declared he was going to stay in Utah until he heard how his son had faired in the trial, as others also remained, retrieved their hidden arms, obtained ammunition from caches and Navajo friends, and hesitated to go to the reservation. Jenkins left them to return on their own, since their livestock was poor, estimating they would be back in a week or ten days.[61] The white community, unhappy that the Indians were still around, felt the whole incident had been handled poorly. As reports of events first in Salt Lake City and then in Denver filtered back, many believed the vocal advocacy of the Indian Rights Association and federal bungling were at the roots of their problems.

When Tedrow was in Bluff on May 6 to collect information for the upcoming trial, he learned that Posey and his group were sullen and outspoken about how they did not want to go to the reservation and did not intend to stay long once they got there. One young warrior grabbed Kumen Jones, a Mormon bishop and elderly advocate for Indians, and shook him with frustration. Still, to their credit, all of the Utes (except Polk) arrived at Towaoc with one day to spare before the appointed time. Ten days later, Jenkins reported that all the Bluff Indians were present for ration day and that the fuss about their being off the reservation was just more "yellow press" encouraged by "vicious white men anxious to make trouble for Indians."[62]

The superintendent changed his tune the next day in a telegram to the commissioner of Indian affairs. That morning, a group of travelers encountered Posey and fifteen Utes leaving the reservation for Allen Canyon and driving their sheep. The agent reported: "He is very untruthful and irresponsible and should be disciplined for breaking parole. . . . Recommend marshal be notified and requested to apprehend Posey and return him to jail. . . . Posey is half Mexican and half Piute; very unpopular with rest of tribe; his arrest and incarceration would have wholesome effect."[63]

To the public, however, Jenkins maintained an image of control. He went on record in mid-June stating that the rumors about friction in Bluff were false and that he had given the Indians permission to go off the reservation temporarily to collect their possessions and pick up their families. But he also "estimated that it may take a year or two to complete the transfer of all effects and people to the agency but it will be accomplished as fast as possible."[64] Besides, he had "many letters from residents of Grayson, Monticello, and other places from people who desired he send them Indians to help on ranches."

Posey and Polk and their bands did not stay on the reservation. Polk, camped near James M. Holley's store in McElmo Canyon, showed up on the reservation for ration day, but the rest of the time went where he wanted. Mancos Jim had left Towaoc with a dozen people in search of water and grass for their livestock. Posey did not even pretend to be on the reservation. Bluff, Allen Canyon, Mexican Hat, Douglas Mesa, and Navajo Mountain—he returned to all of his old haunts with his band of twenty-five to thirty followers and resumed his practices of demanding food at the cabin door or appropriating a cow for dinner. The men in Bluff feared leaving their families to go out on the range to tend cattle and wondered if the previous fight had accomplished anything.[65]

Indeed, from the white man's perspective, the Indians were a nuisance at best and a threat at worst. The recent conflict bore testimony that outside help only made matters more difficult, people beyond the Four Corners area did not really understand the wards they were championing, and the Utes were now more aggressive, since they had beaten the white man on his own terrain: the courtroom. Albert R. Lyman, one of a number of witnesses called to Denver to testify for the prosecution, summarized what he had seen during the trial when he wrote, "All the evidence was minimized, overlooked, or ignored by the daily papers. I was never so thoroughly disgusted with a court procedure in my life.

The Indian Rights people had no eyes to see, ears to hear, nor hearts to consider the sorrowing parents and the broken hearted wife [of Juan Chacon]."[66] No resolution to these problems created what Lyman called "scoff-law killers." Only the future held answers to issues now exacerbated.

As months turned into years and irritations simmered, a final soothing of the friction seemed distant. It came unexpectedly, however, in the form of a small robbery at a sheep camp belonging to a Mexican, Desidirio Chacon (a relative of Juan Chacon). Two young Utes, Joe Bishop's Little Boy and Sanap's Boy, both in their twenties, threw Chacon out of his cabin, took some food and other items, and were eventually arrested for their crime. Sheriff Bill Oliver released the two men on their own recognizance to appear for their day in court, which they did. The trial went without interruption until lunchtime. The jury found the prisoners guilty, and since six hours had to lapse between verdict and sentencing by the judge, Sheriff Oliver waited for the courtroom to clear before taking the defendants to get something to eat. Whether it was the anticipated light sentence of ten days in jail or a desire to push the issue further, the young men changed their attitude of cooperation as they left the basement of the schoolhouse where the trial had been held. Here, the statements of eyewitnesses vary greatly, but the majority of them indicate that Joe Bishop's Little Boy hit Oliver with his stick, the sheriff drew his pistol (which twice failed to fire), and Bishop's Boy grabbed the gun. He then mounted his horse, and as he rode out of town, he turned and fired at the sheriff, wounding the sheriff's horse. Chester Cantsee recalled: "Suddenly there came a rider galloping past me on a horse that looked like it belonged to a white man. It was one of Joe Bishop's boys. In his hand he held a pistol. Following right behind him was the sheriff. He was holding a gun. The sheriff fired a couple of times but Joe Bishop's son got away."[67] Sanap's Boy, in the meantime, went with Posey, who was blamed by most whites as being at the bottom of this incident, since his name had become synonymous with low-grade trouble. Sanap's Boy and Posey fled to Westwater.[68]

The fight was on, and the first shots had been fired. The news spread quickly as "every man dropped what he was doing and ran for his horse and gun then rushed to volunteer."[69] With a nucleus of a half dozen World War I veterans, Oliver sealed off the town and rounded up any Indians within its limits. One man told of how Dave Black brought in Joe Bishop, who insisted he did not want trouble and would make every effort to bring his boy back. Black let Bishop go, but when the Indian thought he was out of sight, "He just whirled and took off as hard as he could ride. Black caught him then commanded, 'You old son-of-a-bitch. You turn

Fig. 35—William Posey, early 1920s. Posey became the most famous of all the Utes in southeastern Utah by chance. Caught in the conflict over loss of land and resources, he defended his rights and property while provoking, irritating, and fighting with those who sought to take them away. The vest with what appears to be a US military belt buckle was one of his trademarks. (Courtesy San Juan County Historical Commission)

around and go back or I'll let your guts out right here.' "[70] A sweep of the area netted about forty Ute men, women, and children: approximately half of the Westwater population, who were caught totally unaware.[71] This counters the belief of many white participants that the entire episode had been planned, with food cached for an anticipated flight and Posey plotting and directing the events. The great Indian uprising, or Posey War (as it is often billed), appears to have been more of a white uprising against the grievances of the past.

Initially, those captured stayed in the basement of the schoolhouse where the trial had been held. Described by Superintendent McKean as "warmed by a furnace and a stove . . . and fairly well-lighted and ventilated," the structure served as a temporary jail until the townspeople completed a 100-square-foot stockade with 10-foot-high barbed-wire walls more central to town. The basement, crammed with forty people inside before the numbers eventually swelled to almost eighty, proved to be close quarters for the Utes, who not-so-lovingly dubbed the edifice The Shithouse, since buckets in the corner were all they had to relieve themselves.[72]

Edward Dutchie remembers the day of his capture and subsequent stay in the basement. As a six-year-old, he had been in town and was on his way home to Westwater with a group of friends when they spied a lot of horsemen approaching through the trees near the Westwater Ruin. The children scattered "just like ants," jumping down into the canyon and scurrying under flat rocks where a space had eroded away. Some white teenage boys appeared, throwing rocks below to scare the Utes out of hiding, but everyone remained under the boulders. After the searchers departed, the children went to their camp, then "a lot of riders came out with their guns. Everybody knew there was trouble then. Some white guys got off and pushed the women around. They pushed us kids around, too."[73] Many of the parents were already in town, but whoever was cornered was brought to the school. Dutchie captured the fear of the moment:

> What I heard as a child was that they were going to take us away from our parents and the older people's heads [would be] cut off. Some of them were crying. One guy said, "What are you people crying for? You are crying because they are going to cut your head off? Why cry for it?" he said. "Let it come. Let them cut your head off and forget about yourselves. Try to be brave," he said, "maybe it won't happen." So everybody quieted down. That was the rumor going on among the Utes.[74]

Local men, with Navajo help, built the World War I-style barbed-wire stockade. The Navajos also constructed two large hogans which, along with several tents, sheltered the eighty captives for a month until Posey's fate had been determined.[75]

Soon after the fracas began, a group of settlers visited Polk's camp in Montezuma Canyon to see if he had any intention of joining Posey's group. He had no desire to be a part of it and told them that "if you fellows shoot Posey, pretty good alright."[76] McKean was convinced that the reason for this response was really because the Ute horses were weakened and in poor condition from the winter range and so could not get the warriors to the scene of conflict. Another reason was that many of the rifles owned by Polk's men were in hock at the Montezuma Canyon Trading Post for supplies already purchased.[77] Polk's response also may have been prompted by a desire to please the posse. At any rate, he never entered the fight.

Members of the Ute community who had not been initially captured began fleeing first to Murphy's Point five miles south of Blanding, thence west, most likely heading for Navajo Mountain, which was a traditional sanctuary during times of trouble. The exodus was not a well-planned retreat. As women and children moved away from Blanding with some of the men, others spread the word to outlying groups while still others served as rear guard. They watched to see if they were being followed, and when they discovered they were, they fought a delaying action. Oliver took the opportunity to make the proceedings legal by saying, "Every man here is deputized to shoot. I want you to shoot everything that looks like an Indian."[78]

Not everyone in the posse shared the same sentiments. Alma Jones was later asked what his feelings were toward Joe Bishop's Little Boy and said, "He was just friendly. He would shake hands with me and talk. . . . I just asked myself, 'What am I doing here? What would I do if I did come face-to-face with that boy and had to choose between shooting him or letting him shoot me.' It would be just like shooting one of your friends."[79] Posey, among others, exchanged shots with his .30-06 rifle, which outgunned members of the posse at Murphy's Point and other places along the route. John D. Rogers had his horse shot out from under him, while three men had a near miss with a bullet that passed through the Ford Model T they were riding in. The day concluded with most of the posse returning to Blanding while ten men remained close to the trail at Fred Lyman's cabin on the road eight miles south of Blanding.[80] Guards stationed there at night spotted cedar-bark torches tossed high in the air to the west of the cabin, signaling other Utes to come and join those who were fleeing. Little did those who were signaling realize that the others were imprisoned in the school basement.[81]

The next day, a posse of about fifty men renewed its efforts with increased determination fostered at the previous night's town meeting. "We all knew that Old Posey wasn't going to be taken alive, and there was not one dissenting vote about what we must do."[82] As they advanced, they occasionally found spots where the Indians had "barricaded themselves behind rocks and banks" to use as fighting positions if the posse approached too close and threatened the escape of the women and children fleeing ahead with the goats and ponies.[83] By noon, the whites spied the Indians' campfires across Butler Wash at the head of what is now called Posey's Trail. The men dismounted, leaving their horses hidden and under guard in Butler Wash. They spread out and moved through the trees toward the camp. Dave Black and Bill Young reached the crest of Comb Ridge ahead as others in their group moved upslope. Below, gunshots rang out, and warriors emerged from the wash, taking the enemy under fire before retreating. Black, as leader of the group, ran downslope to better assess the situation, leaving Young at the top of the ridge. Posey emerged from the north and began firing, then used his horse as a shield and rode in the opposite direction, possibly heading for a trail further north where today's old Highway 95 (which had not yet been built) dropped off Comb Ridge near the mouth of Arch Canyon.[84]

Meanwhile, Bill Young held his position on the crest. He spied Joe Bishop's Little Boy and Sanap's Boy riding toward his location and so moved downslope to avoid detection. The Indians spotted him, whipping their horses into a run. Realizing he could not outdistance them, he moved behind a bushy juniper and waited. The two Utes rode on either side of the tree. Young picked out the button of Joe Bishop's Little Boy's coat through the branches and fired. The Indian toppled off his horse and remained motionless while Young went around the other side of the tree to engage Sanap's Boy, who was in full retreat. Not wanting to kill needlessly, Young let him go, determined that the other man was dead, and rejoined his party. One testimony claimed that Young said, "There's one good Indian up there." Another person said he reported, "It was no fun to kill an Injun." But probably the most realistic and sensitive account came from Alma Jones, who remembered, "It wasn't long until he came down. He was upset. He said, 'I have killed a man.' He just kept saying that. That wasn't like Bill Young at all. He is one of the most calm and collected men that you ever saw. He was really upset."[85]

The men in Butler Wash determined that at least one of the Indians—Jack Fly—had been released from Blanding for some reason. He was in their rear, sporadically firing at targets of opportunity. Fearing that all the Ute prisoners were freed, the posse returned to town to learn that townspeople had turned Fly loose to care for his livestock, but he had later chosen to help those resisting. In the meantime, the Indians returned to the top of Comb Ridge and spent the night reclaiming their livestock and baggage before moving to a more defensible position. A second town meeting reaffirmed the whites' desire to either kill or capture the Indians not already incarcerated and end the issue. The next day, forty men from Blanding rendezvoused with twenty from Bluff, then they all traveled up Comb Wash. Standing at the foot of Posey's Trail, the united party spied the Utes on top of "The Island," a high mesa half a mile wide.

There were only two paths that traversed the mesa's easily defended steep slopes. Splitting the force, the posse sent a handful of men to seal off the trail in the rear while the rest spread out and assaulted the heights. They encountered no resistance. There was only an abandoned camp with cooking fires still burning and food in some frying pans. The Indians had "found a treacherous trail on the opposite side of the mesa, jumping their horses down four- and five-foot ledges, managing to scramble to safety just ahead of us."[86] Oliver reminded his posse, "Now men, when you see the horse tracks separate and the good horses with the big feet go this way, don't follow them. You follow the squaw tracks on the little horses. The bucks come back to them every night."[87] Finding the Indians' trail became increasingly difficult. They had taken every precaution to stay on rock and had eventually descended a steep incline, which was illuminated by cedar torches at night, with only their weapons. The posse at first could find no tracks, making it "look like the red men had simply 'riz' in the air." Eventually, they looked at an impossible place to descend, found a dog who refused to go down, and lowered some of the posse members on ropes before again finding the tracks along the base of the rimrock above the talus slope.[88] The chase continued.

Evening approached. The Utes held the next mesa to the west. On the previous day, Posey had exchanged shots with Black, had been wounded, and had not been seen since. The posse had no desire to wage war in the dark and so spent the night at Frank Karnell's ranch at the mouth of Arch Canyon, sending volunteers to Blanding for food. Sunrise saw the vigilantes riding toward where they had stopped the chase the previous day. The Utes had disappeared through a crack in the rim into Dry Wash. The posse pursued. In the Utes' tracks and tied on trees were white pieces of cloth fluttering in the canyon breeze, indicating a desire for peace. By evening, the whites had the Utes surrounded within a three-mile radius at the head of Dry Wash. A small boy with a white flag approached the camp first. Posse members sent him back with the message that everyone should come down and surrender or else the whites would go up and "kill them all."[89]

That night, the Indians came down from above on different trails. They carried cedar-bark torches to light their way, which the posse interpreted as an attempt to signal Polk in Montezuma Creek to come to their defense. The Indians arrived without weapons. When asked to surrender them, they refused until Anson Posey went back up the hill with Dave Black and showed them where they had been buried or hidden in cracks in the rocks. Black learned that they were totally out of ammunition and could not defend themselves any longer.[90] With that, the Utes settled down for the night around the campfire. Mormon guards kept watch, and all prepared for the next day's march down Dry Wash and into Comb, where trucks were to transport the captives to Blanding via Bluff. The uncertainty of the situation took its toll on the people; they were nervous and afraid of what might happen but also realized resistance was futile. Only one incident marred the truce: when "Sanap's Boy became frightened and suddenly bolted from the fire and escaped into the darkness. John W. Newman from Bluff, who had formerly been sheriff in Arizona, fired a shot at him as he vanished into the darkness. He was quite upset to find that he had missed his mark."[91] The Indian fled all the way to the San Juan River to a Navajo camp where the people took him in.

The next afternoon only one of the two requested vehicles arrived. Oliver squeezed the women and children and as many men as possible into the truck and started it rumbling on its way down Comb Wash. The eight remaining Utes became restless; the sheriff feared trouble. He ordered the remainder of his posse members to get the prisoners moving.

> We lined the Indians up abreast in the bottom of Comb Wash, and a man with a gun got behind each Indian. The sheriff on his horse rode out on one side of the wash, and I [John D. Rogers] on my mule rode out on the other side. We told the Indians that if Posey attacked or any trouble started, the posse men would immediately each kill an Indian without any questions. The sheriff and I were to fire shots if Indians were sighted or any trouble [was] encountered. This would be the signal for the others to shoot the prisoners. If we had fired a shot for any reason at all, those eight Paiutes would have been killed.[92]

Fortunately, after two or three miles, the second truck arrived and took all but the men who remained with the horses to Bluff, where they spent the night. Sixteen-year-old Ellen Lefler remembered walking through the encampment where the captives sat around several campfires. Many of the women cried constantly. "It broke my heart because the tears were streaming down their faces. . . . It was a sad thing. These people had lost some of their loved ones. We walked out among the campfires. We thought maybe some of them would talk to us but they didn't. They hung their heads in grief and kept on crying. Their feet had been bleeding also."[93] Guards remained posted throughout the night.

Fig. 36—Ute prisoners on the march. Instructions to the guards were clear: shoot the man in front of you if there is any sign of danger or if given the command. With that, these Utes made their way down Comb Wash until a truck arrived to transport them to Bluff, then to Blanding and a stockade. (Courtesy San Juan County Historical Commission)

That evening in Bluff, the white men thought it would be useful to interrogate the eight prisoners individually in order to find out where Posey was located. Joe Bishop's Big Boy was the first to be separated from the group and questioned. Next, the men took Anson Posey. His response was immediate: He "braced his hands against the door and refused to go in. The sheriff hit him on the fingers with his gun," four or five men wrestled him down, and then they started the interrogation.[94] He yelled, "'Me know! White man kill Joe Bishop's

Little Boy and skin him now! Mebbe so kill me and skin me too!'"[95] Although no such incident had actually occurred, the Indians viewed their captors as being *capable* of such actions.

Posey, the man whose name became synonymous with this fracas, was still at large. Last seen fighting around the large mesa to the west of Comb Wash, he never surrendered. During the month after the roundup—when the Utes remained in the open stockade in the middle of Blanding—his signal fires appeared on Comb Ridge in the vicinity of where he had disappeared. Posey spent his last days in a small alcove near the mouth of Mule Canyon. Suddenly, the signal fires stopped. His people, thinking he was dead, guided Marshal J. Ray Ward to where he had been hiding and where Ute friends had visited him. He had died of blood poisoning from a gunshot wound through the hip. At least, that was the official explanation. To the Utes, he had been killed by poisoned Mormon flour. Jim Mike, Harry Dutchie, and others believed that the settlers could not find him and so laced a sack of flour with poison so that people released from the stockade to tend Ute animals would give it to him. He had made bread from it and had died. These Utes who visited Posey (including his son Jesse, along with Jack Fly) had unwittingly brought the poisoned flour to his camp. Later, when the settlers found his body, they shot it so they could claim that was how he had died, but the white flour and bread in his hands showed what had really happened.[96]

Ward, along with some Utes who led the marshal to the body, buried Posey secretly. The law officer returned to Blanding and assured the townspeople, "Boys, I want to announce to you that Posey is dead and no other white man will ever know besides myself where he is buried. I buried him today and the tracks are covered up."[97] John Rogers remembers the marshal saying, "I have given the Indians my word that I will not tell where Posey is buried, but I assure you he is dead . . . and I ask that you take my word for it."[98] But the people of Blanding resented the "high-handed manner" with which the law had treated the situation. The next day after a brief search, some townspeople exhumed the body—an event that happened at least three times during the next two weeks: once by Agent McKean from Towaoc and twice by local settlers to verify Posey's death. There also had to be at least one other time, since five years later, the body had disappeared.[99]

As with other recent conflicts, the press had irritated the situation by providing inaccurate, overly dramatic, and inflammatory information. Throughout the month between the initial outbreak and the discovery of Posey's body, the newspapers had a field day. Two reporters—one from the *Chicago Tribune*, and the other from the *Salt Lake Tribune*—fired off press releases with a thin veneer of truth covering a mass of outright lies. Under such headings as "Piute Indians Again on War Path; Attack Southern Community" and "Piute Indians are Reinforced," C. F. Sloane of the *Salt Lake Tribune* had Blanding besieged during "thirty-six hours of terrorism"; Indians in war paint riding the streets; Posey, "the red fox," forming a "mobile squadron"; a well-planned Paiute conspiracy that included robbing the San Juan State Bank; and finally, "sixty men skilled in the art of the mountains awaiting the call of service."[100] In the best tradition of the yellow press and reminiscent of the lively reporting of World War I, the newsmen gave the town a military character: "Blanding since the outbreak has become more or less an armed camp. It wears the aspect of a military headquarters. The arrival and departure of couriers from the front is a matter of public interest."[101] When the citizens of Blanding kidded the reporters for their coverage, they replied, "We're not ready to go home yet and if we don't keep something going, we'll be getting a telegram to come home."[102]

Assured that Posey was dead, the civilian guards released approximately eighty Utes from their month-long confinement in the stockade, or "bullpen" (as some referred to it). This facility, built in the center of town, housed two hogans, some tents, a water spigot, and an outhouse. Guards patrolled its perimeter night and day, townspeople brought food in daily, and occasionally, a Ute received permission to leave the stockade to care for the prisoners' livestock. Agent McKean sent many Ute children to school in Towaoc, a government surveyor quickly surveyed and allotted lands in Allen Canyon to individual Ute families, and a small sub-agency established there assumed responsibility for their welfare. Treated as if they had started the war, these captives were really just victims of circumstance. The conclusion to over forty years of physical conflict between the Utes, Paiutes, and the white man was over, consigned to history.

The Posey "War" was a product of its time, not only as the end of a long chain of events but also as a commentary on contemporary affairs. The dissemination of volatile propaganda, combined with tracking Indians in Ford Model T's, horse-mounted posses, and old-fashioned gunfights, made this outbreak dramatic, if not unique. As the old frontier passed away, modern inventions created a new era dominated by machines and technological advances. Both the equipment and the approach used by men who had been introduced to the military regimen of World War I played a part. While not showing tremendous skill in applying either, there was certainly resolve to bring the existing situation to a close. The last of the Indian fights in southeastern Utah had come to an end for the remainder of the twentieth century.

Fig. 37—Bundled against the cold March weather, women and children receive rations in the stockade. Once released, Agent McKean ensured that some of the children were taken directly from the barbed-wire enclosure to an area where they received a hurried cleaning and haircut before boarding vehicles bound for Towaoc. (Courtesy San Juan County Historical Commission)

Chapter Endnotes

1. Portions of this chapter were previously published in Chapters Eleven and Twelve of *As If the Land Owned Us: An Ethnohistory of the White Mesa Utes* (Salt Lake City: University of Utah Press, 2011).

2. Forbes Parkhill has written an entire account of the 1915 fight in Bluff (*The Last of the Indian Wars* [New York, NY: Crowell-Collier Press, 1961]). Heavily dependent upon newspapers and with no citations, the book introduces a number of errors while also providing new information. It is good for a general overview, but the reader also needs to be careful of some of its detail.

3. Claude C. Covey to commissioner of Indian affairs, White Mesa Ute Oral History Project, American West Center, University of Utah, Salt Lake City, Utah (May 14, 1914) [hereafter cited as WMUHP].

4. Covey to commissioner of Indian affairs, WMUHP (May 18, 1914).

5. Ibid.

6. Ibid.

7. According to Stella Eyetoo, who met Polk and knew of him, he had a "bullet-proof power" (called *tuppwíyu-puwa-ga-pügat*) that ensured that no matter how many times he was shot, the rounds would just bounce off him. Stella Eyetoo, in an interview with the author (December 9, 2008).

8. Covey to commissioner of Indian affairs, WMUHP (June 29, 1914).

9. Kumen Jones, et al. to Cato Sells (September 28, 1914); and Covey to commissioner of Indian affairs, Letters Received—BIA (September 26, 1914).

10. Aquila Nebeker to Covey, Letters Received—BIA (December 4, 1914).

11. William W. Ray to commissioner of Indian affairs, Letters Received—BIA (January 2, 1915).

12. "Investigation into Depredations of Indian is Ordered," *Deseret Evening News* (October 24, 1914), p. 1; Covey to commissioner of Indian affairs, Letters Received—BIA (October 29, 1914); "Colorado State News," *Bayfield Blade* (December 25, 1917), p. 2; and "New Agent at Navajo Springs Takes up Work," *Montezuma Journal* (December 3, 1914), p. 1.

13. "Nebeker in Pursuit of Indians at Bluff," *Salt Lake Herald Republican* (February 17, 1915), p. 1.

14. "Piutes Entrench to Battle Nebeker's Force," *Salt Lake Herald Republican* (February 18, 1915), p. 1; "Posses Seeking Indian Meet Tonight," *Salt Lake Evening Telegram* (February 18, 1915), p. 2; and "Coloradoans Are on Way to Join Nebeker," *Salt Lake Tribune* (February 18, 1915), p. 4.

15. James E. Jenkins to commissioner of Indian affairs, Letters Received—BIA (February 19, 1915).

16. "Nebeker to Demand Surrender of Indian," *Salt Lake Herald Republican* (February 19, 1915), p. 1.

17. Gary L. Shumway, Jay Jones, Kay Jones, and Merle McDonald, *Cowboys and Indians: Interviews and Recollections of Marion Ashton and Alma Uriah Jones* (Flower Mound, TX: Shumway Publishing Company, 2009), p. 44.

18. "May Clash with Redskins Today," *Salt Lake Herald Republican* (February 21, 1915), p. 1.

19. Chester Cantsee interview.

20. "Testimony of Mr. [A. N.] Gingles," WMUHP (March 1, 1915).

21. "Testimony of Mr. [J. B.] Douglas," WMUHP (March 1, 1915); and Ira Hatch, in an interview with author (May 30, 1991).

22. Frank Pyle, "The Uprising of Polk and Posey in 1915," William Evans Collection, Special Collections, Harold B. Lee Library, Brigham Young University, Provo, Utah.

23. Uriah Butt, in an interview with Ruth Meo, O.H. 1628, Southeastern Utah Project, Utah State Historical Society and California State University–Fullerton (May 29, 1978).

24. Shumway, et al., *Cowboys and Indians*, p. 44.

25. Charles Burke, in an interview with Floyd O'Neil and Gregory Thompson, O.H. 374, Doris Duke Oral History Project, American West Center, University of Utah, Salt Lake City (September 13, 1968).

26. Ibid.
27. Edward Dutchie, Sr., in an interview with the author (May 21, 1996).
28. Frank Pyle, "Uprising."
29. "Friendly Utes May Join Polk," *Salt Lake Herald Republican* (March 3, 1915), p. 1.
30. John Perkins, in an interview with Charles S. Peterson, Library, Utah State Historical Society, Salt Lake City, Utah (n. d.).
31. "Testimony of Aquila Nebeker," Letters Received—BIA (n.d.); "Posse of 29 Is on Way to Aid," *Salt Lake Herald Republican* (February 22, 1915), p. 1; "Indians Surround Marshal's Posse," Ibid.; Gregory to Nebeker, Letters Received—BIA (February 26, 1915); "Indian Police Hurry to Bluff," *Salt Lake Herald Republican* (February 25, 1915), p. 3; "Five Indians are Killed in Battle," *Salt Lake Herald Republican* (February 23, 1915), p. 2; "Renegades Still Showing Fight 100 Miles West," *Montezuma Journal* (February 25, 1915), p. 1; and "Postpone Effort to Hunt Out Redskins," *Salt Lake Herald Republican* (February 25, 1915), p. 1.
32. "Ute Reported Slain by Posey for Mutiny," *Salt Lake Herald Republican* (February 27, 1915), p. 1.
33. Lorenzo D. Creel to commissioner of Indian affairs, Letters Received—BIA (April 13, 1915).
34. Ibid.
35. Ibid.
36. Nebeker to attorney general, WMUHP (March 1, 1915).
37. Secretary of war to attorney general (March 2, 1915); Scott to secretary of war (March 2, 1915); Woodrow Wilson to secretary of war (March 2, 1915); and Scott to War Department (telegram), Record Group 94, Adjutant General's Office—Letters Received, National Archives, Washington, DC (March 11, 1915).
38. Attorney general to Dewey C. Bailey, Letters Received—BIA (March 3, 1915); No Title, *Montezuma Journal* (March 4, 1915), p. 2; "Reds Entrench in Narrow Pass," *Salt Lake Herald Republican* (March 5, 1915), p. 1; and "Quintet of Captives Lodged in Local Jail," *Salt Lake Herald Republican* (March 6, 1915), p. 1.
39. Scott to commissioner of Indian affairs (March 11, 1915); Cato Sells to Scott, Letters Received—BIA (March 11, 1915); and "Only Bullets Talk—Polk," *Salt Lake Herald Republican* (March 11, 1915), p. 2.
40. "Scott Unarmed Goes to the Piutes," *Salt Lake Herald Republican* (March 13, 1915), p. 1; and "Indians Will Soon Scatter," *Salt Lake Herald Republican* (March 16, 1915), p. 7.
41. "Scott Fails to Find Renegades," *Salt Lake Herald Republican* (March 17, 1915), p. 1; "Nebeker Posse Ordered Home" (March 19, 1915), p. 1; and Scott to secretary of war, Record Group 94, Adjutant General's Office, Letters Received, National Archives, Washington, DC (March 20, 1915).
42. Hugh Lenox Scott, *Some Memories of a Soldier* (New York: The Century Company, 1928), p. 536. See also "Persons in the Foreground," *Current Opinion* (May 1915), pp. 323–324.
43. "Scott Arrests Renegade Indians," *Salt Lake Herald Republican* (March 21, 1915), p. 1.
44. Scott, *Some Memories*, p. 538.
45. Ibid.
46. John D. Rogers, in an interview with Michael T. Hurst, CRC-J6, Posey War Oral History Project, Charles Redd Center for Western Studies, Brigham Young University, Provo, Utah (April 29, 1972), p. 5.
47. "Redmen Are Lodged in Salt Lake Jail" (March 25, 1915), p. 1; "Indians Will Say Farewell Today to 'Good White Father' General Scott" (March 26, 1915), p. 14; "Scott Bids Reds Farewell" (March 27, 1915), p. 12; "Indian Warwhoops Reverberate Through Corridors of Jail" (March 31, 1915), p. 6 (all from *Salt Lake Herald Republican*); and "Tse-ne-gat Tickled with Hospital," *Denver Times* (April 20, 1915), p. 10.
48. "Sworn Oath," District of Utah, Letters Received—BIA (witnessed April 10, 1915).
49. "Indians Agree to be Peaceful," *Salt Lake Herald Republican* (April 13, 1915), p. 28.

50. Jenkins to commissioner of Indian affairs, Letters Received—BIA (April 14, 1915).
51. Jenkins to Utah attorney general, WMUHP (April 22, 1915).
52. Henry McAllister to US attorney general, Letters Received—BIA (May 6, 1915).
53. Jenkins to commissioner of Indian affairs, Letters Received—BIA (June 5, 1915).
54. Harry B. Tedrow to attorney general, Letters Received—BIA (June 25, 1915).
55. Tedrow to attorney general, WMUHP (July 15, 1915).
56. "Indian Accused of Murder Sits in Court of Paleface," *Denver Post* (July 6, 1915), p. 1; and "Hatch's Counsel Ready to Spring Surprise in Case," clipping found in Letters Received—BIA.
57. Ibid., "Indian Accused."
58. "Tse-ne-gat is Freed by Jury," *Rocky Mountain News* (July 15, 1915), p. 1; and "Jury Frees Tse-ne-gat, Ute Shows no Emotion," clipping found in Letters Received—BIA.
59. "Tse-ne-gat is Acquitted of Murder and Leaves for His Native Hills," *Denver Post* (July 16, 1915), p. 3; and "Enraged Widow Rushes at Piute," *Rocky Mountain News* (July 15, 1915), p. 7.
60. "Tse-ne-gat is Freed by Jury."
61. Jenkins to Scott (April 28, 1915); and A. H. Spencer to Scott, Letters Received—BIA (April 29, 1915).
62. Tedrow to attorney general (May 6, 1915); Jenkins to David S. Cook (May 6, 1915); and Jenkins to commissioner of Indian affairs, Letters Received—BIA (June 1, 1915).
63. Jenkins to commissioner of Indian affairs, June 2, 1915, WMUHP.
64. "Supt. Jenkins Denies Reports of Indian Troubles," *Montezuma Journal*, Letters Received—BIA (June 17, 1915).
65. W. W. McConihe to commissioner of Indian affairs (September 13, 1915 and October 22, 1915); and Jenkins to Indian Office (telegram), Letters Received—BIA (September 23, 1915).
66. Albert R. Lyman, *Indians and Outlaws: Settling of the San Juan Frontier* (Salt Lake City: Publishers Press, 1962, 1980), pp. 164–165.
67. Chester Cantsee, Sr., in an interview with the author (September 6, 1994).
68. Westwater, where the Indians lived in those days, was called Ute Village or Ute Flats and had a race track often used by the community. Living sites extended along the canyon for about a mile, with its northern limit at what was called Big Spring and its southern limit slightly north of the Westwater Ruin made by ancestral Puebloans. George Hurst, in an interview with Michael Hurst, CRC-J7, Posey War Oral History Project, Charles Redd Center for Western Studies, Harold B. Lee Library, Brigham Young University, Provo, Utah (February 24, 1973), p. 4.
69. John D. Rogers, "Piute Posey and the Last Indian Uprising," in Lloyd L. Young File (A2022), Library, Utah State Historical Society, Salt Lake City, Utah, p. 2.
70. George Hurst, pp. 12–13.
71. Billy Mike, in an interview with Gregory C. Thompson and James Schultz, WMUHP (May 22, 1980).
72. McKean (April 9, 1923); and Edward Dutchie, in an interview with the author (May 21, 1996).
73. Edward Dutchie interview.
74. Ibid.
75. McKean (April 9, 1923).
76. Ibid.
77. J. Ray Ward to attorney general, WMUHP (May 1, 1923).
78. George Hurst interview.
79. Alma Uriah Jones, in an interview with Gary Shumway, LDS Polygamy Oral History, CRC-K157, Charles Redd Center for Western Studies, Special Collections, Lee Library, Brigham Young University, Provo, Utah (August 4, 1981), pp. 68–69.
80. The following account is from John D. Rogers, "Piute Posey and the Last Indian Uprising," appendix to John Rogers' interview with Michael T. Hurst, CRC-J6, Charles Redd Center for Western Studies, Special Collections, Lee Library, Brigham Young University, Provo, Utah (April 29,

1972). There are dozens of interviews of people who have their own version of what happened in this fight, but Rogers' is the most complete. He was an active participant throughout the incident and has had additional interviews for clarification of detail.
81. William R. Young, "The 1923 Indian Uprising in San Juan County, Utah," filed in Lloyd L. Young Folder, Library, Utah State Historical Society, Salt Lake City, Utah, p. 2.
82. Rogers interview, p. 22, and Rogers, "Piute Posey," p. 7.
83. Young, p. 2.
84. The conventional wisdom from many involved in the fight was that Posey took the old Indian trail through where Highway 95 would later be built. Another possibility is that he went farther north to another easier and more manageable trail into Comb Wash from Whiskers Draw, since he had just been wounded in the hip by Dave Black.
85. Ibid., p. 34; Fern Oliver Shelley, "The Life Story of William Edward Oliver, 1858–1935" (in possession of James W. Oliver, Jr., Mapleton, Utah); and Alma Jones.
86. Rogers interview, p. 35.
87. Leland W. Redd, in an interview with Louise Lyne, O. H. 1094b, Southeastern Utah Project, Utah State Historical Society and California State University–Fullerton, Salt Lake City, Utah (July 12, 1972), p. 7.
88. Albert R. Lyman, "San Juan and Its Piutes," *San Juan Record* (September 21, 1933), p. 8.
89. Ellen Lefler, "Sheriff Newman and the Posey War," *Blue Mountain Shadows*, Issue 4 (Spring 1989), pp. 24–27.
90. Wiley Redd, "Redd Recalls Indian Uprising, A Personal Experience," *San Juan Record* (June 1969), n.p.
91. Rogers, p. 37.
92. Ibid.
93. Ellen Lefler, "Memories of the Ute Roundup," *Blue Mountain Shadows*, Issue 4 (Spring 1989), p. 28.
94. Wiley Redd interview.
95. Ibid., p. 38.
96. Jim Mike, in an interview with Gary Shumway and Anna Marie Nat, in Duke #550 (June 20, 1968); Harry Dutchie, in an interview with Gary Shumway, in Doris Duke #517, Doris Duke Oral History Project, Special Collections, J. Willard Marriott Library, University of Utah, Salt Lake City, Utah (July 15, 1968); and Clarence Perkins, in an interview with Mary Risher, O. H. 790, Southeastern Utah Project, Utah State Historical Society and California State University–Fullerton, Salt Lake City, Utah (June 29, 1971), pp. 44–45.
97. Leland Redd.
98. Rogers, "Piute Posey," p. 10.
99. Ibid.
100. *Salt Lake Tribune* (March 21–April 5, 1923).
101. "Piute Indians Are Reinforced," *Salt Lake Tribune* (March 24, 1923), p. 1.
102. Rogers interview, p. 22.

Conclusion

John Wayne, speaking of the Monument Valley-Moab corridor, is said to have quipped, "This is where God put the West."[1] Central to that now clichéd image is the cowboy-Indian- cavalry, serving as a core to many of Wayne's films that played across the sunny Utah landscape. *Stagecoach*, *Fort Apache*, *The Searchers*, and *She Wore a Yellow Ribbon* all speak of that mythical West of ranchers, settlers, and Native Americans vying for an unsettled frontier. Entertaining but simple, black and white, right over wrong—the plots were straightforward: find, fix, and defeat the enemy with enough time for some comic relief and a little romance, all in an hour and a half.

While critics might complain about the simplicity of this formula and moviegoers demand more realism, both director John Ford and John Wayne hit on a theme that resonated. They tapped into a very real triad of elements when portraying different cultures struggling in conflict within a dramatic environment. The land, as Everett Ruess pointed out at the beginning of this book, can have an overpowering ability to impress the mind. Equally important is its influence on people living and fighting in the terrain. Beginning with the Anasazi and their defensive alcoves and offensive tactics; looking at the Utes and their superb knowledge and use of the topography to ferret out hiding Navajos and to defend against opposing cowboys and cavalry elements; or studying the religious beliefs associated with Navajo protection ceremonies embedded in various features on the landscape, it becomes evident that geography played a prominent role.

The same is true of a culture's distinctive characteristics. Each society waged war according to its capability, lifestyle, beliefs, and current practices or doctrine. There is no missing the repetitive loss of land, the impoverishment of native cultures, and the subsequent conflict that characterized both the nineteenth century and the first quarter of the twentieth century as soldiers, settlers, and ranchers vied against Native Americans for their holdings. Both factions believed it was their God-given right to use the land as they saw fit. The white man, with his superior technology and overwhelming numbers, seized through force and legislation what had belonged to the Indians for hundreds of years. In less than fifty years, it was lost, and a way of life was over. For the Utes, this meant a widely shrinking land base, with two small reservations in southwestern Colorado; for the Navajos, it meant a rectangular chunk of reservation initially straddling the boundary of New Mexico and Arizona. An expansive people, the Navajos consistently gained additional territory until their reservation mushroomed to over 27,000 square miles—a domain larger than the state of Rhode Island—that included holdings in New Mexico, Arizona, and Utah. How this occurred is another story.

To summarize the story at hand, Native American conflict in the Four Corners region led to a shift in power, accompanied by dramatic change. Beyond the myth of the settlement of the West lies a compelling story of people working and fighting to maintain their way of life and a place to live it.

Chapter Endnotes

1. This quote is cited in Bette L. Stanton, *Where God Put the West: A Moab-Monument Valley Movie History* (Moab, Utah: Canyonlands Natural History Association, 1994), p. 1.

CPSIA information can be obtained
at www.ICGtesting.com
Printed in the USA
FFOW02n1648270218
45321247-45990FF

9 781457 548895